# First World War
## and Army of Occupation
# War Diary
## France, Belgium and Germany

5 DIVISION
15 Infantry Brigade
Cheshire Regiment 1/6th Battalion,
Dorsetshire Regiment 1st Battalion
and King's (Liverpool Regiment) 6th Battalion.
4 August 1914 - 31 December 1915

WO95/1572

The Naval & Military Press Ltd
www.nmarchive.com
Published in association with The National Archives

Published by

## The Naval & Military Press Ltd

Unit 10 Ridgewood Industrial Park,

Uckfield, East Sussex,

TN22 5QE England

Tel: +44 (0) 1825 749494

www.naval-military-press.com

www.nmarchive.com

*This diary has been reprinted in facsimile from the original. Any imperfections are inevitably reproduced and the quality may fall short of modern type and cartographic standards.*

**© Crown Copyright**
**Images reproduced by permission of The National Archives, London, England, 2015.**

# Contents

| Document type | Place/Title | Date From | Date To |
|---|---|---|---|
| Heading | WO95/1572/1 | | |
| Heading | 5th Division 15th Infantry Bde 6th Cheshires Aug 1914 February 1915 | | |
| Heading | 15th Brigade 5th Division Battalion Disembarked Havre 10.11.14. Joined 15th Brigade 17th December 1914 6th Battalion The Cheshire Regiment August To December 1914. | | |
| War Diary | Stock Port | 04/08/1914 | 09/08/1914 |
| War Diary | Shrewsbury | 10/08/1914 | 31/08/1914 |
| War Diary | Northampton | 01/09/1914 | 10/10/1914 |
| War Diary | Great Brinton | 11/10/1914 | 25/10/1914 |
| War Diary | Ston Ham Aspall | 26/10/1914 | 30/10/1914 |
| War Diary | Northampton | 31/10/1914 | 09/11/1914 |
| War Diary | Havre | 10/11/1914 | 14/11/1914 |
| War Diary | St Omer | 15/11/1914 | 20/11/1914 |
| War Diary | Helfaut | 21/11/1914 | 09/12/1914 |
| War Diary | Hazebrouck | 10/12/1914 | 10/12/1914 |
| War Diary | Bailleul | 11/12/1914 | 11/12/1914 |
| War Diary | Neuve Eglise | 11/12/1914 | 29/12/1914 |
| War Diary | Bailleul | 29/12/1914 | 31/12/1914 |
| Miscellaneous | Appendix I | | |
| Miscellaneous | List of Officers 6th Cheshire Regiment App II. | | |
| Heading | 15th Bde 5th Div 6th Cheshires January 1915 | | |
| Miscellaneous | | | |
| War Diary | Bailleul | 01/01/1915 | 04/01/1915 |
| War Diary | Ravelsberg | 05/01/1915 | 16/01/1915 |
| War Diary | St Jans Cappell | 17/01/1915 | 24/01/1915 |
| War Diary | Dranoutre | 25/01/1915 | 31/01/1915 |
| Miscellaneous | Roll of Battle Casualties of The 6th Battn Cheshire Regiment from Nov 10th 1914 to January 31st 1915 App 4. | | |
| Miscellaneous | 6th Cheshire Regiment Record of Gallantry Or Distinguished Conduct App 5 | | |
| Heading | 15th Bde 5th Div Become G.H.Q. Troops March Ist 6th Cheshires February 1915 | | |
| War Diary | Dranoutre | 01/02/1915 | 01/02/1915 |
| War Diary | St Jans Cappel | 02/02/1915 | 09/02/1915 |
| War Diary | Dranoutre | 10/02/1915 | 28/02/1915 |
| Miscellaneous | Record of Gallantry Or Distinguished Conduct | | |
| Miscellaneous | Battle Casualties Feby 1915 | | |
| Miscellaneous | Copy of Telegram | | |
| Heading | 5 Div 15 Bde 6 Cheshire 1915 March 1915 Dec | | |
| Miscellaneous | L of C | | |
| Heading | War Diary of 6th Battalion The Cheshire Regt From 1st March 1915 To 31st March 1915 Vol IV | | |
| War Diary | Pranoutre | 01/03/1915 | 01/03/1915 |
| War Diary | St Omer | 02/03/1915 | 31/03/1915 |
| Heading | War Diary of 6th Batt Cheshire Regt From April 1st To April 30th 1915 (Volume V) | | |
| War Diary | Stomer | 01/04/1915 | 02/04/1915 |

| | | | |
|---|---|---|---|
| War Diary | Havre | 03/04/1915 | 30/04/1915 |
| Heading | War Diary of 6th Batt Cheshire Regt From May 1st To May 31st 1915 | | |
| War Diary | Havre | 01/05/1915 | 31/05/1915 |
| Heading | War Diary of 6th Batt Cheshire Regt From June 1st To June 1915 (Volume VII) | | |
| War Diary | Havre | 01/06/1915 | 30/06/1915 |
| Heading | War Diary of 6th Battn The Cheshire Regt From July 1st 1915 To July 31st 1915 Volume VIII. | | |
| War Diary | Havre | 01/07/1915 | 31/07/1915 |
| Heading | War Diary of 6th Battalion The Cheshire Regiment From 1st August 1915 To 31st August 1915 Volume 9. | | |
| War Diary | Havre | 01/08/1915 | 31/08/1915 |
| Heading | War Diary of 6th Battalion The Cheshire Regt. From 1st September 1915 To 30th September 1915 Volume X. | | |
| War Diary | Havre | 01/09/1915 | 30/09/1915 |
| Heading | War Diary of 6th Battalion The Cheshire Regt. From 1st October To 31st October 1915 Volume XI | | |
| War Diary | Havre | 01/10/1915 | 31/10/1915 |
| Heading | Official War Diary of The 1/6th Battalion The Cheshire Regiment (T) From November 1st 1915 To November 30th 1915 Vol XII | | |
| War Diary | Havre | 01/11/1915 | 30/11/1915 |
| Miscellaneous | Commandant Etaples | 28/12/1915 | 28/12/1915 |
| Miscellaneous | Headquarters I.G.C. | 30/12/1915 | 30/12/1915 |
| Miscellaneous | Memorandum | | |
| Heading | 20th Infy Bde 1/6th Bn Cheshire Regt 1914 Aug-1916 Feb To 39 Div 118 Bde | | |
| Heading | 20th Brigade 7th Division Joined 20th Brigade From G.H.Q.9.1.16.1/6th Battalion Cheshire Regiment January 1916 | | |
| War Diary | Havre | 01/01/1916 | 08/01/1916 |
| War Diary | Pont Remy | 09/01/1916 | 09/01/1916 |
| War Diary | Ailly-L-H-C | 10/01/1916 | 28/01/1916 |
| War Diary | Picquigny | 29/01/1916 | 31/01/1916 |
| Heading | 20th Brigade 7th Division Battalion Transferred To 30th Division 29.2.16 1/6th Battalion Cheshire Regiment February 1916 | | |
| Heading | War Diary of The 6th Cheshire Regt From Feb 1st To Feb 29th 1916 Vol XV | | |
| War Diary | Picquigny | 01/02/1916 | 02/02/1916 |
| War Diary | Cardonette | 03/02/1916 | 03/02/1916 |
| War Diary | Pont Noyelles | 04/02/1916 | 05/02/1916 |
| War Diary | Ville-Sous-Corbie | 06/02/1916 | 07/02/1916 |
| War Diary | Ville-Sur-Corbie | 08/02/1916 | 10/02/1916 |
| War Diary | Ville | 11/02/1916 | 12/02/1916 |
| War Diary | Trenches | 13/02/1916 | 20/02/1916 |
| War Diary | Ville | 21/02/1916 | 26/02/1916 |
| War Diary | Wallon-Cappel | 27/02/1916 | 29/02/1916 |
| Heading | WO95/1572/2 | | |
| Heading | 5th Division 1st Dorset Reg Aug To December 1914 | | |
| Heading | 15th Brigade 5th Division 1st Battalion Dorsetshire Regiment August 1914 | | |
| War Diary | | 04/08/1914 | 31/08/1914 |
| Miscellaneous | 1st Bn Dorsetshire Regiment | | |
| Miscellaneous | | | |

| | | | |
|---|---|---|---|
| Miscellaneous | With Reference To Your Letter No 10 dated 8th August 1914. | 09/08/1914 | 09/08/1914 |
| Miscellaneous | A Form Messages And Signals | | |
| Miscellaneous | 1st Batt Dorset & Norfolk Regts. | 08/08/1914 | 08/08/1914 |
| Heading | 15th Brigade 5th Division 1st Battalion Dorsetshire Regiment September 1914 | | |
| War Diary | | 01/09/1914 | 01/10/1914 |
| Heading | 5th Division 15th Inf. Bde War Diary 1st Dorset Regt. October 1914 | | |
| War Diary | | 01/10/1914 | 12/10/1914 |
| War Diary | Pont Fixe-Givenchy Near La Bassee | 13/10/1914 | 13/10/1914 |
| War Diary | Pont Fixe Near Givenchy | 14/10/1914 | 15/10/1914 |
| War Diary | Festubert | 16/10/1914 | 18/10/1914 |
| War Diary | Rue Douvert | 18/10/1914 | 20/10/1914 |
| War Diary | Rue Du Marais | 21/10/1914 | 22/10/1914 |
| War Diary | Festubert | 23/10/1914 | 25/10/1914 |
| War Diary | Gorre | 26/10/1914 | 26/10/1914 |
| War Diary | Le Touret | 27/10/1914 | 27/10/1914 |
| War Diary | Richebourg L'Avoue | 28/10/1914 | 28/10/1914 |
| War Diary | Richebourg L'Avoue-Richebourg St Vaast | 28/10/1914 | 28/10/1914 |
| War Diary | Rue de L'Epinette | 29/10/1914 | 29/10/1914 |
| War Diary | Calonne | 30/10/1914 | 30/10/1914 |
| War Diary | Strazeele | 31/10/1914 | 01/11/1914 |
| War Diary | Neuve Eglise | 01/11/1914 | 01/11/1914 |
| Heading | 5th Division 5th Inf. Bde War Diary 1st Dorset Regt. November 1914 | | |
| War Diary | Strazeele | 01/11/1914 | 01/11/1914 |
| War Diary | Neuve Eglise | 01/11/1914 | 01/11/1914 |
| War Diary | Neuve Eglise Ploegsteert Wood | 02/11/1914 | 03/11/1914 |
| War Diary | Ploegsteert Wood | 02/11/1914 | 18/11/1914 |
| War Diary | Dranoutre | 19/11/1914 | 23/11/1914 |
| War Diary | Lindenhock | 24/11/1914 | 30/11/1914 |
| Heading | 5th Division 15th Inf. Bde War Diary 1st Dorset Regt. December 1914 | | |
| War Diary | Dranoutre | 01/12/1914 | 11/12/1914 |
| War Diary | St Jans Cappel | 11/12/1914 | 13/12/1914 |
| War Diary | Dranoutre | 14/12/1914 | 14/12/1914 |
| War Diary | Neuve Eglise | 15/12/1914 | 17/12/1914 |
| War Diary | Wulverghem | 18/12/1914 | 29/12/1914 |
| War Diary | Bailleul | 30/12/1914 | 31/12/1914 |
| Heading | 5th Division 15th Infantry Bde 1st Dorsets January To June 1915 | | |
| Heading | 15th Bde 5th Div 1st Dorsets January 1915 | | |
| War Diary | Bailleul | 01/01/1915 | 04/01/1915 |
| War Diary | Wulverghem | 04/01/1915 | 07/01/1915 |
| War Diary | Dranoutre | 08/01/1915 | 10/01/1915 |
| War Diary | Wulverghem | 10/01/1915 | 13/01/1915 |
| War Diary | Dranoutre | 14/01/1915 | 23/01/1915 |
| War Diary | Wulverghem | 24/01/1915 | 28/01/1915 |
| War Diary | Lindenhoek-Neuve Eglise Rudd | 29/01/1915 | 30/01/1915 |
| War Diary | Dranoutre | 31/01/1915 | 31/01/1915 |
| Heading | 15th Bde 5th Div 1st Dorsets February 1915 | | |
| War Diary | Dranoutre | 01/02/1915 | 01/02/1915 |
| War Diary | Bailleul | 02/02/1915 | 08/02/1915 |
| War Diary | Bailleul-Lindenhoek | 09/02/1915 | 09/02/1915 |
| War Diary | Lindenhoek-Wulverghem | 10/02/1915 | 13/02/1915 |

| | | | |
|---|---|---|---|
| War Diary | Dranoutre | 14/02/1915 | 18/02/1915 |
| War Diary | Lindenhoek-Wulverghem | 19/02/1915 | 24/02/1915 |
| War Diary | Lindenhoek | 25/02/1915 | 27/02/1915 |
| War Diary | Bailleul | 28/02/1915 | 28/02/1915 |
| Heading | 15th Bde 28th Div Joined 28th Div. With Bde 3rd March 1916 1st Dorsets March 1915 | | |
| War Diary | Vlamertinghe | 01/03/1915 | 04/03/1915 |
| War Diary | Ypres | 04/03/1915 | 31/03/1915 |
| Heading | 15th Bde 5th Div Left 28th Div & Returned With Bde To 5th Div /4/15 1st Dorsets April 1915 | | |
| War Diary | Ypres | 01/04/1915 | 17/04/1915 |
| Miscellaneous | Reference War Diary for April of 1sty Bn Dorsetshire Regiment | 20/04/1915 | 20/04/1915 |
| War Diary | Ypres | 17/04/1915 | 30/04/1915 |
| Heading | 15th Bde 5th Div 1st Dorsets May 1915 | | |
| War Diary | Ypres Hill 60 | 01/05/1915 | 31/05/1915 |
| Heading | 15th Bde 5th Div 1st Dorsets June 1915 | | |
| War Diary | | 01/06/1915 | 01/06/1915 |
| War Diary | Ypres-Hill 60 | 02/06/1915 | 03/07/1915 |
| Heading | 5th Division 15th Infantry Bde 1st Dorsets July To December 1915 | | |
| Heading | 15th Bde 5th Div 1st Dorsets July 1915 | | |
| War Diary | | 01/07/1915 | 03/07/1915 |
| War Diary | Ypres Hill 60 Sector | 04/07/1915 | 13/07/1915 |
| War Diary | Reninghelst | 13/07/1915 | 21/07/1915 |
| War Diary | Watou | 21/07/1915 | 29/07/1915 |
| War Diary | Pont Noyelle | 30/07/1915 | 01/08/1915 |
| Heading | 15th Bde 5th Div 1st Dorsets August 1915 | | |
| War Diary | Pont Noyelle | 02/08/1915 | 02/08/1915 |
| War Diary | Dernancourt | 02/08/1915 | 02/08/1915 |
| War Diary | Meaulte | 03/08/1915 | 08/08/1915 |
| War Diary | Trenches 76-83 | 09/08/1915 | 15/08/1915 |
| War Diary | Night of Fr Court | 15/08/1915 | 15/08/1915 |
| War Diary | Meaulte and Becordel | 16/08/1915 | 22/08/1915 |
| War Diary | Meaulte | 23/08/1915 | 27/08/1915 |
| War Diary | Etinehem and Chipilly | 28/08/1915 | 31/08/1915 |
| Miscellaneous | Field Return | | |
| Miscellaneous | In The Field | | |
| Miscellaneous | Field Return | | |
| Miscellaneous | For Information of The A.G.'s Office At The Base | | |
| Miscellaneous | Field Return | | |
| Miscellaneous | For Information of The A.G.'s Office At The Base | | |
| Miscellaneous | Field Return | | |
| Miscellaneous | For Information of The A.G.'s Office At The Base | | |
| Miscellaneous | Field Return | | |
| Miscellaneous | For Information of The A.G.'s Office At The Base | | |
| Heading | 15th Bde 5th Div 1st Dorsets September 1915 | | |
| War Diary | Etinehem | 01/09/1915 | 01/09/1915 |
| War Diary | Maricourt | 02/09/1915 | 22/09/1915 |
| War Diary | Carnoy | 23/09/1915 | 24/09/1915 |
| War Diary | Trenches 36 To 48 Inclusive | 25/09/1915 | 30/09/1915 |
| Miscellaneous | Field Return | | |
| Miscellaneous | For Information of The A.G.'s Office at The Base | | |
| Miscellaneous | Field Return | | |
| Miscellaneous | For Information of The A.G.'s Office at The Base | | |
| Miscellaneous | Field Return | | |

| | | | |
|---|---|---|---|
| Miscellaneous | For Information of The A.G.'s Office at The Base | | |
| Miscellaneous | Field Return | | |
| Miscellaneous | For Information of The A.G.'s Office at The Base | | |
| Heading | 15th Bde 5th Div 1st Dorsets October 1915 | | |
| War Diary | Carnoy | 01/10/1915 | 01/10/1915 |
| War Diary | Trenches 36 To 48 | 02/10/1915 | 02/10/1915 |
| War Diary | Bray | 02/10/1915 | 05/10/1915 |
| War Diary | Carnoy Subsector C I | 06/10/1915 | 17/10/1915 |
| War Diary | Bray | 18/10/1915 | 20/10/1915 |
| War Diary | Sailly Laurette | 21/10/1915 | 31/10/1915 |
| Miscellaneous | Field Return | | |
| Miscellaneous | For Information of The A.G.'s Office at The Base | | |
| Miscellaneous | Field Return | | |
| Miscellaneous | For Information of The A.G.'s Office at The Base | | |
| Miscellaneous | Field Return | | |
| Miscellaneous | For Information of The A.G.'s Office at The Base | | |
| Miscellaneous | Field Return | | |
| Miscellaneous | For Information of The A.G.'s Office at The Base | | |
| Miscellaneous | Field Return | | |
| Miscellaneous | For Information of The Officer i/c of A Base Record Office. | | |
| Heading | 15th Bde 5th Div 1st Dorsets November 1915 | | |
| War Diary | Bray | 01/11/1915 | 03/11/1915 |
| War Diary | Sub-Sector C.I | 04/11/1915 | 09/11/1915 |
| War Diary | Bray | 09/11/1915 | 15/11/1915 |
| War Diary | Sub-Sector C.I | 15/11/1915 | 21/11/1915 |
| War Diary | Bray | 21/11/1915 | 26/11/1915 |
| War Diary | Sub-Sector C.I | 27/11/1915 | 30/11/1915 |
| Miscellaneous | Field Return | | |
| Miscellaneous | For Information of The Officer i/c of A Base Record Office. | | |
| Miscellaneous | Field Return | | |
| Miscellaneous | For Information of The Officer i/c of A Base Record Office. | | |
| Miscellaneous | Field Return | | |
| Miscellaneous | For Information of The Officer i/c of A Base Record Office. | | |
| Miscellaneous | Field Return | | |
| Miscellaneous | For Information of The Officer i/c of A Base Record Office. | | |
| Heading | 15th Bde 5th Div Left To Join 95th Bde, Send Div 31.12.15 1st Dorsets December 1915 | | |
| War Diary | | 01/12/1915 | 03/12/1915 |
| War Diary | Bray | 04/12/1915 | 07/12/1915 |
| War Diary | Bray & Etinehem | 08/12/1915 | 08/12/1915 |
| War Diary | G I Subsector | 09/12/1915 | 13/12/1915 |
| War Diary | Bray & Etinehem | 14/12/1915 | 17/12/1915 |
| War Diary | G I Subsector | 18/12/1915 | 22/12/1915 |
| War Diary | Bray & Etinehem | 22/12/1915 | 26/12/1915 |
| War Diary | C I Subsector | 26/12/1915 | 31/12/1915 |
| Miscellaneous | Field State | | |
| Miscellaneous | | | |
| Miscellaneous | Field State | | |
| Miscellaneous | | | |
| Miscellaneous | Field State | | |
| Miscellaneous | | | |

| Type | Description | From | To |
|---|---|---|---|
| Miscellaneous | Field State | | |
| Miscellaneous | | | |
| Miscellaneous | Field Return | | |
| Miscellaneous | For Information of The Officer i/c of A Base Record Office. | | |
| Heading | WO95/1572/3 | | |
| Heading | 5th Division 15th Infantry Bde 1/6 Liverpools Feb To June 1915 | | |
| Heading | 15th Bde 5th Div Disembarked From U.K. 25.2.1915 1/6th Liverpool Regiment February & March 1915 | | |
| War Diary | Canterbury | 01/02/1915 | 24/02/1915 |
| War Diary | Havre | 25/02/1915 | 26/02/1915 |
| War Diary | Bailleul | 27/02/1915 | 02/03/1915 |
| War Diary | Vlamertinghe | 03/03/1915 | 07/03/1915 |
| War Diary | Ypres | 08/03/1915 | 15/03/1915 |
| War Diary | Bosseboom | 16/03/1915 | 21/03/1915 |
| War Diary | Trenches Ypres | 21/03/1915 | 31/03/1915 |
| Heading | 15th Bde 5th Div 1/6th Liverpools April 1915 | | |
| War Diary | Vlamertinghe | 01/04/1915 | 05/04/1915 |
| War Diary | Rosental Chateau | 05/04/1915 | 06/04/1915 |
| War Diary | Ypres (Rosental) | 07/04/1915 | 09/04/1915 |
| War Diary | Rosen Hill | 09/04/1915 | 10/04/1915 |
| War Diary | Ypres | 16/04/1915 | 30/04/1915 |
| Heading | 15th Bde 5th Div 1/6th Liverpools May 1915 | | |
| War Diary | Ypres | 01/05/1915 | 06/05/1915 |
| War Diary | Ouderdom | 07/05/1915 | 15/05/1915 |
| War Diary | E Camp Ouderdom | 15/05/1915 | 15/05/1915 |
| War Diary | Ypres | 15/05/1915 | 17/05/1915 |
| War Diary | E Camp Ouderdom | 18/05/1915 | 20/05/1915 |
| War Diary | W Side Etang de Zillebeke | 21/05/1915 | 31/05/1915 |
| Miscellaneous | A Form Messages And Signals | | |
| Miscellaneous | Messages And Signals | | |
| Miscellaneous | A Form Messages And Signals | | |
| Miscellaneous | A Form Messages And Signals. | | |
| Miscellaneous | | | |
| Miscellaneous | A Coy App VI | | |
| Miscellaneous | The Adjutant 6th Liverpool Ap VII. | 11/05/1915 | 11/05/1915 |
| Miscellaneous | Appendix To War Diary Ap. VIII | 05/05/1915 | 05/05/1915 |
| Miscellaneous | Appendix To War Diary Ap IX | 05/05/1915 | 05/05/1915 |
| Diagram etc | | | |
| Diagram etc | Hill 60 | | |
| Heading | 15th Bde 5th Div 1/6th Liverpools June 1915 | | |
| War Diary | | 01/06/1915 | 03/06/1915 |
| War Diary | E Tang de Zillebeke | 04/06/1915 | 30/06/1915 |
| Miscellaneous | To The Adjutant 6th Bn R.L.R. Ap. I | 23/06/1915 | 23/06/1915 |
| Miscellaneous | A Form Messages And Signals. App II | | |
| Miscellaneous | | | |
| Heading | 5th Division 15th Infantry Bde 1/6 Liverpools July To December 1915 | | |
| Heading | 15th Bde 5th Div 1/6th Liverpools July 1915 | | |
| Heading | War Diary of 1/6th (Rifle) Battn. "The Kings" (L'Pool Regt.) From 1st July 1915 To 31st July 1915 | | |
| War Diary | Etang de Zillebeke | 01/07/1915 | 11/07/1915 |
| War Diary | Reninghelst | 12/07/1915 | 17/07/1915 |
| War Diary | Dickebusch & Rosendahl | 18/07/1915 | 19/07/1915 |
| War Diary | Rosen Hill | 20/07/1915 | 20/07/1915 |

| | | | |
|---|---|---|---|
| War Diary | Abeele | 21/07/1915 | 23/07/1915 |
| War Diary | Godewaersvelde | 24/07/1915 | 30/07/1915 |
| War Diary | Lahoussoye. | 31/07/1915 | 31/07/1915 |
| Heading | 15th Bde 5th Div 1/6th Liverpools August 1915 | | |
| Heading | War Diary of 1/6th (Rifle) Battn. "The King's" Liverpool Regiment. From 1st Augt 1915 To 31st Augt 1915 | | |
| War Diary | Lahoussoye. | 01/08/1915 | 03/08/1915 |
| War Diary | Dernancourt | 04/08/1915 | 06/08/1915 |
| War Diary | Meaulte | 07/08/1915 | 23/08/1915 |
| War Diary | Morlancourt | 24/08/1915 | 31/08/1915 |
| Heading | 15th Bde 5th Div 1/6th Liverpools September 1915 | | |
| Heading | War Diary of 1/6 (Rifle) Battn The Kings Lpool Regt From 1st Sept 1915 To 30 Sept 1915 | | |
| War Diary | Morlancourt | 01/09/1915 | 01/09/1915 |
| War Diary | Suzanne | 02/09/1915 | 02/09/1915 |
| War Diary | Vaux | 03/09/1915 | 09/09/1915 |
| War Diary | Suzanne | 10/09/1915 | 22/09/1915 |
| War Diary | Vaux | 22/09/1915 | 30/09/1915 |
| Heading | 15th Bde 5th Div 1/6th Liverpools October 1915 | | |
| Heading | War Diary of 1/6 (Rifle) Battn The Kings Lpool Regt From 1st October 1915 To 31st October 1915 | | |
| War Diary | Vaux | 01/10/1915 | 31/10/1915 |
| Heading | 15th Bde 5th Div Became Third Army Troops 17.11.15 1/6th Liverpools November 1915 | | |
| War Diary | Vaux | 31/10/1915 | 06/11/1915 |
| War Diary | Vaux Ref Map Vaux G 4 D 10 B | 07/11/1915 | 12/11/1915 |
| War Diary | Vaux | 13/10/1915 | 17/11/1915 |
| War Diary | Suzanne | 18/11/1915 | 18/11/1915 |
| War Diary | Bertrancourt | 19/11/1915 | 30/11/1915 |
| Heading | Third Army Troops Came From 15th Bde. 5th Div 17/11/15.1/6th Liverpools December 1915 | | |
| Heading | War Diary of 1/6 (Rifle) Battn The Kings Liverpool Regt From 1 Dec 1915 To 31st Dec 1915 | | |
| War Diary | Bertrancourt | 01/12/1915 | 31/12/1915 |

WO 95/15721

5th Division

15th Infantry Bde

6th Cheshires

Aug — 1914

~~January~~ — February

1915

15th Brigade
5th Division.
-----

Battalion disembarked Havre 10.11.14.

Joined 15th Brigade 17th December 1914.

6th BATTALION

THE CHESHIRE REGIMENT

AUGUST to DECEMBER 1914.

| Date Place and time | Summary of events and information | Remarks and reference to appendix. |
|---|---|---|
| STOCKPORT 4. Aug. 1914 | The Battalion mobilized | APP. 1. Notes on Mob<sup>n</sup>. " II |
| 5 " " | Remained at STOCKPORT | |
| 6 " " | " " | |
| 7 " " | " " | |
| 8 " " | " " | |
| 9 " " | The Battalion proceeded to SHREWSBURY | |
| SHREWSBURY 10 Aug 1914 | Remained in billets at SHREWSBURY and commenced training | |
| 11 " " | " " | |
| 12 " " | " " | |
| 13 " " | " " | |
| 14 " " | " " | |
| 15 " " | " " | |
| 16 " " | " " | |
| 17 " " | " " | |
| 18 " " | " " | |
| 19 " " | " " | |
| 20 " " | " " | |
| 21 " " | " " | |
| 22 " " | Went into camp at CHURCH STRETTON | |
| 23 " " | Continued training | |
| 24 " " | " " | |
| 25 " " | " " | |
| 26 " " | " " | |
| 27 " " | " " | |
| 29 " " | " " | |
| 30 " " | " " | |
| 31 " " | Moved to NORTHAMPTON | |

| Date, Place and time. | Summary of events and information. | Remarks and reference to appendix |
|---|---|---|

NORTHAMPTON

Sept 1.1914 Battalion remained in billets
" 2 at NORTHAMPTON and
" 3 continued training
" 4 " "
" 5 " "
" 6 " "
" 7 " "
" 8 " "
" 9 " "
" 10 " "
" 11 " "
" 12 " "
" 13 " "
" 14 " "
" 15 " "
" 16 " "
" 17 " "
" 18 " "
" 19 " "
" 20 " "
" 21 " "
" 22 " "
" 23 " "
" 24 " "
" 25 " "
" 26 " "
" 27 " "
" 28 " "
" 29 30 " "

| Date, place and time. | Summary of events and information. | Remarks and reference to appendix |
|---|---|---|
| NORTHAMPTON | | |
| Oct 1. 1914 | | |
| " 2 | | |
| " 3 | | |
| " 4 | | |
| " 5 | | |
| " 6 | | |
| " 7 | | |
| " 8 | | |
| " 9 | | |
| " 10 | Moved to billets at GREAT BRINTON | |
| GREAT BRINTON | | |
| Oct 11 | | |
| " 12 | | |
| " 13 | | |
| " 14 | | |
| " 15 | | |
| " 16 | | |
| " 17 | | |
| " 18 | | |
| " 19 | | |
| " 20 | | |
| " 21 | | |
| " 22 | | |
| " 23 | | |
| " 24 | | |
| " 25 | Moved into billets at STONHAM ASPALL | |
| STONHAM ASPALL " 26 | | |
| " 27 | | |
| " 28 | | |
| " 29 | | |
| " 30 | Returned to billets at NORTHAMPTON | |
| NORTHAMPTON " 31 | | |

| Date, place and time. | Summary of events and information. | Remarks and reference to appendix |
|---|---|---|
| NORTHAMPTON NOV. 1. 1914 | Battalion continued training | |
| " 2 | | |
| " 3 | | |
| " 4 | | |
| " 5 | | |
| " 6 | | |
| " 7 | | |
| " 8 | | |
| " 9 | Proceeded to FRANCE to join Expeditionary Force Strength 26 Officers 1.W.O & 793 other ranks | APP III |
| HAVRE Nov 10. | Landed at HAVRE and remained at rest camp. | |
| " 11 | | |
| " 12 | | |
| " 13 | | |
| " 14 | arrived ST. OMER by rail and occupied barracks | |
| ST OMER " 15 | | |
| " 16 | | |
| " 17 | A detachment from the Battalion under Major ROSTRON attended Funeral procession of the late Earl ROBERTS. The remainder of the Batt: lined the streets | |
| " 18 | | |
| " 19 | | |
| " 20 | B: moved to new billets at HELFAUT and BILQUES South of ST OMER | |
| HELFAUT Nov. 21 | The Battalion continued training | |
| " 22 | " " " | |
| " 23 | " " " | |
| " 24 | " " " | |
| " 25 | " " " | |
| " 26 | " " " | |
| " 27 | " " " | |
| " 28 | " " " | |
| " 29 | " " " | |
| " 30 | " " " | MC |

| Date, Place and time | Summary of events and information | Remarks and reference to appendix. |
|---|---|---|
| HELFAUT Dec 1. 1914 | The Battalion continued training | WK |
| " 2 " | " " " " | WK |
| " 3 " | " " " " | WK |
| " 4 " | " " " " | WK |
| " 5 " | " " " " | WK |
| " 6 " | " " " " | WK |
| " 7 " | " " " " | WK |
| " 8 " | " " " " | WK |
| " 9 " | The Batt⁰ marched to HAZEBROUCK and billetted there one night | |
| HAZEBROUCK Dec 10 1914 | marched to BAILLEUL and billetted there one night | WK |
| BAILLEUL Dec 11 1914 | marched to X roads 2¼ miles S.W. of NEUVE EGLISE B,H,C, & G Companies (Nos. 2 & 4 double Companies) occupied the trenches near WULVERGHEM same night in support of the XIV Inf⁺ Brigade. Strength 350 all ranks. B & H Companies with 1/MANCHESTERS., C & G Companies with 1/D.C.L.I. These Companies were in the trenches for 48 | Strength 27 Officers 1 W.O. 759 others 6/22 |
| NEUVE EGLISE | | |
| Dec 12 " | hours. Casualties 1 man wounded. | WK |
| " 13 " | Nos 1 & 3 Double Companies A,E,D,F. relieved the other ½ Battalion at nightfall and remained in the trenches for 72 hours. Casualties 13th 1. Killed 1 wounded | WK |

| Date, place and time. | Summary of events and information. | Remarks and reference to appendix |
|---|---|---|

NEUVE EGLISE
Dec 14 1914

A E D & F Coys 34T. all ranks remained up in trenches for 72 hours

" 15 "

" 16 "  Casualties 2 wounded (afterwards died)
2 wounded

The Batt: was reorganized on the 4 Company system as follows

A / E } No 1. became A. Co
B / H } No 2     "    B Co
C / G } No 4     "    C Co
D / F } No 3     "    D Co

Company Officers as follows

A Co. Capt. F LEAH (A)  Capt. T. GIBBONS (E)
      Lt. C. NORMAN (A)  Lt. G E HOWARTH (E)

B Co. Capt. KIRK (B)  Lt. J.E. Johnston (H)
      Lt. R NORMAN (B)  Lt. S.A. ALEXANDER (B)
      Lt. H.B BURGESS (H)

C Co. Capt. W.D DODGE (G)  Capt. H COOKE (G)
      2Lieut J.C. HOYLE (C)  Lt. W.R INNES (G)
      2Lieut C.E. BROCKBANK (C)

D Co. Capt A.W. SMITH (D)  Capt C.F WHITE (F)
      2Lt W.L. READ (F)  Lt. R.R. COOKE (D)

| Date, Place and Time. | Summary of Events and Information. | Remarks and reference to appendix |
|---|---|---|
| NEUVE EGLISE | | |
| Dec 16 1914 | A & D. Companies returned to billets from the trenches | nil |
| " 17 " | The Battalion was attached to the XV Inf. Brigade. | nil |
| " 18 " | The Battalion moved into new billets in the town of NEUVE EGLISE. Lt.Col. HEYWOOD was admitted to hospital. The Battalion for trench duties was split up as follows. A & D. Coys under orders of O.C 1/DORSETS, B Coy under 1/BEDFORDS  C. Coy under 1/NORFOLKS | 6/22 nil |
| " 19. | The Battalion continued from 18th at duty in the trenches by alternate platoons, ½ Companies, or Companies | nil |
| " 20. | Casualties  2 Killed | nil |
| " 21. | | |
| " 22 | | |
| " 23 | | |
| " 24 | Casualties 2 Killed | nil |
| " 25 | "  1 wounded | nil |

| Date, Place and Time. | Summary of Events and Information. | Remarks and reference to appendix |
|---|---|---|
| NEUVE EGLISE Dec 26. 1914 | Casualties 3 wounded<br>1 (RAMC attached) wounded | |
| Dec 27 " | | |
| " 28 " | | |
| " 29 " BAILLEUL | The Battalion moved into new billets 1 mile E of BAILLEUL for a period of rest. [The parties in the trenches were relieved that night and arrived at new billets early next morning]<br><br>During the period in the trenches and subsequently during the rest period all men were inoculated against enteric fever who had not previously been done.<br><br>During the period 11th to 29th Dec. over 120 men were admitted to hospital mainly frostbite and rheumatism | |
| Dec 30 | | Strength Officers 26 |
| " 31 | | W.O 1 Other ranks 638 |

# APPENDIX I

Notes on Mobilization, Organization, Education
Training, equipment &c.

Mobilization proceeded smoothly according to the programme. Pay books and identity discs should be kept up to date. The name of a clerk should be registered for use on mobilization, and he should be partially trained in Military work.

The transport was a weak point, the civilian transport was generally unsuitable. No remedy can be suggested for this except the provision of Military Transport.

Much might have been done in the time available for training had not the Battalion been frequently moved from place to place. As it was the training was thrown back several months.

Had the Battalion been encamped instead of being in billets, it would have been much better in the interests of training and discipline & would have inured the men to service conditions. Much useful elementary knowledge can only be taught in barracks.

The practice of cleaning rifles and equipment has not hitherto been a sufficiently important part of the training. It should be the duty of every man to keep his own rifle and bayonet clean.

The number of compulsory drills has not been sufficient. Week end camps should be more frequent and compulsory.

The equipment was very old. It was replaced

APP I 2

only five days before leaving ENGLAND. The men did not know the rifle, the pull off of which was different. The rifles being new required use, practice with dummy cartridge and many minor adjustments before they could be considered thoroughly serviceable.

The first issue of boots was very bad. It appears essential that boots should be kept as an article of Mobilization stores, and the turn over arranged for at the Annual training.

A far greater percentage of Regular establishment is badly needed to ensure the smooth working of discipline & interior economy. The fact that all ranks are drawn from the same district militates against perfect discipline.

The men were mainly young, and many were of only moderate physique. A far stricter Medical Examination would have been advisable.

The methods under which National Reservists were enrolled appear to be in need of revision.

The unequal treatment (financially) of men who rejoined the Colours caused much dissatisfaction.

APP II

## LIST OF OFFICERS -
### 6th. CHESHIRE REGIMENT.

---

Lieut Colonel G B Heywood

Major H Hesse
" R Rostron

Capt. F A Leah
" W D Dodge
" R Kirk
" J M Diggles — Adjutant till Nov. 29
" H Cooke
" A W Smith
" T Gibbons
" C F White

Lieut J C Hoyle
" G E Haworth
" F White — Maxim Gun
" W R Innes
" J E Johnston
" E E Spence — Transport Officer
" R Norman — Scout Officer
" C Norman

2nd Lt. W L Read
" S A Alexander
" H B Burgess
" R R Cooke
" C B Brockbank

Capt & Adjutant M F Clarke — Joined Nov 30 1914
Major & Qm. J Rawlinson
Lieut J. Morris, R.A.M.C.

---

15th Bde.
5th Div.

# 6th CHESHIRES

## JANUARY

## 1915

25th Bde.
5th Div.

1st ROYAL WEST KENT

........................

1 9 1 5

13th Bde.
5th Div.

1st ROYAL WEST KENT

........................

1915

# WAR DIARY or INTELLIGENCE SUMMARY

Army Form C. 2118.

*(Erase heading not required.)*

Instructions regarding War Diaries and Intelligence Summaries are contained in F. S. Regs., Part II. and the Staff Manual respectively. Title pages will be prepared in manuscript.

| Hour, Date, Place | Summary of Events and Information | Remarks and references to Appendices |
|---|---|---|
| BAILLEUL Jan 1. 1915 | The Battalion remained in billets 1 mile W. of BAILLEUL and were exercised in drill, physical training and marching | WK |
| " Jan 2 " | " | WK |
| " Jan 3 " | " | WK |
| " Jan 4 " | The Battalion moved into new billets [at RAVELSBERG] E. of BAILLEUL | WK |
| RAVELSBERG Jan 5 " | Whole four Companies were employed in fatigue at the trenches viz digging redoubts & trenches by night, and carrying tools, parcours, wire &c &c to the trenches. This work necessitated a 6½ mile march every other night for the fatigue parties in so far as to the bivouac at which the stores were collected, thereafter a fatigue of from 3 to 6 hours duration followed by a 6½ mile march home. | WK |
| " 6 " | " | WK |
| " 7 " | " | WK |
| " 8 " | " | WK |
| " 9 " | " | WK |
| " 10 " | The general health of the Battalion improved. When off duty all men were encouraged to play football and watches between different Companies were arranged. Drill & physical exercise were practised as time permitted. | WK |

1247 W 8299 200,000 (E) 8/14 J.B.C. & A. Forms/C. 2118/11.

# WAR DIARY or INTELLIGENCE SUMMARY

*(Erase heading not required.)*

Army Form C. 2118.

| Hour, Date, Place | | Summary of Events and Information | Remarks and references to Appendices |
|---|---|---|---|
| RAVETSBERG | Jan 11. 1915 | 14 men were returned to the base as unfit for service either at the front or on the lines of communication | — |
| " | Jan 12 " | | — |
| " | Jan 13 " | | — |
| " | Jan 14 " | | — |
| " | Jan 15 " | | — |
| " | Jan 16 " | The Battalion moved into new billets near ST JANS CAPPEL for a rest period | Strength of Bn 26 officers n.c. and men |
| ST JAN'S CAPPELL | Jan 17 " | " | — |
| | Jan 18 " | " | — |
| | Jan 19 " | " | — |
| | Jan 20 " | " | — |
| | Jan 21 " | " | — |
| | Jan 22 " | " | — |
| | Jan 23 " | " | — |
| | Jan 24 " | The Battalion moved into new billets between DRANOUTRE | — |

# WAR DIARY
## or
## INTELLIGENCE SUMMARY.

Army Form C. 2118.

(Erase heading not required.)

| Hour, Date, Place | Summary of Events and Information | Remarks and references to Appendices |
|---|---|---|
| Jan 24 | and RAVELSBERG, 2 Companies under Major HESSE (A & C) marched straight to the trenches, the remainder of the Battalion with transport marched to their billet under Major ROSTRON. [Both parties marched past the Coy Commander 83 Coy J.C. FERGUSON outside BAILLEUL.] | w/e |
| DRANOUTRE Jan 25 | The Companies in the trenches remained there until the evening of the 28th when they were relieved by the other two Companies B & D. A Co. and part of C. were in the fire trenches for the first 48 hours, the remainder of C Co. were in support. The men in the fire trenches were then relieved by those in support. | |
| Jan 26 | Casualties A Co. 2 men wounded C Co. 1 Sergt & 1 man wounded | w/e |
| " | A Co. | w/e |
| Jan 27 | 1 Sergt killed 1 man wounded | w/e |

**Army Form C. 2118.**

# WAR DIARY
## or
## INTELLIGENCE SUMMARY.
*(Erase heading not required.)*

Instructions regarding War Diaries and Intelligence Summaries are contained in F.S. Regs., Part II. and the Staff Manual respectively. Title pages will be prepared in manuscript.

| Hour, Date, Place | | Summary of Events and Information | Remarks and references to Appendices |
|---|---|---|---|
| DRANOUTRE | Jan 28 | A.C. Companies were relieved in the trenches by B & D, and marched into billets vacated by the two latter Companies. The weather during the period 24 to 28 Jan. was on the whole good. There was little or no rain, and some frost. The ground was however saturated with water, but the trenches occupied were comparatively dry. The health of the men was excellent. During the nights, they were employed in improving the parapets & bayonets and refilling the trenches. | |
| DRANOUTRE | Jan 29 | Casualties 1 N.C.O. wounded. 4 Officers and 243 N.C.O. & men arrived from the Reserve Battalion | W.E. K.11 W.S. Roll of Battle Casualties to 31st Jan. APP. 4. M. Record of Distinguished Conduct APP. 5. |
| DRANOUTRE | Jan 30 | The weather continued good, the health of the men in the trenches was good, a considerable amount of work was done at night in improving the trenches | |
| " | Jan 31 | & putting up wire entanglements | W.P. Strength of Bn on 31st Jan. included all ranks 30 Officers 826 other ranks |

ROLL of BATTLE CASUALTIES

of

The 6th. Battn CHESHIRE REGIMENT.

From Nov. 10th. 1014 to January 31st. 1915.

AT WULVERGHEM.

| Date G | No | Rank | Name | Casualty | | |
|---|---|---|---|---|---|---|
| Dec 12 | 1797 | Pte | J Espley | Wounded | (Shrapnel) | |
| " | 1091 | " | W Murray | " | " | |
| " | 1524 | " | W Williamson | Killed | (Gunshot) | |
| " 16 | 1708 | " | J Clarke | Wounded | (Shrapnel) | Died of wounds |
| " | 2055 | " | R Bradbury | " | | |
| " | 2232 | " | J Ward | " | (Gunshot) | |
| " 20 | 1626 | " | B Turner | Killed | " | |
| " 21 | 1637 | " | J Price | " | " | |
| " 24 | 2150 | " | H Roberts | " | (Shrapnel) | |
| " | 1436 | " | J Carruthers | " | " | |
| " | 1562 | " | W Platt | Wounded | " | Died of wounds |
| " 25 | 1693 | LcCpl | E Bryan | " | " | |
| " 26 | 1722 | Pte | J Evans | " | " | |
| " | 153- | " | T Walker, RAMC | " | " | |
| " | 130 | Sgt | J Knowles | " | " | |
| Dec 26 | 1388 | Pte | T Croft | " | " | Died of wounds |
| " 23 | 1574 | " | S Hughes | " | " | Slight |
| Jan 25 | 1491 | " | A Asquith | " | " | Died of wounds |
| " | 1154 | " | F Stubbs | " | " | |
| " | 2117 | Sgt | J Goddard | " | " | Died of wounds |
| " | 1753 | Pte | F Booth | " | Gunshot. | |
| " 26 | 1405 | Sgt | W West | Killed | " | |
| " | 1833 | Pte | W Wilson | Wounded | Shapnel | |
| " | 1500 | " | W H Lodge | " | " | Slight. |
| " 29 | 2323 | " | J Brown | " | " | |
| " | 2030 | C.S.M | H Brand | " | Gunshot | |

APP. 5.

## 6th. CHESHIRE REGIMENT.

Record of GALLANTRY or DISTINGUISHED CONDUCT.

| No. Rank and Name | Action | Witnesses |
|---|---|---|
| No. 1554 LcCpl J Cropper | AT WULVERGHEM<br>At dawn on the 20th Dec. 1914 two messengers arrived at the fire trench in which Capt. Martin Leake was - one from O.C. 1st Dorsets: the other, LcCpl Cropper, 6th. Cheshire Regt., from the fire trench on his right. After delivering their messages they left together. They had not gone far when the Dorset messenger was hit and fell helpless with a broken thigh. They were then about six yards from the end of the trench and the fire from the German trench was fairly heavy. LcCpl Cropper, lying flat on the ground, managed to push and roll the wounded man to the end of the trench where both were pulled under cover. The breast pocket of LcCpl Cropper's coat was cut by a bullet. | Capt. W. Martin Leake 1st. Cheshire Regt. |
| No. 1247 Pte Boardman<br><br>No. 1295 Pte J Bennett | AT WULVERGHEM<br>About 9am on the 25th. Jany. 1915 were employed as stretcher bearers with "A" Coy in No. 9 trench, when word came from another trench about 60 yards away that a man (Sgt Goddard) was hit. They ran across the open ground between the two trenches under fire and attended to the case, and returned to their own trench on completion.<br>About an hour later word came from another trench (No. 10) about 100 yards away from their position that two men had been badly wounded. They crossed over a road under fire, having to get through a barbed wire fence. They attended to the two men there and remained there till later on, when, towards evening, while still light, they went back to bring stretchers for the wounded, who were urgent cases. | No. 648 Sgt A. Nield<br><br>Capt. T Gibbons. |

APP. 5.

15th Bde.
6th Div.

Became G.H.Q. Troops March 1st.

6th CHESHIRES.

FEBRUARY
........................

1918

WAR DIARY
or
INTELLIGENCE SUMMARY.

(Erase heading not required.)

Army Form C. 2118.

6/22

| Hour, Date, Place | Summary of Events and Information | Remarks and references to Appendices |
|---|---|---|
| DRANOUTRE Feb. 1. | The Battalion moved up to new billets near ST. JANS CAPPEL. The Companies in the trenches were relieved by troops from the 13th Brigade and marched to the new billets late the same evening | Mr. Strength of Bn including attached 30 Officers 826 other ranks |
| ST. JANS CAPPEL Feb 2. | The Battalion remained in Divisional Reserve for 8 days | w/e |
| " Feb 3. | 29 men were sent to the base for service on the lines of Communication | w/e |
| " Feb 4. | 13 men were sent to the base as unfit for service at the front in any capacity | w/e |
| " Feb 5. | — | w/e |
| " Feb 6. | — | w/e |
| " Feb 7. | — | w/e |
| " Feb 8. | The Batt: with the remainder of the Brigade was inspected by HM the King of the Belgians outside BAILLEUL | w/e |
| " Feb 9. | The Batt: less D.Coy returned to the trenches at WULVERGHEM | w/e |

# WAR DIARY
## or
## INTELLIGENCE SUMMARY.
(Erase heading not required.)

Army Form C. 2118.

| Hour, Date, Place | | Summary of Events and Information | Remarks and references to Appendices |
|---|---|---|---|
| DRANOUTRE | Feb 10 | D. Company went to billets at DRANOUTRE | we |
| " | Feb 11. | 1 wounded | in |
| " | Feb 12. | C. Company went to the trenches relieving B. Co. 1 Killed. 1 wounded (slight) | un |
| " | Feb 13 | B. Company returned to the trenches A Co. went into billet | un |
| " | Feb 14 | 1 wounded  we | we |
| " | Feb 15 | A. Co reinforced the Companies in the trenches and the whole Battalion remained there until the 18th. 1 wounded | up |
| " | Feb 16 | 4 wounded | we |
| " | Feb 17. | | wh |

# WAR DIARY or INTELLIGENCE SUMMARY.

Army Form C. 2118.

(*Erase heading not required.*)

| Hour, Date, Place | Summary of Events and Information | Remarks and references to Appendices |
|---|---|---|
| DRANOUTRE Feb. 18. | Batt: returned to billets at DRANOUTRE | WE |
| " 19 | | we |
| " 20 | | we |
| " 21 | | we |
| " 22 | | we |
| " 23 | Reinforcements coming up of 126 N.C.Os and men arrived. | we 1/2 |
| " 24. | The Batt: including last reinforcements marched to the trenches at WULVERGHEM. Casualties 1 wounded 1 slightly wounded | we |
| " 25 | " 1 wounded | we |
| " 26 | 1 Killed 3 wounded, 2 missing (believed wounded) | we |
| " 27 | 1 Killed 3 wounded The Batt: returned to billets | we |
| " 28. | | we Strength of Bn. including attached officers 30 officers 854 Other ranks. |

RECORD OF GALLANTRY OR DISTINGUISHED CONDUCT.

| Name | Action | Witnesses. |
|---|---|---|
| No 1517 Private G Wood. | Near WULVERGHEM on the 27th February 1915, when the Battalion was holding the Fire trenches, Coy Sergt Major Long of the 6th Cheshire Regiment was wounded behind the trenches, Private Wood, one of the Stretcher Bearers, got out of his trench to attend to him and brought him into the trench under a heavy rifle fire directed on him. The equipment was hit in two places while doing this. He had to about 30 yards under fire. | Captain H Cooke Fire 6th Battn Cheshire Regt. |
| No 1073 Private T Mather. | Near WULVERGHEM on the 27th Feby.1915. when the Battalion was holding the fire trenches, Coy Sergt Major Long of the 6th Cheshire Regiment was wounded behind the trenches, Private Mather got out of his trench and ran to him to render first aid under heavy fire. He was shot in the head whilst doing so and was killed. | Capt. H Cooke 6th Battn Cheshire Regt. |

## BATTLE CASUALTIES.

Feby 1015.

| | | | | |
|---|---|---|---|---|
| 1618 | Pte T Mather | Gunshot | 10.2.15. | WOUNDED. |
| 1592 | " H Smith | " | 11.2.15. | Killed. |
| 1443 | Cpl H Reid | " | 12.2.15 | Slightly wounded. not detained. |
| 1760 | Pte G Hobson. | " | 15.2.15. | WOUNDED. |
| 1330 | " W Delaney | Shrapnel | 16.2.15. | Wounded. |
| 1547 | " W Taylor | " | " | " |
| 1465 | " A Johnson | " | " | " |
| 1553 | " J Unsworth | Gunshot | " | " |
| 1300 | Dmr H Harrop | " | 24.2.15. | " |
| 1505 | Pte Beech | " | " | Slightly wounded not detained. |
| 1211 | Pte A Taylor | " | 25.2.15. | Wounded |
| 987 | Pte W Eaton | " | 26.2.15 | Killed. |
| 1103 | Cpl H Hague | " | " | Wounded. |
| 1540 | Pte T Bolton | " | " | " |
| 2382 | " H Lancashire | " | " | " |
| 1858 | " W Miekle | " | " | Missing |
| 1406 | " W Houlton | " | " | " |
| 1073 | " T Mather | " | 27.2.15 | Killed. |
| 1495 | Lce Cpl G Taylor | " | " | Wounded |
| 2333 | Pte Austin | " | " | " |
| 177 | C.S.M.T Long | " | " | " |

C O P Y.
-------

C.R.No.2663, d/- 25-2-15.
A/0657.

Copy of Telegram.

From:- G.H.Q.   To:- Second Army.

O.A.H.642,   23rd February 1915.

With reference to O.A.H.637 dated 21st February, 6th Cheshire Regt. will move to G.H.Q. at end of this week, inform G.O.C., G.H.Q. Troops date of arrival. This Battn. will relieve 2nd Royal Irish which has been allotted to 12th Infantry Brigade. As 2nd Royal Irish has been much broken up on detached duties whilst here G.O.C., G.H.Q. Troops recommends that they should undergo one week's Battalion training before joining its Bde. Any objections to this training taking place here.

(Sgd.) R.Hutchinson, Major, G.S

--------------

D.A.G.,
   Base.

   For information.

(Sgd.) J.L.Learmonth, Major.
D.A.A.G. for A.G.
G.H.Q.   British Army in the Field.
23-2-15.

---

Commandant,
   Havre.

   For your information.

Lieut-Colonel.
D.A.A.G.
Base,   for D.A.G.G.H.Q., 3rd Echelon.
27-2-15.

5 DIV
15 Bde
6 CHESHIRE

1915 MARCH — 1915 DEC

Box 2403

1343

1247

L of C

105 (Beds & Essex Yeomanry)

Battalion
M.G. Corps

191    to    191

BRIT
B1

CONFIDENTIAL.

WAR DIARY.

of

6th Battalion THE CHESHIRE REGT.

*Army Troops*

from 1st March 1915.   to   31st March 1915.

Vol IV   nil

Army Form C. 2118.

# WAR DIARY
## or
## INTELLIGENCE SUMMARY.
*(Erase heading not required.)*

Instructions regarding War Diaries and Intelligence Summaries are contained in F.S. Regs., Part II. and the Staff Manual respectively. Title pages will be prepared in manuscript.

| Hour, Date, Place | Summary of Events and Information | Remarks and references to Appendices |
|---|---|---|
| PRANOUTRE March 1st | The Battn moved by motor bus to ST. OMIER where they took over the Infantry barracks from the Royal Irish Regiment | Strength of Battn including attached 30 Officers 822 other ranks. |
| ST OMIER March 2nd | The Battn took over the duties of guards &c at ST OMIER. | up |
| March 3rd | — | up |
| March 4th | A guard of honour of 50 men under Capt. LEAH and Lieut HOYLE was furnished for a representative of the French Republic. (General DE LA CROIX) | up |
| March 5th | — | up |
| March 6th | — | up |
| March 7th | — | up |
| March 8th | Pt. E.E. SPENCE was admitted to hospital. | up |
| March 9th | — | up |

Army Form C. 2118.

# WAR DIARY
## *or*
## INTELLIGENCE SUMMARY.
*(Erase heading not required.)*

Instructions regarding War Diaries and Intelligence Summaries are contained in F. S. Regs., Part II. and the Staff Manual respectively. Title pages will be prepared in manuscript.

| Hour, Date, Place | Summary of Events and Information | Remarks and references to Appendices |
|---|---|---|
| STOMER March 10 | | |
| " 11 | | |
| " 12 | | |
| " 13 | | |
| " 14 | | |
| " 15 | | |
| " 16 | | |
| " 17 | | |
| " 18 | | |
| " 19 | | |
| " 20 | | |
| " 21 | | |
| " 22 | | |
| " 23 | | |
| " 24 | | |

Army Form C. 2118.

# WAR DIARY
## or
## INTELLIGENCE SUMMARY.
*(Erase heading not required.)*

Instructions regarding War Diaries and Intelligence Summaries are contained in F.S. Regs., Part II. and the Staff Manual respectively. Title pages will be prepared in manuscript.

| Hour, Date, Place | Summary of Events and Information | Remarks and references to Appendices |
|---|---|---|
| ST. OMER March 25 | | " |
| " 26 | | " |
| " 27 | | " |
| " 28 | | " |
| " 29 | | " |
| " 30 | | " |
| " 31 | | Strength of Batt. infantry included. 28 officers 825 attached. Major & QM. J RAWLINSON absent (sick from Feb 11.15) |

121/5108

## CONFIDENTIAL

# WAR DIARY.

of.

## 6ᵀᴴ Battⁿ Cheshire Regᵗ

from April 1ˢᵗ to April 30ᵀᴴ 1915.

L. of C.

(Volume V).

Army Form C. 2118.

# WAR DIARY
## or
## INTELLIGENCE SUMMARY.
*(Erase heading not required.)*

Instructions regarding War Diaries and Intelligence Summaries are contained in F. S. Regs., Part II. and the Staff Manual respectively. Title pages will be prepared in manuscript.

| Hour, Date, Place | | Summary of Events and Information | Remarks and references to Appendices |
|---|---|---|---|
| 1915. APRIL | 1 ST OMER | Battalion left "C" ST OMER for L. of C. Headquarters + "B" Co proceeded by rail to HAVRE, "A" Co. to ROUEN, Right half "D" Co to DIEPPE, left half Co to ABBEVILLE. | Strength of Battⁿ = 28 Officers 822 Other ranks |
| " | 2 " | — | — |
| " | 3 HAVRE | Headquarters + "B" Co arrived at HAVRE "C" Co left ST OMER for BOULOGNE | Strength 4 Officers 386 other ranks |
| " | 4 " | | " " |
| " | 5 " | | " " |
| " | 6 " | | " " |
| " | 7 " | | " " |
| " | 8 " | Draft of 59 NCOs + men arrived at HAVRE 1 NCO + 19 of draft sent to ABBEVILLE | " " |
| " | 9 " | | " " |
| " | 10 " | 1 " +18 " " DIEPPE. | " " |
| " | 11 " | | " " |
| " | 12 " | | " " |
| " | 13 " | | " " |
| " | 14 " | | " " |

Army Form C. 2118.

# WAR DIARY
## or
## INTELLIGENCE SUMMARY.
*(Erase heading not required.)*

Instructions regarding War Diaries and Intelligence Summaries are contained in F.S. Regs., Part II. and the Staff Manual respectively. Title pages will be prepared in manuscript.

| Hour, Date, Place | Summary of Events and Information | Remarks and references to Appendices |
|---|---|---|
| 1915. | | |
| APRIL 15th HAVRE | — | nil |
| 16 " | — | nil |
| 17 " | — | nil |
| 18 " | — | nil |
| 19 " | — | nil |
| 20 " | — | nil |
| 21 " | — | nil |
| 22 " | — | nil |
| 23 " | — | nil |
| 24 " | — | nil |
| 25 " | — | nil |
| 26 " | — | nil |
| 27 " | — | nil |
| 28 " | 12 men discharged from hospital arrived at HAVRE | nil |
| 29 " | — | nil |
| 30 " | — | Strength 26 officers 857 other ranks. Strength at H.Q. HAVRE 4 officers 312 other ranks |

L of C 121/5614

~~5th Division~~

## — CONFIDENTIAL — 6/22

## WAR DIARY

of

## 6ᵀᴴ Battⁿ Cheshire Regᵗ

## from May 1ˢᵗ to May 31ˢᵗ 1915.

## — (Volume VI). —

Army Form C. 2118.

# WAR DIARY
## or
## INTELLIGENCE SUMMARY.
(Erase heading not required.)

Instructions regarding War Diaries and Intelligence Summaries are contained in F. S. Regs., Part II. and the Staff Manual respectively. Title pages will be prepared in manuscript.

| Hour, Date, Place | Summary of Events and Information | Remarks and references to Appendices |
|---|---|---|
| May 1st HAVRE | — | Strength of 48 — 26 officers 862 other ranks |
| May 2nd HAVRE | — | Strength of H.Q. HAVRE 14 officers 313 other ranks Bris |
| May 3rd HAVRE | — | ”””” |
| May 4th HAVRE | — | ”””” |
| May 5th HAVRE | — | ”””” |
| May 6th HAVRE | — | ”””” |
| May 7th HAVRE | — | ”””” |
| May 8th HAVRE | — | ”””” |
| May 9th HAVRE | — | ”””” |
| May 10th HAVRE | — | ”””” |
| May 11th HAVRE | — | ”””” |
| May 12th HAVRE | — | ”””” |
| May 13th HAVRE | — | ”””” |
| May 14th HAVRE | — | ”””” |
| May 15th HAVRE | — | ”””” |
| May 16th HAVRE | — | ”””” |
| May 17th HAVRE | — | ”””” |

Army Form C. 2118.

# WAR DIARY
## or
## INTELLIGENCE SUMMARY

*(Erase heading not required.)*

Instructions regarding War Diaries and Intelligence Summaries are contained in F. S. Regs., Part II. and the Staff Manual respectively. Title pages will be prepared in manuscript.

| Hour, Date, Place | | Summary of Events and Information | Remarks and references to Appendices |
|---|---|---|---|
| May 18th | HAVRE | | fine |
| May 19th | HAVRE | | fine |
| May 20th | HAVRE | | fine |
| May 21st | HAVRE | | fine |
| May 22nd | HAVRE | | fine |
| May 23rd | HAVRE | | fine |
| May 24th | HAVRE | | fine |
| May 25th | HAVRE | | fine |
| May 26th | HAVRE | | fine |
| May 27th | HAVRE | | fine |
| May 28th | HAVRE | | fine |
| May 29th | HAVRE | | fine |
| May 30th | HAVRE | | fine |
| May 31st | HAVRE | | fine |

Strength of the Battn.
2nd Officers 854 O.R.
Strength at HAVRE
1 Officers 309 O.R.

*L of C*

121/5931

## CONFIDENTIAL

## WAR DIARY

of

6th Battn Cheshire Regt

from June 1st to June 1915.

(Volume VII)

Army Form C. 2118.

# WAR DIARY
## or
## INTELLIGENCE SUMMARY

*(Erase heading not required.)*

Instructions regarding War Diaries and Intelligence Summaries are contained in F. S. Regs., Part II. and the Staff Manual respectively. Title pages will be prepared in manuscript.

| Hour, Date, Place | Summary of Events and Information | Remarks and references to Appendices |
|---|---|---|
| June 1st 1915 HAVRE | | Strength of Bn. 24 officers 854 other ranks. Strength of H.Q. at HAVRE 14 officers 309 other ranks |
| June 2nd 1915 HAVRE | | ,, |
| June 3rd " | | ,, |
| June 4th " | | ,, |
| June 5th " | | ,, |
| June 6th " | | ,, |
| June 7th " | | ,, |
| June 8th " | | ,, |
| June 9th " | | ,, |
| June 10th " | Draft of 1 NCO + 17 O.R. arrived from England + 9 men discharged from hospitals | ,, |
| June 11th " | | ,, |
| June 12th " | | ,, |
| June 13th " | | ,, |
| June 14th " | | ,, |
| June 15th " | | ,, |
| June 16th " | | ,, |
| June 17th " | | ,, |
| June 18th " | | ,, |
| June 19th " | | ,, |
| June 20th " | | ,, |
| June 21st " | | ,, |

Army Form C. 2118.

# WAR DIARY
*or*
# INTELLIGENCE SUMMARY
*(Erase heading not required.)*

Instructions regarding War Diaries and Intelligence Summaries are contained in F. S. Regs., Part II. and the Staff Manual respectively. Title pages will be prepared in manuscript.

| Hour, Date, Place | Summary of Events and Information | Remarks and references to Appendices |
|---|---|---|
| June 22nd HAVRE | | contd |
| " 23rd " | | contd |
| " 24th " | | contd |
| " 25th " | | contd |
| " 26th " | | contd |
| " 27th " | | contd |
| " 28th " | | contd |
| " 29th " | | contd. Strength of Battn. 26 officers 866 O.R. Strength at I.B. 14 officers 373 O.R. contd |
| " 30th " | | |

5th Division  L of C.

B.S. Hahrels

121/6243

6/22

— CONFIDENTIAL —

— WAR DIARY —

— of —

— 6ᵀᴴ Battⁿ The Cheshire Regᵗ —

— from July 1ˢᵗ 1915 to July 31ˢᵗ 1915 —

— (Volume VIII) —

Army Form C. 2118.

# WAR DIARY
## or
## INTELLIGENCE SUMMARY.
*(Erase heading not required.)*

Instructions regarding War Diaries and Intelligence Summaries are contained in F.S. Regs., Part II. and the Staff Manual respectively. Title pages will be prepared in manuscript.

| Hour, Date, Place | Summary of Events and Information | Remarks and references to Appendices |
|---|---|---|
| July 1st 1915. HAVRE | Draft consisting of 94 other ranks arrived from England from 2/6th Battn. | Strength of Battn 26 Officers 994 O.R. |
| 2. " | Draft consisting of 35 other ranks from hospitals arrived from England elsewhere | And. |
| 3. " | | And. |
| 4. " | Sent away 31 other ranks to BOULOGNE & 36 other ranks to ROUEN | And. |
| 5. " | Sent away 27 other ranks to DIEPPE | And. |
| 6. " | — — — — | And. |
| 7. " | | And. |
| 8. " | | And. |
| 9. " | | And. |
| 10. " | | And. |
| 11. " | | And. |
| 12. " | | And. |
| 13. " | | And. |
| 14. " | | And. |
| 15. " | | And. |
| 16. " | | And. |
| 17. " | | And. |

Army Form C. 2118.

# WAR DIARY
## or
## INTELLIGENCE SUMMARY
*(Erase heading not required.)*

Instructions regarding War Diaries and Intelligence Summaries are contained in F. S. Regs, Part II. and the Staff Manual respectively. Title pages will be prepared in manuscript.

| Hour, Date, Place | Summary of Events and Information | Remarks and references to Appendices |
|---|---|---|
| July 18th 1915 HAVRE | 7 Officers (including one from sick leave) arrived from 2/6th Cheshire Regt from England | nil |
| 19th " | | nil |
| 20th " | | nil |
| 21st " | | nil |
| 22nd " | One officer sent to ROUEN | nil |
| 23rd " | 3 officers arrived from 3/6th Cheshire Regt England | nil |
| 24th " | | nil |
| 25th " | | nil |
| 26th " | One officer sent to DIEPPE | nil |
| 27th " | One officer sent to ROUEN, one to ABBEVILLE + one to BOULOGNE | nil |
| 28th " | | nil |
| 29th " | | nil |
| 30th " | | nil |
| 31st " | | nil |

Strength of Battalion
35 Officers 981 O.R.
Strength at H.Q. (Havre)
18 Officers 378 O.R.

- CONFIDENTIAL -

WAR     DIARY

of

6th. BATTALION THE CHESHIRE REGIMENT.
----------------------------------------

From 1st AUGUST 1915 to 31st AUGUST 1915.
-----------------------------------------

(VOLUME 9.)
-----------

Army Form C. 2118.

# WAR DIARY
or
## INTELLIGENCE SUMMARY

*(Erase heading not required.)*

Instructions regarding War Diaries and Intelligence Summaries are contained in F. S. Regs., Part II. and the Staff Manual respectively. Title pages will be prepared in manuscript.

| Hour, Date, Place | Summary of Events and Information | Remarks and references to Appendices |
|---|---|---|
| August 1st 1915 – HAVRE | | Strength of Batt" 36 offers 980 O.R |
| 2nd | 3 officers 79 O.R. sent to Abbeville — — — | at H.Q. 35 offers 980 O.R — 377 " |
| 3rd | " | ins. |
| 4th | One officer sent to Boulogne + one from ROUEN to DIEPPE — | ins. |
| 5th | " | ins. ins. |
| 6th | " | ins. |
| 7th | | ins. |
| 8th | | |
| 9th | | |
| 10th | | |
| 11th | | |
| 12th | | |
| 13th | | |
| 14th | | |
| 15th | | |
| 16th | | |
| 17th | | |
| 18th | | |
| 19th | | |
| 20th | | |
| 21st | | |
| 22nd | | |
| 23rd | | |
| 24th | | |
| 25th | | |
| 26th | | |
| 27th | | |
| 28th | | |
| 29th | | |
| 30th | | |

Strength of Batt" 36 offrs 980 O.R. at J.H.Q. 15 " 287 "
at 31.8.15.

- Confidential -

WAR DIARY

of

6th BATTALION THE CHESHIRE REGT.

From 1st SEPTEMBER 1915 to 30th SEPTEMBER 1915.

(VOLUME X

Army Form C. 2118.

# WAR DIARY
## or
## INTELLIGENCE SUMMARY
*(Erase heading not required.)*

Instructions regarding War Diaries and Intelligence Summaries are contained in F. S. Regs., Part II. and the Staff Manual respectively. Title pages will be prepared in manuscript.

| Hour, Date, Place | Summary of Events and Information | Remarks and references to Appendices |
|---|---|---|
| SEPTEMBER 1st 1915. HAVRE | | Strength of Batty 36 Offrs 980 O.R. |
| 2 " " | | " " H.Q. 15 " 287 " |
| 3 " " | | |
| 4 " " | | |
| 5 " " | | |
| 6 " " | | |
| 7 " " | | |
| 8 " " | | |
| 9 " " | | |
| 10 " " | | |
| 11 " " | | |
| 12 " " | | |
| 13 " " | | |
| 14 " " | | |
| 15 " " | | |
| 16 " " | | |
| 17 " " | | |
| 18 " " | | |
| 19 " " | | |
| 20 " " | | |
| 21 " " | | |
| 22 " " | | |
| 23 " " | | |
| 24 " " | | |
| 25 " " | | |
| 26 " " | | |
| 27 " " | | |
| 28 " " | | |
| 29 " " | | |
| 30 " " | | Strength of Batty 36 Offrs 977 O.R. |
| | | " " H.O. 15 " 285 O.R. |
| | | at 30.9.15 |

- CONFIDENTIAL -

WAR      DIARY

of

6th BATTALION THE CHESHIRE REGT.

From 1st OCTOBER to 31st OCTOBER 1915.

(VOLUME XI)

# WAR DIARY
or
## INTELLIGENCE SUMMARY

*(Erase heading not required.)*

Army Form C. 2118.

| Hour, Date, Place | Summary of Events and Information | Remarks and references to Appendices |
|---|---|---|
| OCTOBER 1st 1915. HAVRE | | N[?] Strength of B.M.? 36 Offrs 977 O.R. Jar/H.Q. 15 " 285 O.R |
| 2 " | | |
| 3 " | | |
| 4 " | | |
| 5 " | -15 O.R. left to join detachment at Abbeville | |
| 6 " | | |
| 7 " | | |
| 8 " | | |
| 9 " | | |
| 10 " | | |
| 11 " | | |
| 12 " | | |
| 13 " | | |
| 14 " | One Officer left to join Collection Guards | |
| 15 " | Two Officers left to join 1st Cheshire Rgt | |
| 16 " | | |
| 17 " | | |
| 18 " | | |
| 19 " | | |
| 20 " | | |
| 21 " | | |
| 22 " | | |
| 23 " | | |
| 24 " | | |
| 25 " | | |
| 26 " | | |
| 27 " | | |
| 28 " | | |
| 29 " | | |
| 30 " | | |
| 31 " | | Strength of B.A.? 33 Offrs 923 O.R. " /H.Q. 16 " 261 O.R. at 31.10.15. |

- OFFICIAL WAR DIARY -

of the

1/6th BATTALION THE CHESHIRE REGIMENT. (T)

From November 1st 1915

to November 30th 1915.

Army Form C. 2118.

# WAR DIARY
## or
## INTELLIGENCE SUMMARY.
*(Erase heading not required.)*

| Hour, Date, Place | Summary of Events and Information | Remarks and references to Appendices |
|---|---|---|
| NOVEMBER 1st, 1915, HAVRE. | | Strength of Batt? 33 Officers 983 O.R. |
| 2nd " | | " at H.Q. 14 " 261 O.R. |
| 3rd " | | |
| 4th " | | |
| 5th " | | |
| 6th " | | |
| 7th " | | |
| 8th " | | |
| 9th " | | |
| 10th " | | |
| 11th " | | |
| 12th " | | |
| 13th " | | |
| 14th " | | |
| 15th " | | |
| 16th " | | |
| 17th " | | |
| 18th " | | |
| 19th " | | |
| 20th " | | |
| 21st " | | |
| 22nd " | | |
| 23rd " | | |
| 24th " | | |
| 25th " | | |
| 26th " | | Strength of Batt? 33 Officers 968 O.R. |
| 27th " | | " at H.Q. 14 " 262 O.R. |
| 28th " | | at 30.11.15. |
| 29th " | | |
| 30th " | | |

Commandant,

Etaples.

---

The 1/6th Cheshire Regiment is about to be relieved on the Lines of Communication by the 1/6th Gordon Highlanders. As this latter Battalion is some 500 less in strength than the 1/6th Cheshire Regiment the following moves will be necessary:-

The 12th Battalion London Regiment will send 3 officers and 100 other ranks to Boulogne. *from Etaples*.

The 13th Battalion London Regiment will arrange to relieve the Railhead Detachments in the 1st Army area, now furnished by the 12th Battalion London Regiment. Total strength amounting to 4 officers and 99 other ranks, and this party will be sent to Boulogne.

Headquarters and One Company of 1/6th Gordons approximate strength 100 will proceed to Havre.

One Company of 1/6th Gordons approximate strength 100 will proceed to Rouen.

Two Companies of 1/6th Gordons approximate strength 200 will proceed to Abbeville. Of these companies a detachment of 50 will proceed to Dieppe.

The 12th Battalion London Regiment will send a detachment of 2 officers and 30 other ranks to Dieppe from Etaples.

Until the 1/6th Gordon Highlanders are brought up to strength it will be necessary at Havre, Rouen and Etaples to make use of reinforcements for guard duties in order to allow the men 2 nights in bed.

Date on which these moves will be carried out will be notified later.

Headquarters, L.G.C.,  Lieut-Colonel,
28th December, 1915.  A.A.G.

Copy to:- B.C. Boulogne: Havre: Rouen: Dieppe.
          C. Etaples: Adv. Base: No. 1 Sec. R.
                                 L. of C.

S E C R E T.

Z.E. 382.

Headquarters,
 I. G. C.
-----------

1.      The further railhead parties called for from the 12th London Regiment under your A.C.2894 of 28th December 1915, and A.C.3447 of 29th December 1915, are :-

|  | Officers. | Other ranks. |
|---|---|---|
| Boulogne | 4 | 100 |
| Dieppe | 2 | 30 |
| Calais | - | 26 |
|  | 6 | 156 |

2.      The present strength of the Detachment at ETAPLES (excluding Officers) is as follows :-

|  | Other ranks. |
|---|---|
| Police | 40 |
| E.A.D.Orderlies. | 3 |
| Battalion Headquarters | 10 |
| Attached R.A.M.C. & A.O.D. | 5 |
| Pioneers | 10 |
| Cooks | 7 |
| Quartermasters Stores | 1 |
| Officers Servants | 19 |
| Postmen (Camp) | 2 |
| Transport (including A.S.C.attached) | 44 |
| Officers Mess | 3 |
| Sergeants Mess | 1 |
| Medical Orderlies | 2 |
| Camp Orderly & Barber | 2 |
| Training Ground | 2 |
|  | 151 |
| Available for duty (including 7 permanently employed as Guard for "B" Details Camp) | 107 |
|  | 257 |

3.      Out of this total the following are available for Detachment duty :-

duty :-

         6 <u>Other ranks.</u>

| | |
|---|---:|
| Duty men | 107 |
| Training Ground | 2 |
| Pioneers (say) | 5 |
| Cooks (say) | 4 |
| Camp Barber | 1 |
| Officers Servants | 4 |
| Medical Orderly | 1 |
| Camp Postman | 1 |
| | 125 |

It will be seen that it is quite impossible to furnish all three detachments, and only barely possible to furnish those for Boulogne and Calais.  The 40 police are absolutely indispensable. It has been found by experience that police obtained from Base Details are absolutely useless.

I beg to recommend that under the circumstances only the Boulogne and Calais Detachments be furnished.

                    Colonel.
                    Commandant.

Etaples,
30 - 12 - 15.

Secret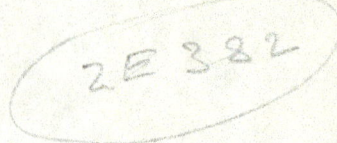

## M E M O R A N D U M.

1. The further Railhead parties called for from the 12th London Regiment under ~~I.G.C. Memos No~~ your A.C.2894 of 28th December 1915 and ~~No.~~ A.C.3447 of 29th December 1915 are:-

|  | Officers. | Other ranks |
|---|---|---|
| Boulogne | 4 | 100 |
| Dieppe | 2 | 30 |
| Calais | – | 26 |
|  | 6 | 156 |

2. The present strength of the Detachment at ETAPLES (excluding Officers) is as follows:-

|  | Other ranks |
|---|---|
| Police | 40 |
| E.A.D. Orderlies | 3 |
| Battalion Headquarters | 10 |
| Attached R.A.M.C. & A.O.D. | 5 |
| Pioneers | 10 |
| Cooks | 7 |
| Quartermasters Stores | 1 |
| Officers Servants | 19 |
| Postmen (Camp) | 2 |
| ~~do. (District)~~ | ~~10~~ |
| Transport (including A.S.C. attached) | 44 |
| Officers Mess | 3 |
| Serjeants Mess | 1 |
| Medical Orderlies | 2 |
| Camp Orderly & Barber | 2 |
| Training Ground | 2 |
|  | ~~161~~ 151 |
| Available for duty (including 7 permanently employed as Guard for "B" Details Camp) | ~~97~~ 107 |
|  | 258 |

3. To allow for possible contingencies when the detachments are actually made up a total of say 165 men require to be readily available, and this figure can be obtained as follows:-

-2-

*From this total the following are available for detachment duty*

|  | Other Ranks |
|---|---|
| Duty men | ~~107~~ 97 |
| Police | 40 |
| Postmen (District Offices) | 10 |
| Training Ground | 2 |
| Pioneers (say) | 5 |
| Cooks (say) | 4 |
| Camp Barber | 1 |
| Officers Servants | 6 |
| | ~~165~~ 123 |

4. In addition to the figures quoted in paragraph 2, the following Railhead parties are furnished from ETAPLES, viz:-

|  | Other ranks. |
|---|---|
| SAMER | 10 |
| MONTREUIL | 10 |
| | 20 |

If these parties can be furnished by another unit, the number of duty men would be increased to 117

Add: Police 40
Postmen 10

making a total of 167

which would suffice.

5. The six Officers called for are available.

A D Bayliffe
LT. COLONEL
COMDG "THE RANGERS" (12TH LONDON REGT.)

~~1st Division~~
~~20th Infy Bde~~

1/6th Bn Cheshire Regt

~~Jan. Feb. Sept.~~
1914 AUG — 1916 FEB

To 39 DIV 118 BDE

20th Brigade
7th Division.

Joined 20th Brigade from G.H.Q. 9.1.16.

2

1/6th BATTALION

CHESHIRE REGIMENT

JANUARY 1916.

Army Form C. 2118.

# WAR DIARY
## or
## INTELLIGENCE SUMMARY.
(Erase heading not required.)

Instructions regarding War Diaries and Intelligence Summaries are contained in F.S. Regs., Part II. and the Staff Manual respectively. Title pages will be prepared in manuscript.

| Hour, Date, Place | | Summary of Events and Information | Remarks and references to Appendices |
|---|---|---|---|
| January 1st 1916 | HAVRE | CAPT COOKE rejoined from Hospital | fmd |
| " 2 " | " | One O.R. rejoined from Hospital, 4 other ranks sent to Base for munition work, one O.R. admitted to Hospital | fmd |
| " 3 " | " | | fmd |
| " 4 " | " | | fmd |
| " 5 " | " | One O.R. admitted to Hospital | fmd |
| " 6 " | " | CAPT KIRK admitted to Hospital + one O.R. to Hospital | fmd |
| " 7 " | " | Two O.R. sent to Base "T.B". 3 O.R. to hospital | fmd |
| 7.35 pm " 8 " | " | Battalion left return Base entrained for PONT REMY, except ABBEVILLE detachment who marched by road. Lt ALEXANDER left behind with Base Details | fmd |
| 7.0 am " 9 " | PONT REMY | Battalion detrained + marched into billets at AILLY-LE-HAUT-CLOCHER Joined 20th Bde 7th Division | fmd |
| " 10 " | AILLY-L-H-C | Battalion Commanded Company training 30 R.M. Hopkin | fmd Strength 30 Offrs 910 O.R. |
| " 11 " | " | Training continued — Lt HAWORTH + C. NORMAN to O.R. left for hospital | fmd |
| " 12 " | " | Training continued. 10 O.R. rejoined from hospital. 7 Sgts + Sgt Major returned from leave | fmd |
| " 13 " | " | Training continued. 5 O.R. to hospital. 1 O.R. admitted to Hospital | fmd |
| " 14 " | " | Training continued Lts HINTON + CHANDLER rejoined from hospital. 2 O.R. admitted to Hospital | fmd |

# WAR DIARY or INTELLIGENCE SUMMARY.

Army Form C. 2118.

| Hour, Date, Place | | Summary of Events and Information | Remarks and references to Appendices |
|---|---|---|---|
| January 15th 1916. AILLY L.H.C. | | Training continued. 2 OR to Hospital + 8 OR to Base Depot discharged Time Expired | |
| " 16 " | | Training Continued, 4 OR admitted to Hospital. Capt COOKE | |
| " 17 " | | Training continued. 2 Lt JONES joined from England. Lt HR YORKE + 6 OR left for 1 OR returned from hospital. Lt HINTON Leave from training at PONT REMY. 5 Officers (Lts HINTON CHANDLER, RIGBY, F. YORKE, S. WALKER + 83 OR left for Course at Bom 13 SCHOOL at PONT REMY. 6 OR left for Signalling School at PONT REMY | |
| " 18 " | | Training continued | |
| " 19 " | | Training Continued. 5 OR admitted hospital, 2 returned from hospital | |
| " 20 " | | Training continued Lt PARKHURST + 6 OR left for Candle in LEWIS Gun at PONT REMY  2 Lt HR YORKE + 6 OR rejoined 9 OR admitted to hospital | |
| " 21 " | | Training continued. 1 OR admitted to hospital 3 OR rejoined from hospital | |
| " 22 " | | Training continued. 2 OR rejoined from hospital 3 OR left for Base Time expired. Capt KIRK rejoined from hospital | |
| " 23 " | | 10 OR rejoined from hospital. 1 OR admitted hospital Training continued. 3 OR rejoined from hospital | |
| " 24 " | | Battalion practised in attack. 1 OR returned from hospital | |
| " 25 " | | 1 OR + 1 OSut to Divisional Baths | |

Army Form C. 2118.

# WAR DIARY
## or
## INTELLIGENCE SUMMARY

*(Erase heading not required.)*

3

| Hour, Date, Place | Summary of Events and Information | Remarks and references to Appendices |
|---|---|---|
| 26.1.1916 AILLY-L-H-C. | Brigade Training | Nil |
| 27.1.1916 " | Standing to for move – 1 man reported from hospital. 80 O.Ranks (draft from England 3/6th Cheshires Regt) arrived from Base | Nil |
| 9.0am 28.1.1916 " | Battalion moved from AILLY-LE-HAUT-CLOCHER & arrived at PICQUIGNY went into billets. 4 men admitted to hospital | Nil |
| 29.1.1916 PICQUIGNY | Lt C.R. NORMAN & 9 O.R. left for WISQUES for service from Corps. 2 O.R. admitted to hospital | Nil |
| 30.1.1916 " | 2 OR admitted to hospital | Nil |
| 31.1.1916 " | 3 OR reported from hospital | Nil, Strength 36 Officers 962 O.R. |

20th Brigade.
7th Division.

Battalion transferred to 39th Division 29.2.16.

1/6th BATTALION

CHESHIRE REGIMENT

FEBRUARY 1916

G.140/39

Confidential —

20/7    Feb    B.15
                7 sheets

War Diary
of the 6th Cheshire Regt

From Feb 1st to Feb 29th
1916

Vol XV

VIIth Divn
[Compared to XXXXth Divn Feb 29th]

**Army Form C. 2118.**

# WAR DIARY
## or
## INTELLIGENCE SUMMARY
*(Erase heading not required.)*

Instructions regarding War Diaries and Intelligence Summaries are contained in F.S. Regs., Part II. and the Staff Manual respectively. Title pages will be prepared in manuscript.

| Hour, Date, Place | Summary of Events and Information | Remarks and references to Appendices |
|---|---|---|
| February 1st, 1916 PICQUIGNY | Orders received for move to CARDONETTE. 2 men left for discharge. 1 man admitted hospital. | |
| 9 am 2nd " | Battalion marched from PICQUIGNY into billets at CARDONETTE. 2 O.R. admitted to Hospital. | Fine. |
| 10 am 3rd CARDONETTE | Battalion marched from CARDONETTE into billets at PONT NOYELLES. 1 O.R. admitted to Hospital. | Fine. |
| " 4th PONT NOYELLES | Battalion rested. Inspection of first gas helmets & equipment generally. 1 O.R. admitted to Hospital. | mud. |
| " 5th " | Battalion marched from PONT NOYELLES into new billets at VILLE-SOUS-CORBIE about 5 miles behind firing line. 1 O.R. admitted to hospital, LtCl CL.E. MARSDEN taken on the strength and marched to hospital. | mud F.A.P. |
| " 6th VILLE-SOUS-CORBIE | Battalion rested. 1 O.R. admitted to hospital. | mud |
| " 7th " | 7.30 am 1st officers parade. 9. Officers go under Lt. MERICOURT. "A" Coy (about 1.30) dinner. 1.60 dinner under 2nd Lt. Franklin. 2 Platoon to 1st Border in D.3. Subsection. 2 Platoon to 8th Devon in D. 3. Salvation. Parade 9 a.m. "B"  "C"  "D" Coys carry on with training. New Lewis gun marked one Lieut. Coy. (D[?] Instalment). MAJOR F.A. LEAH F.g.c.m. at MEAULTE. Casualties. 3 O.R. admitted to Hospital. 1 O.R. returned from Hospital. Orders. No men to leave village except for training. Attention drawn to 3rd Army Trained Orders. Paras 3 (a) (b) 1 (c). 2nd Trees to be stopped on cut down. "Stand to" 5.50 a.m & 4.30 p.m. | |

Army Form C. 2118.

# WAR DIARY
## or
## INTELLIGENCE SUMMARY.
*(Erase heading not required.)*

Instructions regarding War Diaries and Intelligence Summaries are contained in F.S. Regs., Part II. and the Staff Manual respectively. Title pages will be prepared in manuscript.

| Hour, Date, Place | Summary of Events and Information | Remarks and references to Appendices |
|---|---|---|
| February 8th VILLE-SUR-CORBIE. 11. A.M. | 1. "B" Coy: (strength 4 Officers 220 other ranks) relieve "A" Coy: in trenches. Parade 9. a.m. 2. C.O., Adjutant, M.O., & M? Transport Officer make reconnaissance of trench line. 3. "C" & "D" Coys carry on with Training. 4. Orders = (a) Defensive measures against Gas attack. (b) Discontinue against gas unit marked L.G.B.L.222 to be worn on O.O. 1. F.B & Time exp. Strength = 2 Officers 2 other ranks to be sent from each establishment to D.3. H.Q. to THE TAMBOUR. 6. 2nd Lieut. HOLMES and 25 other ranks to carry. Establishment Waggon to carry 1 gun 1 ammunition from The Citadel to MEAULTE. for 16th T.M. Battery. | F.A.R. |
| Feb 9th VILLE-SUR-CORBIE. | 1. "C" Coy. (strength 6 Officers, 166 O.R.) relieved "B" Coy. 2. "A" & "B" Coy. continue training. Fatigues — (a) N.C.O. 24 Men about F.2. R.E. dump F.7.B. 6.30 A.M. (b) N.C.O. 120 Men report 9.5" Field Coy. 4.30 p.m. 3. Casualty — 1. O.R. discharged from Hospital. | |
| Feb. 10th " " | 1. "A" Coy. relieved "C" Coy: in trenches. 2. (a) Fatigues – 120 Men with Shovels & Sachers for unloading Road Metal & cleaning road – about road crossing VILLE-MEAULTE Road @ 9.a.m. (b) N.C.O. & 24 Men 95" Field Coy. R.E. 8.30. a.m. (c) N.C.O. 120 Men on job 183. 2/9.2.16. (d) 2. Officers depart on leave. | |

Army Form C. 2118

# WAR DIARY
## or
## INTELLIGENCE SUMMARY
(Erase heading not required.)

Instructions regarding War Diaries and Intelligence Summaries are contained in F.S. Regs., Part II. and the Staff Manual respectively. Title Pages will be prepared in manuscript.

| Place | Date | Hour | Summary of Events and Information | Remarks and references to Appendices |
|---|---|---|---|---|
| VILLE | 11-2-16 | - | Orders received for Battn to relieve 8th Devons in Trenches on 12th | 
| " | 12.2.16 | 1 p.m. | Battalion relieved 8th Devons in D 2 subsector of the trenches opposite FRICOURT. 2 men killed - Battn employed at night in wiring improving trenches | 
| TRENCHES B5/6 | 13/2/16 |  | Heavy bombardment of trenches all afternoon one man killed one man wounded one man admitted hospital, destruction of two companies A+B in front line one coy "C" in support, Coy D in reserve. Trenches starting to crumble owing to rain. Battalion employed in rebuilding parapets, wiring | 
| " | 14/2/16 |  | Raining, trenches getting very wet needing a lot of repair, an enemy wiring party dispersed by our fire. Quiet day | 
| " | 15/2/16 |  | Still raining, many landslides in trenches. Battalion busy all day and night repairing. 1 man killed. 3 men admitted hospital. Patrols sent out but encountered nothing. Quiet day. | 
| " | 16/2/16 |  | Raining very hard & only with very hard work could trenches be kept both repair of landslides. Quiet day. 1 man admitted hospital after relief of companies | 
| " | 17/2/16 |  | Weather improved, work of repairing trenches carried on. 8 men admitted to hospital. Quiet day. | 
| " | 18/2/16 |  | Quiet day. 3 men admitted hospital |

# WAR DIARY or INTELLIGENCE SUMMARY

Army Form C. 2118

| Place | Date | Hour | Summary of Events and Information | Remarks and references to Appendices |
|---|---|---|---|---|
| TRENCHES | 19/2/16 | - | Very wet day. Battalion employed in repairing damage done during the night. 2 wounded. In morning 2 wounds of front attempted. I man killed, 2 wounded owing to heavy machine gun fire at 7 p.m. Night reconnaissance of German sap undertaken. Unit successful & party returned at 9.45 p.m. all safe. 3 O.R. admitted to hospital. | (Sgd) |
| " | 20/2/16 | - | Battn. relieved by 8 R. Devons in trenches. Evacuated tracks to billets at VILLE-SUR-ANCRE. 2 O.R. admitted hospital. | (Sgd) |
| VILLE | 21.2.16 |  | Battn. in reserve, occupied on fatigues in trenches, on road running to 3 O.R. admitted hospital sick. 2 O.R. wounded by shrapnel in support trenches. |  |
| " | 22.2.16 |  | Battn. in reserve occupied on fatigues in trenches, reports to 3 O.R. admitted hospital sick, 1 wounded. 2 O.R. rejoined from hospital. |  |
| " | 23.2.16 |  | Battn. in reserve occupied on fatigues in trenches. At 5.30 p.m. 22nd received order to stand to arms as enemy expected to attack. At 9.15 p.m. instructed to fall out. The attack had been made & repulsed. |  |
| " | 24.2.16 |  | Instructions received for battn. to move to St OMER on 25th. Day utilised in preparing for move. 1 O.R. admitted hospital sick. |  |
| " | 25.2.16 |  | Paraded 9.0 a.m. marched to LA HOUSSOYE where met by motor lorries & conveyed to LONGUEAU station which reached c. 3.0 p.m. Heavy fall of snow considerably impeded transport which left VILLE 8.30 a.m. & arrived LONGUEAU 6.30 p.m. Entrained at LONGUEAU & left 8.0 p.m. 1 O.R. rejoined from hospital. |  |
| " | 26.2.16 |  | On arrival at St OMER received instructions from GHQ for RTO to continue by rail to HAZEBROUCK which reached 6.30 am. Detrained & marched via St omer Caestre roads to farm billets at WALLON CAPPEL. 1 O.R. rejoined from hospital. |  |

Army Form C. 2118

# WAR DIARY
## or
## INTELLIGENCE SUMMARY

(Erase heading not required.)

Instructions regarding War Diaries and Intelligence Summaries are contained in F. S. Regs., Part II. and the Staff Manual respectively. Title Pages will be prepared in manuscript.

| Place | Date | Hour | Summary of Events and Information | Remarks and references to Appendices |
|---|---|---|---|---|
| MALLON-CAPPEL | 27.2.16 | | Battn. occupied in cleaning &c. C.O. & Regtl Staff reported to GHQ personally. | |
| " | 28.2.16 | | Instructional classes for Officers & NCO's, & as far as weather permitted outdoor training. 1 O.R. admitted hospital. | |
| " | 29.2.16 | | Battn. taken on line of march by the 118th Infantry Brigade commanded by Maj Genl BROMILOW. Instructional classes & outdoor training. | |

WO 95/15712

5th Division

1st Dorset Reg.

Aug ~~October~~ to December

1914.

—

Dec 1918

15th Brigade.

5th Division.

-------

1st BATTALION

DORSETSHIRE REGIMENT

AUGUST 1914.

Original

War Diary of 1/Bn Dorset Regt.
from 4th Aug. 1914 to –

Volume I.

**Tuesday
4th Aug 1914**

5.39 pm.  Order to mobilize Received – Wed
5th Aug. 1st Day of Mobn. Acknowledged.

8. pm.  Detachments for WOODBURN and
STONEYFORD despatched.

9.30 pm  Lt PITT, 2/Lt CHAPMAN and 3 NCOs
left for DORCHESTER to conduct Reservists
taking Colours with them –

auth

**Wednesday
5th Aug.**

9. am.  Medical Inspection of Serving Soldiers.
Men not for service – (under age) taken
over by temporary O.C. Details (Capt.
HYSLOP.

5 pm  Railway Staff under /Lt GRANT-DALTON
despatched to G.N.Ry 8th BELFAST.

? pm.  Orders received from War Office to
include men between 19 & 20 years of
age who have pred Table A. in numbers
to proceed on service –

Appointments – Captain A.L MOULTON-
BARRETT – Staff Captain 15th Inf Bde.
Lt MARGETTS – Bn Transport Officer

auth

| | |
|---|---|
| Thursday 6th Aug. | Hr. |
| 7.30 am | The following party arrived at BELFAST from LIVERPOOL from DORCHESTER. |
| | Capt. I. H. KITCHIN |
| | Capt A. R. M. ROE |
| | Lt J. R. Turner |
| | Lt G. A. BURNAND. |
| | 2/Lt G. S. SHANNON. |
| | 96 Reservists and 2 men to join Details. |
| 9 am. | Capt. KITCHIN took over command of Details from Capt HYSLOP. |
| 9. am | Medical Inspection of Officers & men not previously inspected & of men between 19 & 20 years of age. |
| | Postings. |
| | A. Coy - Lt F D S KING (joined at 1 am) |
| | - 2/Lt G. S. SHANNON |
| | B Coy - Lt J. R. TURNER. |
| | C Coy - Lt G A BURNAND. |
| | Attached to Details |
| | Capt A. R. M ROE |
| | Capt W F G WILLES } joined today |
| | Capt A. B PRIESTLEY } |
| 1 am | Lt T. S. RENDALL reported his arrival and shortly afterwards received orders to be ready to return to India sailing 11th Aug. |

| | | |
|---|---|---|
| Friday 7th Aug. | The following party arrived at Great Victoria St. Stn about 4.30 pm from DORCHESTER <br> Lt PITT <br> Lt CLARKE <br> Lt GREGORY <br> Lt CLUTTERBUCK ⎫ To Return to <br> 2/Lt PRICE ⎭ Dorchester on completion. <br> 2 Conducting NCOs and 440 Reservists <br><br> Postings <br> A.Coy — 2/Lt G.S Shannon <br> C.Coy — Lt G.A Burnand <br><br> Attached to Details <br> Captain W.F.G. Willes <br> Capt A.B. Priestley <br><br> ~~The following~~ | and |
| Saturday 8th Aug. | Detachments at GREENORE, KILROOT, CARRICKFERGUS, and WOODBURN returned to Head Qrs. | |
| 11.15 pm | The following party left for Dorchester to act as instructors for a new unit to be raised under War Office authority — <br> Captain W.F.G Willes <br> Lt A.R.S Clarke    Lt T.H Gleeson <br> Lt A.S Gregory,   Lt H.J. Clutterbuck <br> 10 NCOs (one to proceed later). | |

| | |
|---|---|
| Sat<sup>d</sup> 8 Aug (cont) | Lt C.H. Woodhouse assumed duties of M.G. Officer. |
| | Captain A.B. Priestley appointed to command the First Reinforcement |
| 4 pm | Party of 27 Regular Establishment (Depot) and 32 Reservists arrived at Great Victoria St. Stn. BELFAST under command of Lt T.H Clemson. |
| | Orders received pm A.D. to withdraw spare khaki suit and pair of boots from troops of Expeditionary Force |

Sunday 9<sup>th</sup> August

| | |
|---|---|
| 10.30 am | Bn paraded for inspection by the C.O. |
| 11.30 am | Divine Service. |
| 2.30 pm | Route March — 2 hours. |

Monday 10<sup>th</sup> Aug.

| | |
|---|---|
| 8 am to 5 pm | B<sup>n</sup> trained on CAVE & SQUIRES HILLS. |

| | | |
|---|---|---|
| Tuesday 11th Aug | | |
| 8 AM to 4 PM | Bn trained on McILWHANS & SQUIRES HILL | |
| | Major & QM. Kearney reports his arrival. | and |
| Wednesday 12th Aug | Bn carried out field firing at McILWHANS. | and |
| Thursday 13th Aug | | |
| 12 noon | Bn attended Divine Service at BELFAST CATHEDRAL. | and |
| Friday 14th Aug | Bn embarked on S/S "ANTONY" as follows | |
| 8. AM | Transport embarked — completed 1.30 pm Only 2 horse "cradles" were available and only 1 crane. | |
| 1.30 PM | Personnel embarked. | |
| 3.25 PM | Sailed Weather very fine and hot. | and |
| Saturday 15th Aug | At Sea. Early morning very wet. Passage - good. | and |

**Sunday 16th Aug.**

1st 5 pages Extd. and sent to M.

4 pm — Arrived at HAVRE. Commenced disembarkation — Disembarkation of horses & vehicles very slow — owing to one crane being available and it being strong enough to take heavy wagons.

8 pm — Marched to No 8 Rest Camp. Leaving Transport behind and 2 platoons A Coy.

10 pm — Bn reached Rest Camp.

10 pm — Transport left quay, but could not reach camp owing to being blocked by 1st Cheshire Regts transport.

12 mn — Relieved 2 platoons A Coy by 2 Sections B Coy.

Weather — Fine, but camp very wet and muddy — soil clay.

Casualty — One man sick — Pte Hibbs A Coy to Hospitale Militaire. HAVRE.

auds

**Monday 17th Aug**

3 pm — Received orders to entrain at 8 PM at Gare de MARCHANDISE. Captain ROE conveyed orders to Bn Transport Officer — the transport being still on the road between HARFLEUR and HAVRE — as he knew the exact position.

6 pm — Bn marched from Camp.

7.40 pm — Reached Station

see over

| | |
|---|---|
| 12 pm | Orders received for Bn to find 2 posts as follows, to guard against possible hostile cavalry :— |
| | 1. Road Star ¼ mile E of the last L of POMMEREUIL |
| | 2. Point where road crosses the railway almost 1 mile NE of R in ORS |
| | These posts were found by A Coy. |

Wednesday
19th Aug — Remained in billets at ORS.
10 am — Posts of A Coy relieved by B Coy.
2 pm — Posts taken over by D Coy as they are close to that Coy's billets.
Sick. Nil.
Weather — Very fine.

Thursday
20th Aug. — Remained in billets
10.30 am — Major Genl. Sir C. Ferguson Cg. 5th Divn visited ORS and addressed the Battalion.
1 pm. — Informed verbally by Brigadier General that Brigade would move tomorrow.

Monday
17 Aug (cont)

(Bn + Batta)
Vehicles entrained by C Coy and 2 Sections of B Coy in 35 minutes —

This time was stated by the R.T. Staff Officer to be the best fancy unit by 10 minutes so far.

Entrainment of personnel was delayed as D Coy. could not find sufficient accommodation.

[Note. Carriages etc as marked by Officer taking over train must be adhered to and this Officer must make ample allowance for overlapping.]

11 pm — Train departed.

Casualties.
    Absentees 9 – (8 Rejoined)
    Sick    2 (Left at HAVRE)

Weather — Fine.

Tuesday
18th Aug

4.30 am — Issue of coffee to all ranks at ROUEN.
2.20 pm — Reached BUSIGNY and received billeting orders.
3.20 pm — Reached LE CATEAU and detrained. Vehicles detrained by 2 platoons of D Coy in 25 minutes.
4 pm — Marches complete.
5.50 pm — Reached ORS.
6 pm to 9 pm — Billets allotted by Major Roper.

Weather — Fine — Casualties — Nil

**Friday**
**21st Aug.**

Bn being advanced guard.
Marched via R of RAUCOURT – P of POTELLE to GOMMEGNIES where Bde halted. Battalion found out posts from about LE CHEVAL BLANC to PREUX with C, A, & B Coys.
Brigade billeted at GOMMEGNIES, A & C Coys being relieved from outposts by 14 Inf Bde withdrew to billets.
Weather fine and hot.
Distance – 15 miles.

**Saturday**
**22nd Aug.**

3.30 am  Marched via BAVAI – HOUDAIN – ATHIS to DOUR, where Bn billeted, remainder of Bde being at BOIS DE BOUSSI.
Weather – fine and very hot. Very trying for marching
Distance. 15 miles.

**Sunday**
**23rd Aug.**

Remained in billets at DOUR during morning.

12 noon  Orders received for ½ Bns of Bde to proceed as follows at once taking all tools for entrenching
½ Bn Norfolks – HALTE
½ Bn Cheshires – HORNU
½ Bn Bedfords ⎱ R⁷ Bde ½ m. N of W of
½ Bn Dorsets ⎰ WASMES

12.30 pm  C & D Coys with Tool limbers but no ammunition carts marched to HALTE

|        | and thence via Railway line to rendezvous. Tool limber of Bde HQrs which had been ordered to follow the Dorsets did not join and was not heard of afterwards. |
|---|---|
|        | As soon as tool limbers could be brought up – they having been delayed on the railway line – C Coy commenced entrenching on the left of the Bedfords – D Coy remaining temporarily in reserve. Later D Coy was ordered to entrench on the right of the Bedfords. |
| 4.10 pm | Message received from 15th Bde that 3rd Divn was retiring to a position South of MONS and that 15 Bde was to block the MARIETTE – PATURAGES Road. |
| 5 pm    | Enemy opened artillery fire but shells passed over trenches |
| 5.30 pm | O.C. D Coy reported Bn of enemy's infantry 1000x North of his trenches. |
| 6 pm    | Message sent to Brigade asking for S.A.A. Carts. |
| 7.10 pm | O.C. C Coy reported enemy's infantry scouts approaching his trenches. |
| 7.15 pm | Enemy's infantry seen in front of D Coys trenches |
| 7.30 pm | Heavy shelling by enemy of street just South of Ry Bridge – no casualties. |
| 8.30 pm | Major Roper with Bn Hd Qrs, A & B Coys & M.G. Section, and 1st line Transport arrived at Railway Bridge. |
|         | "A" Coy sent to prolong left of C Coy – 2 platoons being subsequently withdrawn |

to the Rly Bridge
B Coy were ordered to proceed at dawn
to get touch with Cheshires about HORNU.

**Monday
24th Aug**

2am — Orders received from 15th Bde (timed 11.55 pm) ordering Bn to move to P of PATURAGES as soon as relieved by a unit of 13th Inf Bde.

4am — Our guns opened - followed by those of enemy

6am — D Coy relieved by a Coy West Riding Regt and rejoined at Rly Bdge.
Subsequently C Coy & the 2 platoons A Coy relieved by same Bn, but instead of rejoining at Rly Bdge these units with the exception of about 1 platoon under Major Saunders retired to position occupied by B Coy. (see below) and ~~took~~ took part in the retirement with that Coy.

6.30 am — Message received from Capt. Williams Comdg B Coy, (timed 4 am) that he was at Bridge 600x W.N.W of W in WASMES in touch with A Coy, but not in touch with the Cheshires.

about 8 AM — Bn Hd Qrs with 2 platoons A Coy, D Coy and MG Section & 1st Line Transport marched to P of PATURAGES where Bde Hd Qrs was established.
The 2 platoons of A Coy were at once sent

to support the Bedfords in a square near the Church –

1st Line Transport was directed to retire first but in order to avoid steep hill through PETIT WASMES, was sent by Brigadier by a more Southerly Road.

10.30 am (about) 1st Line Transport ambushed by hostile infantry – All vehicles escaped except No 2 SAA Cart owing to coolness of Lieut Margetts – Transport Officer – who held back the enemy with his revolver, though himself wounded.

11 am (about) General retirement of Bedfords & Dorsets viâ PETIT WASMES – WARQUIGNIES to BLAUGIES

3 pm Halted for 1 hour at BLAUGIES There joined by bulk of B and C Coys and 2 platoons A Coy

[ Diary of events as far as B Coy is concerned –

B Coy moved at dawn into a railway cutting by a bridge 600x W.N.W. of W of WASMES. 2 platoons were pushed forward to entrench – About 6 am the whole Coy went into the trenches, having part of A Coy on their right and a part of C Coy on their left. The enemy's infantry advanced supported by heavy artillery fire to within 400x, but were repulsed. A lull of about 1 hour followed. The enemy then opened a heavy rifle and artillery fire – It was seen that the enemy had worked round both flanks

About 2pm the Coy was ordered to retire and fell back in the direction of BLAUGIES.

After the remainder of the Coy had fallen back Captain Williams collected about a Dozen men & returned. It was largely due to his energy and example that the retirement of the rest of the Bde was carried out successfully.]

General retirement continued to neighbourhood of ST. WAAST LES BAVAY where Brigade bivouacked.

Casualties
    Officers
Wounded - Capt HYSLOP.
    Lieut Margetts
    Lieut Leishman
Missing - Lieut Burnand.

    Other Ranks
Killed — 12
Wounded — 49
Missing — 69.

This battle will be known as the Battle of MONS.

Weather — very fine & hot.

**Tuesday 5th Aug**

2 A.M. Brigade continued retirement via BAVAI – NW edge of FORET DE MORMAL to LE CATEAU.

2 P.M. Brigade bivouacked at pt 116, 1 mile E of TROISVILLE.

3 P.M. Trenches which had been partially dug reconnoitred –
A Coy placed on outpost near road junction ½ m NE of LA SOTIERE and entrenched –
5 Hostile aeroplanes made reconnaissance while Bde was in bivouac.
Weather – Fine in morning
Thunderstorm in evening.
Rain during night.

**Thursday 26th Aug**

1 am. Orders received from Brigade for Bn to stand to arms as Bedfords outpost Coys had fallen back – Bn fell in at once – "B" and "C" lining NE boundary of bivouac, other being in support.
All quiet and troops ordered to fall out.

4 am. Orders received for retirement to be continued to ESTREES, but these were cancelled as information had been received that 2 German Divisions were at LE CATEAU.

5 am. Bn occupied trenches just to N of wood LA SOTIERE and that village – disposed

as follows:—
Reading from right to left.
In trenches. D Coy, 2 platoons C Coy
B Coy.
2nd line - A Coy.
Bn H.Qrs + 2 platoons C Coy at LA of LA SOTIERE, this point being strongly fortified and entrenched.
Attack by enemy simultaneously on 13th & 14th Inf Bdes on our right and on the 3rd Divn on our left.
Our part of the line was not directly attacked.

11 am — Firing slackened on our left and it appeared that the 3rd Divn had beaten back the attack, & and that enemy could not get out of BEAUMONT-INCHY

12 noon (about) — Permission asked from Bde to counter attack towards - BEAUMONT - INCHY in conjunction with 3rd Divn
Reply received that if counter attack was made it was not to proceed further than the "poplar road"

1 pm to 2 pm — Very heavy gun & rifle fire heard from direction of our right -

3.10 pm — Message received from Brigade timed 2.50 pm to effect that our right was falling back & that if obliged to do so Dorsets were to retire slowly in S.S.W. direction via BERTRY-MARETZ-ESTREES also that four guns (Major Ballards battery) were retiring ½ -

| | |
|---|---|
| 3.10 – 4.15 pm | Bn remained in its position less 1st Line Transport which was sent ahead at once. |
| | Enemy brought a machine gun to the poplar road, but made no serious attempt to attack with infantry. |
| 4.20 pm to 5 pm | Machine Guns under Lieut C.H. Woodhouse did splendid work at this period covering the retirement which commenced at 4.20 pm. The enemy were gradually getting the range with their guns, but had not quite done so, when last party of Bn retired through TROISVILLES covered by B Coy who had taken up a covering position. |
| 5 pm 627 | Retirement continued via BERTRY – MARETZ. Battalion came under artillery fire 3 times during retirement, which though well directed it caused few casualties. Bn billeted at GENÈVE uncomfortable night without supplies. |

Casualties

    Officers Nil
    Other Ranks –
Wounded – 14
Missing – 21


Weather – very fine shot
    Drizzle during night.

| | | |
|---|---|---|
| Thursday 27th Aug. | | |
| | 3am | Marched via ESTREES — ~~POZEEN~~ BELLENGLISE — ST QUENTIN |
| | 1pm | Halted for 1hr at ST. QUENTIN. |
| | 2pm | Retirement continued to EAUCOURT 1 mile WSW of OLLEZY where Bde bivouacked — 3rd 4th + 5th Divns were all concentrated at OLLEZY. Weather fine & hot Distance marched — 23 miles. |
| Friday 28th Aug | | Retirement continued via CUGNY — BERLANCOURT — NOYON to PONTOISE where Brigade bivouacked. Sir John French addressed troops as they passed during march. Weather fine & hot Distance marched — 20 miles Road very hilly — N of NOYON. |
| Saturday 29th Aug. | | ~~Rest Day~~. Rest Day. |
| | 5pm | Marched to CARLEPONT to billet — Much delay caused by billets of 14th 75th Brigades being interchanged Eventually the Bde bivouacked at the Church. Weather — fine & hot Distance marched — 4 miles. |

Sunday
30th Aug

Retirement continued via ATTICHY to
CROUTOY —
8am — Halted in open field ½ m. S. of CROUTOY
Very hot and no shade — Supplies had not
arrived
12 noon — Returned to CROUTOY and billeted —
Billets very comfortable —
Weather — fine and very hot
Distance marched — 12 miles                    and/

Monday
31st Aug    Retirement continued to CREPY, where
Brigade went into bivouac.
Weather — fine & hot
Distance marched. — 15 miles                   and/

# 1st Bn Dorsetshire Regiment.

## Nominal Roll of Officers. Headquarters.

| Rank. | Name. |
|---|---|
| Commanding Officer. | Lieut Colonel. L.J. Bols. D.S.O. |
| Senior Major. | Major R.T. Roper. |
| Adjutant. | Captain A.L. Ransome. |
| Quartermaster. | Major J. Kearney. |
| Machine Gun Officer. | Lieutenant .C.H. Woodhouse. |

### A. Coy.

| | |
|---|---|
| Commander. | Captain W.A.C. Fraser. |
| Second Captain. | Captain R.G.B.M. Hyslop. |
| Subalterns. | Lieutenant J.M. Pitt. |
| | Lieutenant C.O. Lilly. |
| | Lieutenant. F.D.S. King. |
| | 2/Lieutenant G.S. Shannon. |

### B. Coy.

| | |
|---|---|
| Commander. | Captain H.S. Williams. |
| Second Captain. | Captain A.R.M. Roe.  B.M.G. Off. |
| Subalterns. | Lieutenant .C.F.M. Margetts. (Transport Officer) |
| | Lieutenant.J.R. Turner. |
| | 2/Lieutenant.C.G. Butcher. |
| | 2/Lieutenant. H.L. Chapman. |

### C. Coy.

| | |
|---|---|
| Commander. | Major C. Saunders. |
| Second Captain. | Captain. J. Kelsall. |
| Subalterns. | Lieutenant. A.S. Fraser. |
| | Lieutenant W.A. Leishman. |
| | Lieutenant G.A. Burnand. |
| | 2/Lieutenant. L. Grant-Dalton. |

### D. Coy.

| | |
|---|---|
| Commander. | Captain. W.T.C. Davidson. |
| Second Captain. | Captain. F.H.B. Rathborne. |
| Subalterns. | Lieutenant. R.E. Partridge. |
| | Lieutenant. A.K.D. George. |
| | Lieutenant. A.E. Hawkins. |
| | 2/Lieutenant. E.B. Walker. |

### Attached.

| | |
|---|---|
| Medical Officer. | Captain Dunbar. R.A.M.C. |
| | First Reinforcement. |
| Commander. | Captain A.B. Priestley. |
| | Details. |
| Commander. | Captain. I.H. Kitchin. |

Belfast.
9/8/18

L.J. Bols.
Commanding 1st Bn Dorset Regiment. Lt Colonel.

**Note.** I have officers, as above, viz. complete war Est., 2: Lieuts: Chapman & Walker having been posted to me by W.O. yesterday. If I have to go at W.E. (less one Capt: & 2 subalterns) as stated in W.O. Telegram, I would leave these two subalterns and Capt: Roe; the latter who was on sick leave, was passed fit at Dorchester Depot and sent here to join

over

as he had, previous to his sick leave, been attached to this Battalion pending embarkation to India –

I would like to know whether, having these three officers available, the Battalion should, or should not still start short of them.

Belfast.
9. Aug: 1914.

L J Bols. Lt. Col.
Comdg: 1 Bn. Dorset: Regt.

To,

    Headquarters,

        15th Infantry Brigade,

            <u>Belfast</u>.

With reference to your letter No 10 dated 8th August, 1914, I beg to report as follows:-

1. Battalion is up to War Establishment in all respects.
2. First Reinforcement requires 32 to complete Establishment.
3. The following personnel are remaining with the Details:---

    Recruits........189.

    Medically Unfit. 16.

Number of reservists in excess of number required-NIL.

A Nominal Roll of Officers is attached.

Belfast.
9-8-1914.

                Lieut Colonel,
Commanding 1st Bn Dorsetshire Regiment.

"A" Form.  
Army Form C. 2121.  
MESSAGES AND SIGNALS.  
No. of Message_____

| Prefix_____ Code_____ m. | Words | Charge | This message is on a/c of: | Recd. at_____ m. |
|---|---|---|---|---|
| Office of Origin and Service Instructions. | | | | Date_____ |
| | Sent | | _____Service. | From_____ |
| | At_____ m. | | | |
| | To_____ | | | By_____ |
| | By_____ | | (Signature of "Franking Officer.") | |

TO { Commanding Cheshires  
     Commanding Depots }

| Sender's Number | Day of Month | In reply to Number | AAA |
|---|---|---|---|
| 6004 | 8-8-14 | | |

| | | | | |
|---|---|---|---|---|
| 6004 | Require | written | report | by |
| Monday | morning | stating | whether | up |
| to | war | establishment | in | all |
| details | explaining | deficiencies | if | any |
| AAA | give | also | nominal | excess |
| Reservists | nominal | roll | of | Officers |
| and | numbers | of | recruits | unfits |
| and | others | left | behind | AAA |
| Compensation | for | clothing | and | boots |
| without | will | be | given | AAA |
| expect | you | to | your | best |
| to | get | battalion | to | work |
| together | during | time | left | |
| | | | 7.50 pm | |

From: Brigadier  
Place:  
Time:  

The above may be forwarded as now corrected. (Z)  
Censor. Signature of Addressor or person authorised to telegraph in his name.  
* This line should be erased if not required.

XV Bde
No 10

Officer Commanding,

  1st Batt. Dorset & Norfolk Regts.
-------------------------------------------------

  You will report in writing to this office by 10 a.m. on Monday morning whether your battalion is accurately up to War Establishment in all details and, if not, explain any deficiencies or other matters calling for remark.

  You will also give the numbers of recruits, unfit men and others left behind, the number of reservists in excess of numbers required, and give a nominal roll of officers.

  Compensation will be given for clothing and boots withdrawn.

(Sd) J.T. Weatherby

BELFAST.                     Captain.
8-8-1914.          Brigade Major, 15th Infantry Brigade.

15th Brigade.

5th Division.

---------

1st BATTALION

DORSETSHIRE REGIMENT

SEPTEMBER 1914.

| | |
|---|---|
| Tuesday 1st Sept. | Orders for march cancelled and Bn moved with rest of Brigade to DUVEY. After forming up at DUVEY information was received that our 4th Divn was engaged with the enemy about ROCQUEMONT. Bn ordered to proceed to ROCQUEMONT to support 4th Divn. Bn deployed B and D Coys being in front line and A & C in support. Formed bodies of enemy's Cavalry reported moving to across our front. Bn ordered to retire to DUVEY covered by Norfolks. Bn shelled at DUVEY Ch. by own guns. Brigade moved to ORMOY where it halted till 2 a.m. B and D Coys entrenching. |

| | |
|---|---|
| 2 pm | Retirement of Brigade continued to NANT-EUIL. where Bde furnished outposts as follows: A, B, & C Coys from NANTEUIL-LEVIGNEN Road to NANTEUIL-ORMOT Road. But Hdqrs & D Coy being in bivouac ½ mile N of N of NANTEUIL.<br>Casualties - Nil.<br>Weather - fine & hot.<br>Distance marched including operations:-<br>12 miles. |
| Wednesday<br>2nd Sept.<br>7 am | Retirement continued to MONTGE where Bde billeted<br><br>Weather fine & hot<br>Distance marched. |
| Thursday<br>3rd Sept. | Retirement continued via TRILBARDOU - ESBLY (where Brigade halted for one hour) - COUILLY to MONT PICHET (3m NW of CRECY) where Bde bivouacked.<br>Good nights rest.<br>Weather - fine & hot<br>Distance marched. |
| Friday<br>4th Sept<br>11.45 pm | Brigade remained in bivouac at MONT PICHET.<br>Retirement continued<br>Weather - fine & hot. |

War Diary of 1/Bn Dorset Reg't
from 4..8..14 to

**Saturday**
**5th Sept.**
8 to 9 am — Retirement continued in early morning. Brigade billeted at GAGNY.
Good billets in stables of Chateau.
Weather — fine & hot.
Distance marched.

3.30 pm — 1st Reinforcement under Capt. Priestley, strength 2 Sgts 1 Cpl & 87 Privates, joined.

~~Sunday~~
~~6th Sept.~~
~~2 am~~ — ~~Orders received that Div'n would resume the offensive~~

9 pm — Orders received that Div'n would reassume the offensive tomorrow marching about 5 am.

**Sunday**
**6th Sept.**
5 am — Bde marched to VILLENEUVE. Distant gun fire heard on both flanks.
Bn formed Advanced Guard to Bde.

55 pm — Vanguard reached OBELISQUE (2 m. W. of MONTCERF)
Advance continued to MONTCERF where Bde halted, the Bn finding outposts. with C & D Coys in line LA MALMAISON F'm ST ANNE'S Cross Roads.

6.45 pm — Advance continued via LA CELLE, the Bn finding Advanced guard, having orders to occupy high ground about the line LE CHARNOIS – GUERARD.
Approach to position very difficult in

darkness and narrow streets of village. No opposition encountered except one hostile patrol which retired after firing a few shots –

| | |
|---|---|
| Monday 7th Sept. | Bn remained just South of VILLENEUVE covered by A Coy. |
| 2am | Heavy firing on right front – but Bn did not fire a shot – |
| 4am | Officers patrols sent to CHARNOIS and CARROUGE just E of D of GUERARD |
| 5am | Report to Bde – all quiet. |
| 8am | Report to Bde that Bn was in touch with 7th Brigade on right and 13th Bde on left. |
| 9am | Message to Bde asking for orders. |
| 9.30am | Further message asking for information of situation and when Bde was to move. |
| 10.35am | Message from Bde that no orders to move had been received – |
| 10.30am | Message received that orders for advance would shortly be issued. |
| 12.45pm | Bn marched to TRESMES where it joined the remainder of the Bde. March continued towards MOUROUX. |
| 3pm | Just West of MOUROUX Column came under shell fire – Verbal orders received to halt – |
| 3.45pm | Message to Bde asking for orders – Reply received that Bde was awaiting orders |
| 4.45pm | March continued via COULOMMIERS |

to BOISSY LE CHATEL where Bde
bivouacked.
Weather - fine & hot.
Distance marched 6th & 7th Sept. =

**Tuesday 8th Sept**

March continued via ST GERMAIN to
DOUE where Bde halted in support
of 13th Bde which was attacking St
CYR -
Moved to MAUROY
Continued march via ST CYR
Sounds of heavy gun & rifle fire on
both flanks.
Halted about LES HAMEAUX till 5.30pm.

6.30pm  Bn billeted CHARNESSEUIL.
Weather - fine & hot in morning -
rain in afternoon.
Distance marched - 10 miles -
Casualties - Nil.

**Wednesday 9th Sept**

Advance continued via SAARCY - crossing
R. MARNE. E. of MERY.
Halted at P. of PASSY.
Heavy gun fire in front.

? 12 noon  Advance continued - When head of 15th
Bde had reached about N of LE LIMON.
that part of column which was
then crossing open space just S of N of
LE LIMON came under heavy shell
fire from a battery about pt 189. LES
MAILLONS. This Battery had been reported
as deserted, but it continued to cause
considerable loss throughout the day

Bn moved under cover into low ground
near N of LE LIMON on west side of
road.
B Coy detached to march in front of
Bde Hdqrs.

1 pm — Bn formed up at Farm ½ mile N of
LE LIMON, with orders to attack pt. 189
(on the suggestion of Lt Col Bols) the Brigadier
also ordering the Norfolks to support.
Bn deployed — D Coy on right and C Coy
on left forming firing line & support
and A Coy and HQ Section being in reserve. B Coy was
still detached from remainder of Bn.
1st Line Transport remained at Farm

1 – 2 pm — Bn moved forward through woods and by 2 pm were
in position just N of road between
words PISSELOUP and GENEVRAIS
the left of C Coy being in touch with
mixed units of 14th Inf Bde (Suffolks and
Manchesters).

2.20 pm — Following message sent to 15th Bde.
"I will attack shortly. What artillery
support may I expect?"

2.40 pm — Message to Bde for S.A.A. Carts.

2 to 3 pm — Bn moved gradually forward to a line
about 500x N of word PISSELOUP.
B Coy has now left Bde Hdqrs and has
moved to the western edge of the BOIS DES
ESSERTIS being in touch with D Coy.

From 3 pm — Firing line subjected to heavy gun, rifle
and machine gun fire.
2 Coys. Norfolks sent into BOIS DES ESSERTIS
to support our right.
Remainder of Norfolks were in wood
just S of 2nd P of PISSELOUP

During the whole of this time the attack received no artillery support, although under heavy shell fire, and the firing line was consequently unable to get forward.

| | |
|---|---|
| 5.30 p.m. | Lt Col Bols received verbal orders from the Brigadier that the Bn was to retire after dark to an entrenched position just west of BEZU in conjunction with rest of Brigade. |
| 6.30 pm | Firing ceased and Bn withdrew to trenches which were occupied by A & C Coys — B and C Coys being in reserve. |
| ? 9 pm | Message received from Brigade that enemy was retiring North, and that Bde would stand to arms at 4.30am and advance on MONTREUIL. |

Casualties.

Officers
Wounded.  Major C. Saunders  C Coy — Slightly
Capt A R H Roe ×  B Coy
Capt A B Priestley ×  B Coy.  } Severely
Lieut A K D George.  D Coy

× Since died of wounds.

NCOs and men

Killed    7
Wounded  31
Missing   4

Weather — Fine but colder.

**Thursday 10th Sept.**

3.45 am — Brigade, with Dorsets as Advanced Guard, moved to road junction immediately South of HALOUP, as support to 13th Inf Bde who were expected to occupy MONTREUIL at 4am. This was done without opposition.

Advance continued via DHUISY and GERMIGNY, where Brigade was covered by 2 Cavalry Brigades.

Advance continued via GANDELU – BRUMETZ – CHEZY

There was no opposition to advanced guard, but every sign of a hurried German retreat i.e. hastily vacated bivouacs, deserted transport etc.

Brigade moved to ST QUENTIN, but was delayed going into billets by one gun which persistently shelled woods round village till sunset.

Billeted at ST QUENTIN.

7.30 pm — 2nd and 3rd Reinforcement strength 187 under Lieut J.A.F. Parkinson and L/A J. Clutterbuck joined.

<u>Casualties</u> – Nil.

<u>Weather</u> – Fine & cooler. Some showers.

Distance marched – 16 miles.

**Friday 11th Sept.**

7.45 am — Advance continued via MARIZY ST GENEVIEVE – MARIZY-ST.MARD – CHOUY – BILLY to ST REMY where Brigade billeted. Bn in very comfortable billets. No opposition during day.

Casualties – Nil.
Weather – Afternoon very cold & wet.
Distance marched. – 11 miles.

**Saturday 12th Sept**

4.50am  Advance continued via HARTENNES-
NAMTEUIL – many halts.
Heavy gun fire on left.
Brigade made long halt just South of
Ferme de l'Epitaphe.

6pm  Bn returned to NAMTEUIL and billeted.
Casualties. Nil.
Weather – Very cold & wet.
Distance marched. – 10 miles

**Sunday 13th Sept.**

4am  March continued.
5am  Brigade formed up at MONT DE SOISSONS
Farm as support to 13th Inf Bde, who were
attacking MISSY Bridge.
8am  Moved to road junction at 2nd S of
SERCHES where Bde formed up.
2.15pm  Bn moved back about 300x to avoid
shells aimed at our heavy battery.
9pm  Marched – Dorsets leading – to Mon DES
12 m/n  ROCHES and crossed R AISNE on
rafts – Brigade bivouacking on the
north bank –
Casualties – Nil
Weather. morning very cold & wet.
Later – finer.
Distance marched – 12 miles

Monday
14th Sept

4 am — Brigade moved (Dorsets finding Advanced guard) via BUCY-LE-LONG to Ste MARGUERITE where the Brigade came under shell fire.

7 am — Bn moved for cover into sunken road running N.W. through M of MARGUERITE. the rest of the Brigade taking cover in village
Village continually under shell fire.

12 noon — 15th Bde (less Dorsets who remained in sunken road) moved to attack ~~MISSY~~ CHIVRES Spur.
Bn was in touch with 14 Inf Bde on its right and Essex Regt on its left.
Ste MARGUERITE very heavily shelled all afternoon — 3 shells dropping into the sunken road & causing casualties. Firing ceased on both sides at dusk.

6.30 pm — Message received from 15th Bde that Bn was to billet at Ste MARGUERITE and that attack on CHIVRES Spur had failed — the remainder of the Bde being on railway with its right on MISSY Stn.

7. pm — Bn went into billets in Ste MARGUERITE
Casualties.
　　NCos and men.
　Killed　　1
　Wounded. 20
　Missing.　—
Weather — Fine, with showers — cold and windy.

**Tuesday 15 Sept**

4 am — Bn left billets "C" and "A" and Bn Hdqrs moving back to sunken road and "B" and "D" entrenching on slope in rear of sunken road.

5 am — Received message from brigade that attack on CHIVRES Spur was to be resumed at 6 am in conjunction with 13th Inf Bde. Dorsets to remain in reserve.

9.30 am — Very heavy shrapnel fire over sunken road — several casualties. Shellfire continued all morning.

1 pm — Received an order from Br Genl ROLT Comdg 14 Inf Bde that Bn was to join the rest of 15 Inf Bde which was at MISSY.

2 pm — The Bn moved to Farm (Genl Rolts Head Quarters). Thence A Coy was sent to occupy a green hill 600x E of this farm. C Coy being in support, while the remainder of the Bn in single file moved across the fields following stream running through SS of MISSY and 1st A of LA BEZAIE Fm.

A Coy came under oblique machine gun fire and suffered about a dozen casualties before dark.
"B and D" meanwhile entrenched themselves along the stream.

5 pm — Orders received for Bn to hold entrench line from Farm N of word MISSY — LA BEZAIE Fm.

line occupied as follows:—
B Coy from LA BEZAIE Fm to about LA of LA BEZAIE. D Coy from this point to Railway. C Coy on left of D Coy.

9 pm. Orders received from 15th Bde that Bde would retire via pontoon bridge at M^{lin} DES ROCHES and billet about LE MESNIL — Bns to retire independently.

10 pm. Bn concentrated on track 300x S of LA BEZAIE F^{m} and crossed by the pontoon bridge. Enemy's search light played on ground to west of Bn's line of march and heavy rifle fire was heard at MISSY, but the march was not disturbed.

Casualties.
    NCos & men.
Killed — 1
Wounded — 21
Missing — 4
Weather — Fine.

**Wednesday 16th Sept**

1 am. Bn reached JURY where it went into billets — where it remained throughout the day.
Weather — cold & showery.

**Thursday 17th Sept**
**Friday 18th Sept**
**Saturday 19th Sept**

Bn remained at JURY — Coys being engaged in digging trenches along SOISSONS—SERMOISE Road covering crossings of R. AISNE and preparing position on line 2^{nd} S of SERCHES — LE PAVILLON F^{m}
Weather unsettled, but improving.

**Sunday**
**20th Sept**

Remained in billets at JURY.
More work on LE PAVILLON 7th position

7.30pm — Bn ordered to fall in at once to proceed to SERMOISE. Order immediately afterwards cancelled.

Weather — Showery.

and

**Monday**
**21st Sept**

Remained in billets at JURY.

5.30pm — C and D Coys to man trenches (usual routine in Brigade)

7.45pm — Orders received from Bde for Bn to assemble at once at RAPREUX Fm

8.10pm — Bn Hdrs, A & B Coys, M.G. Section & 1st Line Transport marched to Farm

10.30pm — Orders received for Bn to bivouac at RAPREUX Fm and to be prepared to move to MISSY early the following morning.

10.30–11.15pm — A & B Coys & Hdrs billeted in barns at RAPREUX Fm

11.30pm — Orders received for Bn to return to billets as soon as CO. pleased.

11.30pm — Coys returned independently to billets. C and D having rejoined.

Weather fine.

and

**Tuesday**
**22nd Sept**

Orders received for Bn to proceed to MISSY after dark to relieve East Surreys.

12.30pm — Colonel Bols, Capts Fraser & Kitchin to MISSY to reconnoitre.

| | | |
|---|---|---|
| 2.30 pm | Orders for move to MISSY cancelled in anticipation of forward move tomorrow. | |
| | Weather fine | and |

**Wednesday 23rd Sept**

| | | |
|---|---|---|
| 10 am | Orders received to proceed to MISSY after dark | |
| 2.30 pm | Col. Bols, Capts Fraser & Kitchin to MISSY to complete reconnaissance. | |
| 6.10 pm | Bn under command of Major Roper and guided by Major Saunders crossed R. AISNE by pontoon bridge at M<sup>n</sup> DES ROCHES and marched to MISSY. A & B Coys occupied advanced trenches and C & D Coys were in reserve, relieving the East Surreys. | |
| | Colonel Bols took over command of No 2 Section of the Defences, consisting of Dorsets and West Riding Regt in MISSY village. | |
| | Whole move completed without mishap or firing by Enemy. | |
| | Weather fine | |
| | [4th Reinforcement joined about 5.30pm & was left at JURY] | and |

**Thursday 24th Sept**

Reported to 14/Bde
"All quiet during night — Trenches held by W. Riding Regt damaged yesterday by shell fire".
Coys engaged at improving trenches.
Quiet day — usual sniping.
Weather fine
W. Riding Regt relieved by K.O.Y.L.I

and

**Friday 25th Sept**

Reserve Corps engaged at improving the breastwork defences.
Quiet day.
Weather - fine.

5.15 pm  Following received from 15th Bde (who relieved 14th Bde H.Q. yesterday)
"In view of possibility of German counter attack during next 48 hours every possible precaution is to be taken"
Quiet night.

**Saturday 26th Sept.**

Quiet day.
Corps engaged at deepening trenches & digging communication trenches.
Quiet night.
Weather - fine.

**Sunday 27th Sept**

3.35 am  Message received from Col Martin Comdg No 1 Section of Defences that W. Riding Regt at GOBINNE Wood reported enemy crossing CONDÉ Bdge in large numbers at 1.40 am

4 am  Message from Bde "Stand to arms at once. The enemy is crossing the bridge at CONDÉ".

About 4.30am but untimed  Message from Bde "CONDÉ alarm unconfirmed - appears to be false"

10.45 am  Very heavy shelling which continued till dark - both shrapnel & high explosive.
Weather - fine.
Quiet night.  Casualties - Nil (notwithstanding heavy shelling)

Monday
28th Sept.
9.45am   Shelling commenced and continued
intermittently during the day - but
not nearly so heavily as yesterday.
Quiet night.
Weather fine but windy
Casualties   nil                                   and

Tuesday
29th Sept
9 am   Shelling commenced, but our guns
replying, it died away.
A few high explosives dropped over
the village at intervals - as usual.
Quiet night
Weather - fine.
Casualties - nil.                                  and

Wednesday
30th Sept.   Quiet day - slight shelling.
A few high explosive shells passed
over village, being directed at
SERMOISE village.
Quiet night -
Weather - fine
Casualties - nil.                                  and

Thursday
1st October   Quiet day.
About 7.30 p.m. a verbal order
were received that the Bⁿ
would be relieved by the
Essex Regt & would return to
                JURY.

5th Division
15th Inf.Bde.

WAR DIARY

1st DORSET REGT.

OCTOBER

1914.

39

| | |
|---|---|
| Thursday Oct 1st contd. | Quiet night. [Weather - fine] Casualties - Nil |
| Friday Oct 2nd | Bn. left MISSY at 12.35. A.M. [and concentrated by Companies at LA BEZACE FARM. "A" Coy proceeded independently from the hill having been relieved by the KING'S OWN. Bn. [then] marched to JURY [crossing R. AISNE by pontoon bridge at M͟s͟n͟ DES ROCHES & occupied its old billets.] ~~Remained there that day~~ ~~Weather, fine and night~~ ~~Distance~~ Weather ~~fine.~~ ~~Casualties~~ Nil. |
| ~~Saturday~~ ~~Oct 4th~~ 2nd | Bn. spent the day in billets. Paraded 4.0 pm & marched to [via. SERCHES - NAMPTEUIL - DROIZY -] LAUNOY. Reached LAUNOY about 12. mid-night [& went into billets. Weather fine. Casualties - Nil. ] |
| ~~Sunday~~ ~~Oct 4th~~ Saturday Oct 3rd. | Spent the day in billets. Instructions were received that baggage wagons would accompany Battalion. Bn. paraded at 6.0 pm & marched via HARTENNES - PARCY TIGNY - |

MONTREMBOEUF F". – LONG PONT –
CORCY. – Reached CORCY about
12. M.N [ & billeted
    Distance
    Weather        fine ]
    Casualties    Nil.

~~Monday Oct 4th~~

Sunday Oct 4th.

Remained in billets during the day.
B". Paraded at 9.0 p.m and marched to FRESNOY LA RIVIERE. During the march we were held up for two hours by long convoy of French troops in motor wagons.

5.15 am Reached FRESNOY ~~at 6 & went into billets~~

Monday Oct 5th

5.15 am B" reached FRESNOY [ & went into billets ]
    Weather fine
    Casualties ——— Nil
    Distance.

Tues

B" [remained] in billets all that day & night. Good night with following notice appeared in Routine orders
"Lt. Col L. J. Bols D.S.O. now commanding 1st B" Dorsetshire Reg" to be A.A. & Q.M.G. 6th Div vice Colonel W. Campbell D.S.O. dated 1st Oct 1914.

| | |
|---|---|
| Tuesday 6th Oct. | Bn paraded at 2.45 pm with orders to march to BETHISY. On arrival there further orders were received that the Bn would go to billets in VERBERIE. All the way from BETHISY the Bn was held up by the 14th Bde & it took about 3 hours to go 4 miles. Great Secrecy again observed. |

[ Weather     Fine.
  Casualties  Nil
  Distance.           ]

| | |
|---|---|
| 11.30 p.m | Orders were received that the Bn would entrain at COMPIEGNE & would be there at ~~7.0 pm~~ 7.0.a.m. |
| Wed 7th | Paraded at 3.0.a.m marched via the BOIS DE COMPIEGNE. (great secrecy) |
| 7.15 a.m | Arrived COMPIEGNE Stn |
| 7.30 a.m | Began loading the transport. Accommodation was good for this purpose. |
| 10.0 a.m | Troops all entrained |
| 10.0 am | Train left. |
| 12.2 pm | Arrived at AMIENS & left at once. Arrived at ABBEVILLE [ & were told |
| Thurs 8th | that we had come too far & were sent back to ~~PONT REME~~ PONT REMY [R.T.O there said that we ought to go back to ABBEVILLE. This was eventually found impossible so Bn ] Detrained. Great difficulty about transport as there were little or no facilities |
| 2.0 A.M | Detrainment of transport finished by 2.0 A.M. |

Thurs 8th
cont'd.

3.0.a.m  B'n paraded and marched to NEUILLY &
billeted. via ABBEVILLE
~~Weath~~

6.0 p.m.  B'n paraded. marched to/via AGENVILLERS -
CAPENNES - NOYELLE - GUESCHART. -
BOUFFLERS -] GENNE IVERGNY. [Maj
Roper was sent on to arrange the
billets.]

11.45 P.M  Arrived [& went into Billets.
Weather - fine.
Distance marched.]

Friday
9th Oct

5 p.m.  Marched leaving all vehicles except Supply wagons
in billets via LE PONCHEL to HARAVESNES where
B'n billeted preparatory to being conveyed forward
in motor omnibuses.
[Weather - fine
Distance marched.]

Saturday
10th Oct

3 am  Moved to high ground 1 mile NNE of HARAVESNES to
wait for motors.

4 am  Ordered to return to billets as motors would not arrive
till about 11.am - B'n returned to billets.

10.30 am  B'n returned to ~~billets~~ high ground 1 mile NNE of HARAVESNES

2.30 p.m  Motors arrived and B'n embarked (less 1 platoon C Coy and
D Coy - proceeding via ST POL

5.30 p.m  Reached LA THIEULOYE and billeted.
Weather - fine

Sunday
11th Oct

7.50 AM   Marched via BRUAY to BETHUNE
B and C Coy on outposts along line of canal
from GORRE to Ferme du ROI. The remainder
of Bn being in BETHUNE near B of BETHUNE

7 pm   Bn (less outpost Coys) billeted in street in
BETHUNE.

and

Monday
12th Oct

? am   Bn marched with 15th Bde via GORRE towards
FESTHUBERT. Bn halted on RUE DE BETHUNE
owing to shell fire and then moved South
to Canal, thence along canal towpath to
PONT FIXE. A & D Coys were ordered to occupy
positions South & North of the bridge A Coy being
on the South and D Coy on the North.
One machine gun was placed on the 1st floor of
a big unfinished factory just North of the
canal bank.
There was no immediate German advance
but the machine gun in the factory opened
on Germans debouching from Lichfeld
near H of CUINCHY. The German firing line
was checked by this fire. Later a movement
of Germans was detected just S of U of CUINCHY
but their advance presented a good target
to the machine gun and the Germans fell back

4 pm   General advance of Dorsets ordered in conjunction    objective
(about)   with French on right and 1/Bedford Regt on the        LA BASSÉE
left A Coy moving on ~~right~~ South bank of

of the canal and D Coy on the South bank forming the firing line was B & C Coy being in reserve. The machine gun was ordered to support the attack.

A Coy moved up the South bank under cover of high bank and did not come under fire from CUINCHY (although held by the enemy) and subsequently inflicted severe loss upon Germans North of CUINCHY. Meanwhile D Coy. advancing from the factory towards a small farm about 200 yds East of it came under heavy cross fire from snipers on the high canal bank (South side) and suffered casualties – Major Roper was killed at this farm about 4.30 pm.

Attack had made excellent progress, and a line had been established from LA BASSÉE Canal to large farm South of GIVENCHY. Dispositions for night.

B and C Coys entrenched on rise upon which above mentioned Farm stood.

A Coy withdrawn to PONT FIXE and with D Coy and Bn H.d Qrs billeted there.

Casualties 11 killed 30 wounded 2 missing

# WAR DIARY
## or
## INTELLIGENCE SUMMARY.
(Erase heading not required.)

Army Form C. 2118.

Instructions regarding War Diaries and Intelligence Summaries are contained in F.S. Regs., Part II. and the Staff Manual respectively. Title pages will be prepared in manuscript.

| Hour, Date, Place | Summary of Events and Information | Remarks and references to Appendices |
|---|---|---|
| 13th Oct 1914 PONT FIXE - GIVENCHY. Near LA BASSEE 5.30AM | In accordance with Bde orders Bn moved at 5.30 am as follows: Firing line B and C Coys. Support A Coy. Reserve A Coy. Machine guns were in position in house on North bank of canal near 1 of PONT FIXE. Advance was slow owing in part to fire units on right and left trying to get in line. | Reference ARRAS map. 12-13 OCT. Note O C Coys were as follows:- A. Captain W A C FRASER B. Captain I H KITCHIN C. Major C SAUNDERS D. Captain W T S DAVIDSON Machine Gun Officer Captain A L RANSOME |
| 7.20AM | Report to Bde that Bn had reached line 200X East of track running South from E of GIVENCHY, and that advance had been checked to enable troops on right and left to come up into line. Also that there appeared to be little opposition in front. | Bn on right  1 Bedfords Bn on left  2 K.O.S. Borderers aul |
| 9.10AM | Situation remained the same till 9 am; the village of CUINCHY on South bank of canal being in cleared of the enemy. O.C. Coys reported situation to Bde Hdrs Bn fourteen was the same as reported at 7.20 am. | |

Army Form C. 2118.

# WAR DIARY
## or
## INTELLIGENCE SUMMARY.
(Erase heading not required.)

Instructions regarding War Diaries and Intelligence Summaries are contained in F. S. Regs., Part II. and the Staff Manual respectively. Title pages will be prepared in manuscript.

| Hour, Date, Place | Summary of Events and Information | Remarks and references to Appendices |
|---|---|---|
| 13ᵗʰ Oct (cont) | | |
| 11.20 am | Enemy shelled B Coy heavily from a North East'ly direction. | |
| 12 noon | Hostile machine gun opened heavy enfilade fire at short range on our right flank – near Canal Bank. B Coy commenced to withdraw as their right was exposed. OC Dorsets reported situation and asked for artillery support | B Coy lost Capt Kitchin & 2/Lt Wheeler wounded and Lt Turner and 2/Lt Smith killed. |
| 12.30 pm | Enemy's artillery machine gun fire increased in volume and firing line gradually fell back on trenches occupied by supports. | |
| 12.45 pm | Major SAUNDERS sent to dispose reserve Company and inform artillery commander of situation | |
| 1.45 pm | Germans advanced from East end of GIVENCHY, some carrying lances. About 250 suddenly appeared from the left rear of C Coy. These were mistaken for French cavalry and fire was not opened on them. About a Battalion appeared about 900ˣ from left of C Coy. out |

# WAR DIARY or INTELLIGENCE SUMMARY.

*(Erase heading not required.)*

Army Form C. 2118.

| Hour, Date, Place | Summary of Events and Information | Remarks and references to Appendices |
|---|---|---|
| | As soon as it was seen that there were Germans & fire was opened on them. The Germans advanced holding up their rifles in both hands. This was taken as a sign of surrender. Some men left the trench to go towards the Germans, who then closed in rapidly driving in our men and enfilading the trench. The position of remaining men was hopeless untenable. Lt Col BOLS and Lt and Adjt PITT remained in the trench in which they had been all day. Col Bols was severely wounded in attempting to get away. Lt Pitt killed. The retirement was skilfully covered by the Reserve Company (A Coy) under Captain W. A. C. Fraser, who in turn retired to a position in buildings about PONT FIXE – and a new line was established from PONT FIXE to factory, the line being thus continued by 2 Coys. 1st DEVONS along PONT FIXE – FESTUBERT Road. Enemy made two attacks on A Coy 1st DEVON Corps during the night but was repulsed. | C Coy lost Lt Fraser wounded and missing Captain Kellock, Lt Grant, Oarleman Lt Cluttenbuck missing<br><br>D Coy lost Capt Davidson and Lt Parkinson killed and Capt Rothman wounded<br><br>Colonel Bols was taken prisoner by the Germans. Who told him to wait for the Ambulance. He waited till dusk and then returned to our lines.<br><br>Command of Battalion devolved upon Major C. Saunders |

Casualties:- 51 Killed, 52 Wounded, 21 ? Missing.

Army Form C. 2118.

# WAR DIARY
## or
## INTELLIGENCE SUMMARY.
(Erase heading not required.)

| Hour, Date, Place | Summary of Events and Information | Remarks and references to Appendices |
|---|---|---|
| 14th Oct.<br>PONT FIXE<br>near GIVENCHY. | Position of Bn. at daylight<br>A Coy holding factory at PONT FIXE with 2 Coy DEVONS on their left.<br>B, C, & D Coys formed up in one Company under Captain H. BEVERIDGE were moved at daylight down South of Canal to a position about ½ mile west of PONT FIXE<br>A Coy under heavy shell fire all day in Factory.<br>Message received from 13th Bde. "PONT FIXE must not be given up. I know I can rely on you to stick to it with the help of the Devons."<br>2 pm. French attack on VERMELLES twice to commence.<br>5 pm. Advice to Atty. to support attack by 2 Coy DEVONS but not to move till advance by 13th Bde on South South of Canal commenced.<br>Enemy attacked 13th Bde on South Bank of Canal | Reference ARRAS map.<br><br><br><br><br><br><br><br><br><br><br><br><br><br><br><br>out |

Army Form C. 2118.

# WAR DIARY
## or
## INTELLIGENCE SUMMARY.
*(Erase heading not required.)*

Instructions regarding War Diaries and Intelligence Summaries are contained in F. S. Regs., Part II. and the Staff Manual respectively. Title pages will be prepared in manuscript.

| Hour, Date, Place | | Summary of Events and Information | Remarks and references to Appendices |
|---|---|---|---|
| PONT FIXE – 15th Oct. GIVENCHY | 8.30pm | Enemy attacked our line and were repulsed. Casualties 3 wounded | Reference ARRAS map. |
| | 7.30pm | Bn removed at PONT FIXE. Also shelled in morning. Bn relieved by DEVON Regt. Bn marched via Canal Bank to LOISNE where it went into billets. | and |
| FESTUBERT 16th Oct | 6am | Bn rendezvous'd at least E. of RUE DE BETHUNE. Coming under orders of 13th Bde – turning Div's coal Resolve with 1. Riding Regt. Billets at FESTUBERT. | and |
| 17th Oct | 7am | Bn assembled at least E. of RUE DE BETHUNE where it remained all day. Billets at FESTUBERT | and |
| 18th Oct | 6am | Fell in on alarm posts and were then dismissed | and |

(9 29 6) W 2794  100,000  8/14  H W V    Forms/C. 2118/11.

**WAR DIARY** or **INTELLIGENCE SUMMARY.**

(Erase heading not required.)

Army Form C. 2118.

Instructions regarding War Diaries and Intelligence Summaries are contained in F. S. Regs., Part II. and the Staff Manual respectively. Title pages will be prepared in manuscript.

| Hour, Date, Place | | Summary of Events and Information | Remarks and references to Appendices |
|---|---|---|---|
| RUE D'OUVERT | 18th Oct (cont) 10am | Moved with 16 RIDING Regt to RUE D'OUVERT. On came under high explosive shell fire on road to RUE OUVERT. | |
| | 6pm | Bn turned up in reserve behind bank about ¼ mile S.W. of C of CHLLE ST ROCH. | |
| | 6pm | Billeted in RUE D'OUVERT | |
| — — | 19th Oct 5am | Returned to position occupied on 18th | |
| | 6pm | Billeted at RUED'OUVERT | |
| — — | 20th Oct 5am | Returned to position occupies on two previous days. | |
| | 2/3pm | Bn advanced to move to a position near d' of 9 RUE D'OUVERT. A Coy occupying ridge and C composite Company being in line | |
| | 7pm 11pm | found in position by relief Aln and entrenched. Bn withdrawn and moved to RUE DU MARAIS, where it went into billets. | auR |
| | | Casualties — one wounded. | |

# WAR DIARY
## INTELLIGENCE SUMMARY.
*(Erase heading not required.)*

Army Form C. 2118.

| Hour, Date, Place | Summary of Events and Information | Remarks and references to Appendices |
|---|---|---|
| RUE DU MARAIS. 21st Oct. | | Reference ARRAS map. |
| 3.30pm | Heavy firing in direction of VIOLAINES. A Coy moved to a position in rear of BEDFORDS on road running S.W. from VE of RUE D'OUVERT | |
| 4.30pm | Report received CHESHIRES retiring from VIOLAINES. | |
| 5.pm | CHESHIRE retirement checked. Report referred to me Trench only. | and |
| 6.45pm | Adv's sent to A Coy to entrench position to the front not by Officer of R.E. | |
| 22nd Oct. | | |
| 2.30am | Heavy firing from direction of LORGNIES. A Coy report position of trenches very exposed and vulnerable by day. Advs sent to A Coy that trenches must be occupied. Difficulties of A Coy reported to 13th Bde. | and |

Forms/C. 2118/11.

Army Form C. 2118.

# WAR DIARY
## or
## INTELLIGENCE SUMMARY

(Erase heading not required.)

| Hour, Date, Place | Summary of Events and Information | Remarks and references to Appendices |
|---|---|---|
| 22nd Oct (cont) 5.50am | Enemy attacked VIOLAINES and carried CHESHIRES trenches cheering loudly. Reserve platoon placed in position astride RUE DU MARAIS. VIOLAINES and one machine gun placed South of road. Efforts were made to collect men & reinforce who were coming back through RUE DU MARAIS. One machine gun had been sent forward under Lt C.H. WOOD HOUSE before daylight to find a position to sweep road running North and South through VIOLAINES. Lt WOOD HOUSE was unable to reach position before German attack succeeded and was last seen firing his revolver. His gun and tripod was lost. | Note. 3 platoons of Lonsdales Company has been sent up to its position as previous day. |
| 6.45am | Enemy brought machine gun to north end of VIOLAINES and enfilades trenches held C. composite Coy, rendering them untenable. One platoon of A Coy (under 2/Lt G.S SHANNON) remained in its position till dusk forming touch with K.O.S.B. on its left. | Captain Beverage and Butcher was wounded. Lt King was who wounded. and |

Army Form C. 2118.

# WAR DIARY
## or
## INTELLIGENCE SUMMARY.
(Erase heading not required.)

Instructions regarding War Diaries and Intelligence Summaries are contained in F. S. Regs., Part II. and the Staff Manual respectively. Title pages will be prepared in manuscript.

| Hour, Date, Place | Summary of Events and Information | Remarks and references to Appendices |
|---|---|---|
| 22nd Oct (cont) | From reports received it appeared that attainment of CHESHIRES when trenches were visited reached pre by DORSET Coy who were digging. Reserve platoon under C.S.M. HOLLOWAY maintained its ground at RUE DU MARAIS. | |
| 7am — 11 am | A second position was gradually taken up at LA QUINQUE RUE behind which men were collected. A Coy and machine gun were then placed in position along main road first South of QUIN of LA QUINQUE RUE, where men of CHESHIRES BEDFORDS and part of Coy. Compts. Coy DORSETS has been collected, the MANCHESTERS having come up to RUE DU MARAIS. Remainder of day quiet. German advance | |
| 8pm | checked - | |
| 8pm | Bn withdrawn to FESTUBERT. Casualties. Captain H. BEVERIDGE wounded and missing Lt F. D. S. KING and 2nd Lt C.G. BUTCHER wounded Lt C.H. LINDAHOUSE missing. Casualties. 4 killed, 22 wounded, 107 missing | (over) |

(0 29 6) W 2791 100,000 8/14 H W V Forms/C. 2118/11.

# WAR DIARY
## or
## INTELLIGENCE SUMMARY.
(Erase heading not required.)

Army Form C. 2118.

| Hour, Date, Place | | Summary of Events and Information | Remarks and references to Appendices |
|---|---|---|---|
| FESTUBERT. 23rd Oct | 6.30pm | Bn. bivouaced in billets about ½ mile west of RUE DE BETHUNE. Bn. with CHESHIRES assembled in field at back E. of RUE DE BETHUNE and bivouaced. | Reference ARRAS map. and |
| 24th Oct | | | |
| FESTUBERT | 6am | Bn. returned to billets | |
| | 6.30pm | Bn. with CHESHIRES assembled as previous evening. Road through FESTUBERT repaired. Bn. ordered to return to billets but to be ready to turn out at a moment's notice. | and |
| FESTUBERT 25th Oct | | Remained in billets | |
| | 4pm | Orders received to stand to arms. Bn. moved to position about ½ mile west of last E. of RUE DE BETHUNE | |
| | 6pm | All quiet. Batt'n returned to billets | and |

Army Form C. 2118.

# WAR DIARY
## or
## INTELLIGENCE SUMMARY.
(Erase heading not required.)

| Hour, Date, Place | | Summary of Events and Information | Remarks and references to Appendices |
|---|---|---|---|
| GORRE | 26th Oct | Day spent in billets at GORRE. Bn found working parties under R.E. | Reference ARRAS map. |
| | 6pm | Bn moves to old billets near last E. of RUE DE BETHUNE | |
| LE TOURET | 27th Oct | | |
| | 6 am | Bn marched via RUE de L'EPINETTE to billets at LE TOURET | |
| | 4 pm | Reinforcement of 5 Officers and 310 men joined. | |
| | 6.15 pm | Bn ordered to move to Road junction 200x west of R ni RUE de l'EPINETTE. | |
| | 6.30 pm | Bn marched to RICHEBOURG - L'AVOUÉ. CHESHIRES, D.C.L.I., and 2 Coys BEDFORDS also assembled in RICHEBOURG, with a view to intended night attack on NEUVE CHAPPEL. Bn remained all night by road side. | Reference LILLE map. |
| RICHEBOURG L'AVOUÉ | 28th Oct | | |
| | 6 am | Owing to difficulties of ground & fact that enemy posture at | |

# WAR DIARY or INTELLIGENCE SUMMARY

Army Form C. 2118.

| Hour, Date, Place | Summary of Events and Information | Remarks and references to Appendices |
|---|---|---|
| RICHEBOURG 28th Oct x L'AVOUE — RICHEBOURG ST VAAST. | NEUVE CHAPPEL had not been reconnoitred, night attack was abandoned, and DORSETS BEDFORDS, CHESHIRES, and 2E L1 moved into position as support to 7th Bde and into of Indian Brigade who were to make a day attack. | Reference LILLE and ST OMER – ARRAS 1/40/40 |
| 7am | Bn moved into cover inside in a ditch running NW and SE through V of NEUVE CHAPPELLE. Bn remained in this position throughout day. Certain amount of Shelling – Casualties – nil. Weather – fine. | |
| 10pm. | Bn moved into billets at ST VAAST. Joined there by Captain Fraser and Reinforcement which had come up during the day from LE TOURET. | auth |
| 29th Oct RUE de L'EPINETTE. 4.15am | Marched via RICHEBOURG ST VAAST to Cnr de L'EPINETTE (14th Bde HdQrs) advise to billet at RUE DE L'EPINETTE. | auth |

Army Form C. 2118.

# WAR DIARY
## or
## INTELLIGENCE SUMMARY.
(Erase heading not required.)

| Hour, Date, Place | Summary of Events and Information | Remarks and references to Appendices |
|---|---|---|
| RUE de L'EPINETTE. 29 Oct (cont) | Reinforcement distributed to Companies. | Reference ARRAS map. |
| 7.30 a.m. | Received order to be ready to move at a moments notice. | |
| 9.30 a.m. | To LT LAVENTIE RUE to support MANCHESTERS — Order cancelled — all quiet. | |
| 11.30 a.m. | A and B Coys ordered to last E of RUE DE BETHUNE and were come under zero of 13th Bde. | and |
| 6.30 p.m. | A and B Coys returned to billets as Bn has received orders to collect at RUE DE L'EPINETTE. Casualties — Nil. 3 men wounded | |
| | ~~RUE DE L'EPINETTE~~ Quiet day. | |
| 8 p.m. | Relief of Burnhill by Indian Bde commenced. Evening very wet. Heavy firing during night. Received no orders to move next day. | |

# WAR DIARY or INTELLIGENCE SUMMARY.

(Erase heading not required.)

Army Form C. 2118.

| Hour, Date, Place | | Summary of Events and Information | Remarks and references to Appendices |
|---|---|---|---|
| CALONNE. | 30th Oct 2 p.m. | Bn marched to CALONNE and billeted. Distance - 12 miles. Weather - wet. | Reference: ST OMER map and |
| STRAZEELE. | 31st Oct 9.30 a.m. | Bn marches to STRAZEELE and billeted. Distance - 13 miles. Weather - fine. | Reference OSTEND map. and 39 M |
| STRAZEELE | 1st Nov. 7.30 a.m. 10.10 a.m. | Received orders to be ready to move at nearly hrs. Gen Sir H Smith-Dorrien Cmdg II Corps address Officers @ 1.18th | — |
| NEUVE EGLISE. | 10.15 a.m. | Bn left in motor buses. 1st Line Transport follows. Proceeded via BAILLEUL - DRANOUTRE - LINDEN HOCK to NEUVE EGLISE | — and |

5th Division
15th Inf. Bde.

# WAR DIARY

## 1st DORSET REGT.

## NOVEMBER

## 1914

WAR DIARY (Original with Diary for October 1914.)

STRAZEELE  1st Nov.
 7.50 a.m.   Received orders to be ready to move at once by bus.

 10.10.a.m.  General Sir H.Smith-Dorrien Comdg.II Corps addressed officers of battalion.

 10.15.a.m.  Battalion left in Motor Busses. 1st Line Transport followed. Proceeded
NEUVE        via BAILLEUL-DRANOUTRE-LINDENHOCK to NEUVE EGLISE.
EGLISE

Army Form C. 2118.

# WAR DIARY
## or
## INTELLIGENCE SUMMARY.
*(Erase heading not required.)*

| Hour, Date, Place | Summary of Events and Information | Remarks and references to Appendices |
|---|---|---|
| NEUVE EGLISE. 12 Nov (cont) | | Reference OSTEND MAP. |
| 1 pm. | Formed up in field. | |
| 3.30 pm. | Moved into billets at NEUVE EGLISE | |
| 5 pm. | Following out dispositions ordered. | |
| | B Coy. outposts from Road Junction 1 mile South B.W. of WULVERGHEM to NEUVE EGLISE – WULVERGHEM Road. Both inclusive. | |
| | C and D Coys to extend position astride above road about ¾ mile N.E. of INN. | 39 |
| | A Coy. Reserve in billets. | |
| 6 pm. | Above cancelled. B Coy withdrawn less 1 Platoon on WULVERGHEM Road. Quiet night. Bm came under orders of 4th Division. | aut? |

Army Form C. 2118.

# WAR DIARY
## or
## INTELLIGENCE SUMMARY.
(Erase heading not required.)

Instructions regarding War Diaries and Intelligence Summaries are contained in F. S. Regs., Part II. and the Staff Manual respectively. Title pages will be prepared in manuscript.

| Hour, Date, Place | | Summary of Events and Information | Remarks and references to Appendices |
|---|---|---|---|
| NEUVE EGLISE 2nd Nov. | | | Reference OSTEND map |
| PLOEGSTEERT Wood | 2 pm | Bn ordered to move via PETIT PONT to Road Junction at 1st S of BOIS DE PLOEGSTEERT. Moved to this point. | |
| | 4 pm | Bn moved back about half a mile and cooked. | |
| | about 6 pm | A Coy moved to road about ½ mile west of LE GHEER as support to Battalion in trenches in that locality. B and D Coys moved to entrench in PLOEGSTEERT woods South of CHATEAU on PLOEGSTEERT — MESSINES Road. C Coy remained in reserve. | 39 ct our |
| — 3rd Nov. | | B, C & D Coys occupied trenches in PLOEGSTEERT wood along hedge of Bois de PLOEGSTEERT. A Coy remained at LE GHEER. Intermittent shelling throughout day. | |
| | 4 pm | A was sent to Coy that Battalion was relieving Royal | |

Forms/C. 2118/11.

Army Form C. 2118.

# WAR DIARY
## or
## INTELLIGENCE SUMMARY.
(Erase heading not required.)

Instructions regarding War Diaries and Intelligence Summaries are contained in F. S. Regs., Part II. and the Staff Manual respectively. Title pages will be prepared in manuscript.

| Hour, Date, Place | Summary of Events and Information | Remarks and references to Appendices |
|---|---|---|
| PLOEGSTEERT WOOD | Inniskilling Fusiliers. | Reference OSTEND map. |
| 6 p.m. | Relief commenced, the bn taking over line as follows — C.Coy astride PLOEGSTEERT – MESSINES Road – A Coy – B Coy – D Coy whose left rested near River DOUVE. Quiet night. | |
| 4th Nov. | Quiet morning. | 39 |
| 1.20 p.m. | Reports to Colonel BUTLER (O.C. Section) that French were retiring from direction of INSTITUTE ROYALE and that counter attack seemed probable. | ault |
| 3.15 p.m. | Reports to Colonel BUTLER situation satisfactory. | |
| 6 p.m. | Reported situation quiet – Patrol sent to gain touch with French right. | |
| 9.15 p.m. | Order sent to D Coy to gain touch with Cavalry in its left. | ault |

Army Form C. 2118.

# WAR DIARY
## or
## INTELLIGENCE SUMMARY.
*(Erase heading not required.)*

Instructions regarding War Diaries and Intelligence Summaries are contained in F.S. Regs., Part II. and the Staff Manual respectively. Title pages will be prepared in manuscript.

| Hour, Date, Place | Summary of Events and Information | Remarks and references to Appendices |
|---|---|---|
| PLOEGSTEERT WOOD 5th Nov. | | Reference OSTEND map. |
| 6.45am | Report to Colonel BUTLER. Situation quiet — no attack last night. | |
| 10.5am | Reported to Colonel BUTLER that patrol was in touch with French troops just South East of Point 25. French expected to attack MESSINES. | 39 |
| 5.30pm | Were moved further to remain in its present position. | |
| 6pm | Information received from Colonel BUTLER of intended French advance — All Companies warned. | |
| 7pm | Heavy rifle fire from our trenches near MESSINES Road. Also heavy German rifle fire. Report brought in that Germans has broken through. Report sent to SOMERSET L.I. to this effect. Reserve trench by Battalion occupied and preparations made to counter attack with C. Coy. | aus |
| 7.30pm | Fire slackened — no sign of enemy. | |

Army Form C. 2118.

# WAR DIARY
## or
## INTELLIGENCE SUMMARY.
(Erase heading not required.)

Instructions regarding War Diaries and Intelligence Summaries are contained in F. S. Regs., Part II. and the Staff Manual respectively. Title pages will be prepared in manuscript.

| Hour, Date, Place | Summary of Events and Information | Remarks and references to Appendices |
|---|---|---|
| PLOEGSTEERT WOOD. 5th Nov. | | Reference OSTEND map. |
| 8 p.m. | Reported to Colonel BUTLER situation satisfactory. Fog very thick — quiet night. | over |
| 6th Nov. | Quiet morning. | |
| 8.25 p.m. | Reported situation satisfactory — certain amount of fire. | 39 |
| 9 p.m. | Machine gun placed in A Coy line. | |
| 7th Nov. 12.30 a.m. 1.30 a.m. | Heavy rifle fire. Reported situation quiet. | over |
| 8.30 a.m. | Information received that general attack by Germans was probable — All Companies warned to instant readiness. | |
| 12 noon | Reported little activity in either trench afternoon. | |
| 3.35 p.m. | Similar report sent in. | |

Army Form C. 2118.

# WAR DIARY
## or
## INTELLIGENCE SUMMARY.
(Erase heading not required.)

Instructions regarding War Diaries and Intelligence Summaries are contained in F. S. Regs., Part II. and the Staff Manual respectively. Title pages will be prepared in manuscript.

| Hour, Date, Place | Summary of Events and Information | Remarks and references to Appendices |
|---|---|---|
| PLOEGSTEERT WOOD. 8th Nov. 9a.m. | Quiet day - nothing unusual | Reference OSTEND map 39F and |
| 9 a.m. 10th Nov. | — Casualties 1 killed 2 wounded | and |
| 9 a.m. | Report situation satisfactory and connection maintained -ed with French | |
| | Quiet day Intermittent shelling during night - | and |
| 11th Nov. 7.25 a.m. | Repeated situation quiet - French positions unchanged | |
| 9 a.m to 12 noon 8.25 p.m. | Considerable shelling by German light gun. Reported "D" Coy withdrawn - situation quiet | and |
| 12th Nov | Troubled by German light gun at battalion's dug out. B Coy engaged at digging during night | and |

(9 29 6) W 2794 100,000 8/14 H W V Forms/C. 2118/11.

Army Form C. 2118.

# WAR DIARY
## or
## INTELLIGENCE SUMMARY.
(Erase heading not required.)

| Hour, Date, Place | Summary of Events and Information | Remarks and references to Appendices |
|---|---|---|
| PLOEGSTEERT Wood 13th Nov. | Intermittent shelling | Reference OSTEND map |
| 5.30 pm | D Coy ordered to dig under orders of R.E. | |
| 10.53 pm | A Coy sent to B Coy to withdraw to Hun Road S.W. of Pt 63 before daylight. Blue ready for digging by daylight. Casualties. Two killed, one wounded | 3 copies and |
| 14th Nov. 7 am | Report battery to Chateau Lodge S.E. of Pt 63. Intermittent shelling | |
| 4.55 pm | Orders sent to B Coy to relieve C Coy in trenches after dark. C Coy to move to Hun Road S. of Pt 63 for digging. | |
| 8 pm | Moved Buttles to Chateau Lodge ¼ mile South of Pt 63. one killed. Other ranks Casualties. Major Ounders wounded. has wounded. Major Fraser assumed command of B⁴ | and |
| 15th Nov. 6 am | Reported Situation quiet. | |
| 9 am | Orders received for Captain Withdraw to take Command after | |

Army Form C. 2118.

# WAR DIARY
## or
## INTELLIGENCE SUMMARY.
*(Erase heading not required.)*

Instructions regarding War Diaries and Intelligence Summaries are contained in F. S. Regs., Part II. and the Staff Manual respectively. Title pages will be prepared in manuscript.

| Hour, Date, Place | Summary of Events and Information | Remarks and references to Appendices |
|---|---|---|
| PLOEGSTEERT WOOD. 15 Nov. | Battalion rec'd Major Gras as appointed Brigade transport officer. Quiet day. A + B Coy still in trenches. D Coy advised to open out their men in pits along their own and B Coy old front. C Coy engaged at digging | Reference OSTEND 20p. Auth |
| 16 Nov. 12.5 am | Moved to B Coy to concentrate at Bn Hd Qrs at 5.30 am Machine gun also withdrawn from A Coys trench. | |
| 4 am | Reported situation quiet | |
| 6 am | Bn (less A + B Coys) concentrated at Bn Hd Qrs | |
| 2 pm | Report received that part of platoon of B Coy buried by high explosive shells | |
| 2.30 pm | Two platoons of C Coy advised to support B Coy. | |
| 6 p.m. | Orders sent to A + B Coys to withdraw to Bn Hd Qrs as soon as relieved in trenches | |
| 6.30 pm | Orders sent cancelling above. | |

**Army Form C. 2118.**

# WAR DIARY
## or
## INTELLIGENCE SUMMARY.
*(Erase heading not required.)*

Instructions regarding War Diaries and Intelligence Summaries are contained in F.S. Regs., Part II. and the Staff Manual respectively. Title pages will be prepared in manuscript.

| Hour, Date, Place | Summary of Events and Information | Remarks and references to Appendices |
|---|---|---|
| PLOEGSTEERT WOOD 16th Nov (cont) | | Reference OSTEND map |
| 6.35 pm | Orders issued to C Coy to relieve A Coy in trenches. Casualties. 5 killed, 2 wounded. | ant |
| 17th Nov | | |
| 4.35 am | Reported situation quiet. | |
| 10 am | A and D Coys found working parties for digging in PLOEGSTEERT Wood. | |
| 5.45 pm | D Coy sent to A Coy 10/find working party to dig trench connecting ?????? HASSNECK & 2nd RIFLE BRIGADE and ROYAL SCOTS. | ※ |
| 16th Nov. | Orders sent to B Coy to withdraw to Battalion after relief by LANCASHIRE Fusiliers. Remaining Companies detailed for digging for digging in & digging at night. Casualties — nil | ant |
| 18th Nov. | | |
| 12 noon | A and B Coys employed at digging | ↓ |

# WAR DIARY
## or
## INTELLIGENCE SUMMARY

*(Erase heading not required.)*

Army Form C. 2118.

| Hour, Date, Place | | Summary of Events and Information | Remarks and references to Appendices |
|---|---|---|---|
| PLOEGSTEERT WOOD | 18th Nov (cont) | Address to relief of Bn by R. IRISH. FUS. received | Reference OSTEND map auth 1 |
| | 19th Nov | | |
| | 5 am | Bn concentrated near PETIT PONT | |
| | 7 am | Bn marched via NEUVE EGLISE to neighbd of DRANOUTRE where it went into billets in area S and SE of DRANOUTRE. Companies were very scattered. Major Fraser resumed Command of Bn. Bn came under orders of 14th Bde. | |
| DRANOUTRE | 20th-21st-22nd-23rd Nov. | Bn remained in billets at DRANOUTRE. Bn inspected and addressed by General Sir H. Smith-Dorrien Comdg II nd Corps on 22nd. On 23rd moves for III rd Army away to shell fire. | and 1 |
| LINDENHOCK | 24th Nov 4 pm | Bn marched to via LINDENHOCK to billets East Sunep in trenches near Point 75, 1 mile S.W. of WYTSCHAETE | and 1 |

# WAR DIARY
## or
## INTELLIGENCE SUMMARY.
(Erase heading not required.)

Army Form C. 2118.

| Hour, Date, Place | Summary of Events and Information | Remarks and references to Appendices |
|---|---|---|
| LINDENHOEK 25th Nov. | | Reference OSTEND map. |
| 2.10am | Relief of 2nd Surreys completed. | |
| 5.10am | Situation quiet - snipers very active | |
| 9am | Memo received re active counter sniping from 14th Bde. | |
| 6.40pm | Report to 14th Bde. Twelve shells 9mm guns. Situation quiet - still unconnected by telephone. Casualties 2 killed, 2 wounded. | Auth. |
| 10pm | Outburst of rifle fire. | 39 A |
| 26th Nov. | | |
| 2.20am | Heavy rifle fire - Germans used machine gun - no hostile advance | |
| 7.20am | Reported situation quiet to 14th Bde. | |
| 6pm | British Bde. ad. us received re counter sniping. Sapping etc. Reports to Bde. all quiet - Large number of unexploded shells noticed. Casualties 3 killed, 4 wounded. | Auth. |
| 27th Nov. 6am | Reported to 14th Bde. quiet night - no movement of trenches carried out | |
| 11am | Heavy shell fire in trenches | |
| 6pm | Reported to Bde. Situation quiet. Casualties - 1 killed, 3 wounded. | Auth. |
| 28th Nov. 6.30am | Reported to 14th Bde. quiet night - less sniping | |

## WAR DIARY

| Hour, date, Place | Summary of Events and Information | Remarks |
|---|---|---|
| 28th Nov (cont). | Quiet day. | Reference OSTEND map. |
| 29th Nov. | 15th Bde took over command of sector from 10th Bde. Orders received to ascertain whether German trenches weakly held. | |
| 6 p.m. | Reported all quiet; two attempts of rifle fire during night. | |
| 30th Nov. | | |
| 5 a.m. | Reported situation quiet. German trenches strongly held. | |
| 5.30 p.m. | Relief of Bn by R. SCOTS FUSILIERS began. - BEDFORDS taking over part of right of line. | |
| 11.30 p.m. | Relief completed - delayed by late arrival of relieving BEDFORD Coy. Bn returned to billets at DRANOUTRE. | |

5th Division
15th Inf.Bde.

WAR DIARY

1st DORSET REGT.

DECEMBER

1914

# WAR DIARY
## or
## INTELLIGENCE SUMMARY.
(Erase heading not required.)

Army Form C. 2118.

Instructions regarding War Diaries and Intelligence Summaries are contained in F. S. Regs., Part II. and the Staff Manual respectively. Title pages will be prepared in manuscript.

| Hour, Date, Place | Summary of Events and Information | Remarks and references to Appendices |
|---|---|---|
| DRANOUTRE. 1st Dec. 1914. 3.30pm | Bn marched via NEUVE EGLISE to WULVERGHEM and relieved East Surreys in trenches in the North of the WULVERGHEM-MESSINES Road. | Reference OSTEND map |
| 2nd Dec. | Quiet day except for heavy shelling of our trenches by C Coy. | auth |
| 3rd Dec. | Bn relieved by Norfolks, and returned to billets at DRANOUTRE. | auth |
| 4th Dec. 5th Dec. 6th Dec. 7th Dec. 4.15pm | Bn remained in billets at DRANOUTRE. A Coy and 1 Platoon B Coy marched via LINDENHOEK to relief bodys in trenches with left Point 75, 1 mile S.O. of WYTSCHAETE and to come under orders of the O.C. K.O.S. Borderers | auth |

Army Form C. 2118.

# WAR DIARY
## or
## INTELLIGENCE SUMMARY.
*(Erase heading not required.)*

Instructions regarding War Diaries and Intelligence Summaries are contained in F. S. Regs., Part II. and the Staff Manual respectively. Title pages will be prepared in manuscript.

| Hour, Date, Place | Summary of Events and Information | Remarks and references to Appendices |
|---|---|---|
| DRANOUTRE. 8th Dec 1914 | | |
| 4 p.m. | (less A Coy) Platoon (B Coy) Bn marched via LINDENHOEK and relieved K.O.S.Bs in trenches - | Reference OSTEND map. K.O.S.Bs |
| 9 p.m. | Relief completed. Casualty. one wounded | |
| 9th Dec. | Quiet day. Repeated no change in situation - | |
| 7.15 am | Quiet day. - Casualties Captain H. M. Powell. S. Stafford shire Regt att'd to Bn Killed. Other ranks - 4 killed, 1 wounded - | 37 |
| 10th Dec | Quiet day Bn relieved by K.O.Y.L.I. and marched via DRANOUTRE to ST JANS CAPPEL - Relief delayed by bad weather conditions Casualty - one wounded - | |
| 11th Dec 2 am | Bn reached ST JANS CAPPEL and billeted - | |

Army Form C. 2118.

# WAR DIARY
## or
## INTELLIGENCE SUMMARY.
(Erase heading not required.)

Instructions regarding War Diaries and Intelligence Summaries are contained in F. S. Regs., Part II. and the Staff Manual respectively. Title pages will be prepared in manuscript.

| Hour, Date, Place | | Summary of Events and Information | Remarks and references to Appendices |
|---|---|---|---|
| ST JANS CAPPEL | 11th Dec (Cont) | Bn remained in billets at ST JANS CAPPEL | |
| | 12th Dec | Major E WALSHE E. Staffd. Regt assumed command of the Bn. | ant |
| | 13th Dec | | |
| | 14th Dec | Bn marched with remainder of 15th Bde to DRANOUTRE & as it turned up in a field just west of that place – | 39 |
| DRANOUTRE | | Bn remained in field till after dark when it moved into billets at NEUVE EGLISE – owing to bad condition of ground and dark nor great difficulty was experienced in clearing the field. | |
| NEUVE EGLISE | 15th Dec | Bn remained in billets with orders to be in readiness to move at 10 minutes notice | ant |
| | 16th Dec | Bn remained in billets as before | ant |
| | 17th Dec 3.50pm | Bn marched to WULVERGHEM to relieve East Surreys in trenches South of WULVERGHEM – MESSINES Road | |

# WAR DIARY
## or
## INTELLIGENCE SUMMARY.
*(Erase heading not required.)*

Army Form C. 2118.

| Hour, Date, Place | Summary of Events and Information | Remarks and references to Appendices |
|---|---|---|
| 1914 17th Dec (cont) | The 1st Cheshire Regt & 2 Coys 6th Cheshire Regt were attached to the Bn for trench duty | Reference OSTEND map |
| 9.55pm | Relief completed. Casualties – Nil | auR |
| WULVERGHEM. 18th Dec 3am | Orders received to threaten firing line as 2 Coys Bedfords and Norfolks had been ordered to occupy reserve trenches | |
| 5am | Reported to Bde. Situation quiet. | |
| | Quiet day. Casualties — one killed, 11 wounded. | auR |
| 19th Dec 8.20am | Reported to Bde as follows. Situation quiet. Patrols report German trenches strongly held. Bn cooperated with mortars "by rapid fire at intervals" during day. | |
| 7pm | Three Bn Headquarters about ½ mile South of Signal headquarters in WULVERGHEM – MESSINES Road. | |
| | Casualties – 2 killed, 1 wounded | auR |

Army Form C. 2118.

# WAR DIARY
## or
## INTELLIGENCE SUMMARY.
*(Erase heading not required.)*

Instructions regarding War Diaries and Intelligence Summaries are contained in F.S. Regs., Part II. and the Staff Manual respectively. Title pages will be prepared in manuscript.

| Hour, Date, Place | Summary of Events and Information | Remarks and references to Appendices |
|---|---|---|
| 1914 | | Reference. OSTEND map. |
| WULVERGHEM 20 Dec | | |
| 2.45 am | Orders sent to Coys to work on similar lines as yesterday | |
| 9.10 am | Reported to Bde - Situation Quiet. | |
| 6.10 pm | Reported to Bde - Situation Quiet. | |
| 10 pm | Orders to tomorrow - Heavy bursts of rifle fire at intervals - | and |
| 21st Dec | | |
| 9.10 am | Reported to Bde - Situation Quiet. Details reports forwarded. | |
| 6.55 pm | Reported to Bde - Trenches heavily shelled in new battery about Due North of M I M INN ½ mile S W of M B MESSINES | |
| 22nd | | |
| 10.55 pm | Orders issued for tomorrow - Same lines as today - our guns will shell new battery - Casualties - 6 wounded. | and |
| 22nd Dec | | |
| 9 am | Reported to Bde Situation Quiet. | |
| 7 pm | Reported to Bde - Situation Quiet - Slight shelling during day Casualties - one killed | and |

# WAR DIARY
## or
## INTELLIGENCE SUMMARY.

*(Erase heading not required.)*

Army Form C. 2118.

| Hour, Date, Place | Summary of Events and Information | Remarks and references to Appendices |
|---|---|---|
| WULVERGHEM 1914 23rd Dec | | Reference OSTEND map. |
| 8.15am | Reported to Bde - Situation quiet | |
| 9am | One shell fell dangerously near our trenches | |
| 7.8pm | Reported to Bde - Quiet day Casualties - nil - | and |
| 24th Dec | | |
| 6.40am | One shell again dangerously near our trenches | |
| 8.50am | Reported to Bde - Situation quiet - Snipers very active - also machine gun. Movement of enemy transport heard | |
| 10.47am | Reported to Bde that too in of the trenches considerable report regarding movement of transport - | and |
| 25th Dec | Quiet day Nothing to report Casualties nil. | and |
| 26th Dec | Quiet day Nothing to report. | and |
| 8pm | Reported to Bde - Situation unchanged - no shelling Few small enemy [?] parties heard towards German trenches through field Casualties - Nil | Give 2nd Batn no shot fired at enemy. |

Army Form C. 2118.

# WAR DIARY
## or
## INTELLIGENCE SUMMARY.
*(Erase heading not required.)*

Instructions regarding War Diaries and Intelligence Summaries are contained in F. S. Regs., Part II. and the Staff Manual respectively. Title pages will be prepared in manuscript.

| Hour, Date, Place | Summary of Events and Information | Remarks and references to Appendices |
|---|---|---|
| WOLVERGHEM | | Reference OSTEND map. |
| 27th Dec 1914 | Reported to Bn — Situation unchanged — Patrols report | |
| 8.25am | everything very quiet | |
| 5.25pm | Reported to Bde — Situation unchanged — Fairly heavy Shell fire. Casualties — Nil — | and |
| 28th Dec. | | |
| 9.45am | Reported to Bde — Situation quiet — Patrols nothing to report | |
| | Quiet day — | |
| 29th Dec | Situation quiet | and |
| 2.30pm | Bn (less Coy and details) marches to billets at BAILLEUL. | |
| 6.50pm | Reported to Bde — Situation quiet | |
| 7.8pm | Relief of Coy by W. Riding Regt completed | |
| | Coy marched via NEUVE EGLISE to billets at BAILLEUL | and |

**WAR DIARY**
or
**INTELLIGENCE SUMMARY**
(*Erase heading not required.*)

Army Form C. 2118.

| Hour, Date, Place | Summary of Events and Information | Remarks and references to Appendices |
|---|---|---|
| BAILLEUL 1914. 30th Dec. 31st Dec. | Bon remained in billets at BAILLEUL. | Reference OSTEND map. |

5th Division

15th Infantry Bde.

1st Dorsets

January to June

1915

15th Bde.
5th Div.

1st DORSETS

JANUARY

1915

Army Form C. 2118.

# WAR DIARY
## of
## INTELLIGENCE SUMMARY.
*(Erase heading not required.)*

Instructions regarding War Diaries and Intelligence Summaries are contained in F.S. Regs., Part II. and the Staff Manual respectively. Title pages will be prepared in manuscript.

| Hour, Date, Place | Summary of Events and Information | Remarks and references to Appendices |
|---|---|---|
| BAILLEUL. 1st Jan 1915. 2nd Jan 3rd Jan 4th Jan | Bn remained in billets at BAILLEUL. | Reference OSTEND map. 39 |
| WULVERGHEM. 5th Jan 9.35 a.m. 9.38 a.m. 5.55 p.m. | Bn marched via DRANOUTRE - Road Junction L8 LINDENHOEK to WULVERGHEM and took over "D" Sector from East Surrey Regt. Relief completed - Good deal of sniping - Casualties - Nil. Reported to Bde. Situation unchanged - Sniping on left. Reports to Bde Quiet day except for shelling of left trenches by German light guns. Casualties  One killed. | ditto ditto |
| 6th Jan 8.28 a.m. 5.5, 5.30 p.m. 5.7 p.m. | Reports to Bde Quiet night, except for sniping Enemy shelled WULVERGHEM - LINDENHOEK Road | ditto |

(73989) W4141—463. 400,000. 9/14. H.&J., Ltd. Forms/C. 2118/10.

Army Form C. 2118.

# WAR DIARY
## INTELLIGENCE SUMMARY.
(Erase heading not required.)

| Hour, Date, Place | Summary of Events and Information | Remarks and references to Appendices |
|---|---|---|
| WULVERGHEM. 6th Jan 1915 | | Reference OSTEND map and |
| 7.3 pm | (Reported to Bde) - Very quiet day Casualties - 2 killed | |
| 7th Jan morning | | |
| 8.15 am | Report delayed by faulty telephone | |
| 9.45 am | Reported to Bde - Quiet night - Weather | |
| 7.45 pm | For Relief of Bn by Bedfords complete. Bn went into billets about DRANOUTRE. | and |
| DRANOUTRE. 8th Jan / 9th Jan | Bn remained in billets at DRANOUTRE. | and |
| 10th Jan | Bn relieved Bedfords in C & D Sector. | and |
| WULVERGHEM. | | |

**WAR DIARY**
**INTELLIGENCE SUMMARY.**
*(Erase heading not required.)*

Army Form C. 2118.

| Hour, Date, Place | Summary of Events and Information | Remarks and references to Appendices |
|---|---|---|
| WULVERGHEM. 1915 | | Reference OSTEND MAP |
| 11th Jan. 8.10am | [Reported to Bde] - Quiet night. | |
| 9 am | D Coy shelled by light gun. | |
| | Quiet day. | |
| 12th Jan. | Quiet day - situation unchanged. | |
| 13th Jan. | Quiet night. | |
| | Bn relieved by Bedfords | auth |
| | Bn moved into billets about DRANOUTRE. | |
| DRANOUTRE, 14th Jan | Bn remained in billets at DRANOUTRE. | auth |
| 15th Jan | | |
| 16th Jan | Bn moved into BAILLEUL. | auth |
| 17th Jan | | |
| 18th " | | |
| 19th " | Bn remained in billets at BAILLEUL | auth |
| 20th " | | |
| 21st " | | |
| 22nd " | | |

# WAR DIARY / INTELLIGENCE SUMMARY

Army Form C. 2118.

Instructions regarding War Diaries and Intelligence Summaries are contained in F.S. Regs., Part II and the Staff Manual respectively. Title pages will be prepared in manuscript.

(Erase heading not required.)

| Place | Hour, Date | Summary of Events and Information | Remarks and references to Appendices |
|---|---|---|---|
| WULVERGHEM. | 24 Jan | Bn marched via LILLE road and NEUVE EGLISE to WULVERGHEM and relieved 1st Riding in C Sector and bath'n D Sector – 2 Coys. 6th Cheshires were attached for | Reference OSTEND map |
|  | 7.45pm | Relief completed. Casualties – Nil | Au3 |
|  | 25th Jan | Reported to Bde } Quiet night |  |
|  | 8.15am |  |  |
|  | 6.55pm | Reported to Bde – very quiet day. Casualties – Nil | Au3 39 |
|  | 26th Jan |  |  |
|  | 3.30am | 2/Lt MORLEY with patrol got up to two German Saps. Found earth newly turned. On his way back he disturbed a sniper's dug out. |  |
|  | 8pm. | Reported to Bde – Quiet night Enemy's transport heard towards MESSINES. |  |
|  | 9.10 am | Trenches shelled by light gun. | Au3 |

Army Form C. 2118.

# WAR DIARY
## INTELLIGENCE SUMMARY.
*(Erase heading not required.)*

Instructions regarding War Diaries and Intelligence Summaries are contained in F.S. Regs., Part II. and the Staff Manual respectively. Title pages will be prepared in manuscript.

| Hour, Date, Place | Summary of Events and Information | Remarks and references to Appendices |
|---|---|---|
| WULVERGHEM. 1915. | | Reference OSTEND Map. |
| 26th Jan. (cont) | | |
| 7.35pm | Reported to bde - Situation unchanged. | |
| 10.30pm | Orders received to be prepared for attack at any time. Firing line to be thickened - | |
| 11.30pm | 1/2 platoons D Coy ordered to reinforce B Coy and 1 platoon A Coy to reinforce C Coy - Casualties - one killed | ans. 39 |
| 27th Jan. | | |
| 1am 3am 5am | Coys reported all quiet, except for heavy rifle fire at 4am. | |
| 6am. | Draft arrived and came under orders of O.C. Dublins. | |
| 6pm. | D Coy (two 1/2 platoons) moving into HQ Farm | |
| | G.O.C. IInd Corps (Lt Gen Sir C. Ferguson) visited Sectn. | |
| 8pm | Reported to Bde) Quiet day - no change - | |

# WAR DIARY of INTELLIGENCE SUMMARY.

*(Erase heading not required.)*

Army Form C. 2118.

| Hour, Date, Place | Summary of Events and Information | Remarks and references to Appendices |
|---|---|---|
| WULVERGHEM. 1915 28th/Jan | | Reference OSTEND map. |
| 1 am | Cps up ntrd / all quiet | |
| 3 am | | |
| 5 am | | |
| 8.10am | Reported to Bde - Quiet night - | |
| 6 pm | Relief of Bn by Bedfords commenced. | |
| 6.30pm | Pon (Cos A + D Coy) who remained under orders of O.C. Bedfords x hrs/Cos respectively) went into billets in LINDENHOEK - NEUVE. EGLISE Road. | |
| LINDENHOEK. - NEUVE EGLISE Road 29th/Jan | Bn remained in billets - | ansr |
| 30th/Jan | Bn relieved by Cheshires. Pon (Cos A + D Coy) moved to DRANOUTRE and billets - A + D Coy rejoining later. | ansr |
| DRANOUTRE 31st/Jan | Bn remained in billets at DRANOUTRE | ansr |

15th Bde.
5th Div.

Bde. attached to 28th Div 17.2.15.

1st DORSETS

FEBRUARY

1 9 1 5

Army Form C. 2118.

# WAR DIARY
## or
## INTELLIGENCE SUMMARY.
(Erase heading not required.)

Instructions regarding War Diaries and Intelligence
Summaries are contained in F.S. Regs., Part II.
and the Staff Manual respectively. Title pages
will be prepared in manuscript.

| Hour, Date, Place | | Summary of Events and Information | Remarks and references to Appendices |
|---|---|---|---|
| DRANOUTRE. | 1915<br>1st Feb.<br>2 p.m. | Bn marched to BAILLEUL and billeted | Reference to trench map<br>and S.Ward map 20,000<br>auth |
| BAILLEUL. | 2nd Feb.<br>3rd<br>4th<br>5th<br>6th<br>7th<br>8th | Bn remained in billets at BAILLEUL | auth |
| BAILLEUL —<br>LINDENHOEK. | 9th Feb.<br>2 p.m. | Bn marched via LILLE Road and NEUVE EGLISE and WULVERGHEM and relieved K.O.S. Borderers in E. Sector | 3 9<br>auth |
| | 11 p.m. | Relief completed<br>Casualties - one wounded. | |
| LINDENHOEK —<br>WULVERGHEM. | 10th Feb.<br>8 a.m. | Reported to Brigade - Quiet night - Approaches to trenches difficult owing to lack of paths | |
| | 7.15 p.m. | Reported to Brigade - Musketry fight (enemies dioxide firing so "sniping") continued all day, increasing in volume at dusk, and am continuing at intervals left of Sector shelled during afternoon | |
| | 11 p.m. | Patrol reported hostile machine gun emplacement established in N.30.C. (map 20,000) in IN DE KRUISSTRAAT CABARET — IN DE SPANBROEK CABARET Road at west end of cutting & 50 yds further South West. Asked that our guns shell it thereon<br>Casualties - 1 killed, 3 wounded - | auth |

# WAR DIARY
## or
## INTELLIGENCE SUMMARY.
*(Erase heading not required.)*

Army Form C. 2118

Instructions regarding War Diaries and Intelligence Summaries are contained in F.S. Regs., Part II. and the Staff Manual respectively. Title pages will be prepared in manuscript.

| Hour, Date, Place | Summary of Events and Information | Remarks and references to Appendices |
|---|---|---|
| **LINDENHOEK — WULVERGHEM.** 1915 | | Reference OSTEND a et f Squared Map 2.0. o.oro |
| 11th Feb. 8am | Reported to Bde. Latter part of night quiet. Work and carrying parties delayed by darkness and rain. Enemy shelled Supporting Point with high explosives. | |
| 10.15am and 3 pm | | |
| 7.10pm | Reported to Bde. Quiet day as regards rifle fire. 4 casualties caused by high explosive shells on Supporting Point and dugouts. Casualties 2 killed, 6 wounded. | auR. |
| 12th Feb. 7.45am | Reported to Bde. Fairly quiet night. Patrols nothing to report. | |
| 6pm | Reported to Bde. Quiet day. Casualties: 2 killed, 4 wounded. | auR. 3.f. |
| 13th Feb. 8.25am | Reported to Bde. Considerable rifle fire all night. | |
| 5.35pm | Quiet day, except for artillery duel. | |
| 8.40pm | Relief of Bn by Norfolks completed. Moved Bn marched to DRANOUTRE | auR |
| | Casualties - one wounded. | auR |
| **DRANOUTRE** 14th Feb. 15th Feb. 16th Feb. | Bn remained in billets at DRANOUTRE | |

Army Form C. 2118.

# WAR DIARY
## or
## INTELLIGENCE SUMMARY.
*(Erase heading not required.)*

Instructions regarding War Diaries and Intelligence Summaries are contained in F.S. Regs., Part II. and the Staff Manual respectively. Title pages will be prepared in manuscript.

| Hour, Date, Place | | Summary of Events and Information | Remarks and references to Appendices |
|---|---|---|---|
| DRANOUTRE | 17th Feb. 1915 | | Reference OSTEND map and Special map 1/40,000. |
| | 11.30am | Orders for move of 15th Bde to BAILLEUL. Bn remained at DRANOUTRE. | |
| | 18th Feb. | | |
| | 9.35am | Orders received that move to BAILLEUL would take place as advised on 17th. | |
| | 11.5am | Orders received cancelling move to BAILLEUL | |
| | 11.50am | Orders received for Bn to relieve Norfolks in trenches in 2nd Corp evening, and 2 Coys Bedfords in Sec C in night. | |
| | 12.30pm | | |
| | 5pm. | H.Q. Recce C Coy and Machine Guns moved to relieve Norfolks and A and D Coys to relieve Bedfords, coming under orders O.C. Bedfords. | |
| | 9.30pm | Relief of Norfolk Coy in E Sector completed - Casualties. Nil. | and |
| DEN HOEK — ULVERGHEM. | 19th Feb. | | |
| | 8.30am | Reported to Bde - Quiet night. Telephone cut off from fire trenches since 6.10 am. Telephone still not working? | |
| | 9.35am | | |
| | 7.15pm | Reported to Bde - Quiet day - wire in front of 15s trench much broken. Casualties. One killed, 3 wounded — | and |

Army Form C. 2118.

# WAR DIARY
## or
## INTELLIGENCE SUMMARY.
*(Erase heading not required.)*

Instructions regarding War Diaries and Intelligence Summaries are contained in F.S. Regs., Part II. and the Staff Manual respectively. Title pages will be prepared in manuscript.

| Hour, Date, Place | | Summary of Events and Information | Remarks and references to Appendices |
|---|---|---|---|
| LINDENHOEK – WULVERGHEM. | 1915. 20th Feb. 7.50am | Reported to Bde. Enemy fired about 10 bombs about 10 pm but missed trenches and did no damage. Afterwards quiet night. | Reference OSTEND map and Squared map 40, own |
| | 6.45pm | Considerable German shell fire off and on all day on trenches and supp nts, which caused no casualties, otherwise average day. | |
| | 10.40pm | Relief of Norfolk Regt by A & D Coys (relieved from attachment to Bedfords) complete. Casualties – 3 women killed. | and |
| | 21st Feb. 6.35pm | Reported to Bde – Airship seen. 10.30pm Snng East. Enemy sent up coloured light at same time – | 3.4 " |
| | 6.40am | A by asked for verification of airship and why no report was sent in at the time. | |
| | 7.15am | Reported to Bde – Only one man saw airship, and he failed to report till this morning – | |
| | 7.45am | Reported to Bde. Considerable rifle fire all night and several very heavy bursts. Greater volume of fire by units of 3rd Div (on our left) – | |
| | 6.10pm | Reported to Bde – During 19/20 50 yards of barbed wire put up – Germans suspected doing same work and were stopped by | |

# WAR DIARY
or
INTELLIGENCE SUMMARY.
(Erase heading not required.)

Army Form C. 2118.

| Hour, Date, Place | Summary of Events and Information | Remarks and references to Appendices |
|---|---|---|
| LINDEN HOEK - WULVERGHEM. 1915. | on fire - | Reference OSTEND map and Squared map 40,000 auth |
| 22nd Feb. | Casualties. one killed, one wounded - | |
| 7.55am | Quiet night - Patrols nothing to report - | |
| 10.30am | Staff Officer visited Sn Pn's visited trenches during fore. | |
| 6.5pm | Thick mist all day, increased in evening. Mine sniping | |
| | than usual. | |
| | Casualties - 3 wounded | auth |
| 23rd Feb. | Reported to Bde. Occasional bursts of rifle fire in our front. | |
| 7.35am | Reported to Bde - Very quiet day - Trenches and farms | |
| 6.5pm | shelled late in afternoon. | |
| 9.30pm | Bn relieved Norfolks and withdrew to Plns :- | |
| | HQ, A and D Coys. M.G. Section - "BUS" Farm | |
| | B Cy - "DRESSING" Farm | |
| | C Cy - PACKHORSE Farm. | |
| 24th Feb. | Casualties - 2 killed 6 wounded | auth |
| | Bn remained in Farms above mentioned. | |
| | Lieut Colonel Bois appointed to command 84th Infantry Brigade | auth |

Army Form C. 2118.

# WAR DIARY
or
## INTELLIGENCE SUMMARY.
*(Erase heading not required.)*

Instructions regarding War Diaries and Intelligence Summaries are contained in F.S. Regs., Part II. and the Staff Manual respectively. Title pages will be prepared in manuscript.

| Hour, Date, Place | Summary of Events and Information | Remarks and references to Appendices |
|---|---|---|
| LINDENHOEK 1915 25th Feb 26th Feb 27th Feb 1200am 7.30 pm | Bn remained in Farms as described. Bn relieved by 1st Suffolks and proceeded to billets at BAILLEUL. | Reference OSTEND map and Enlarged map of do. etc. att att att |
| BAILLEUL 28th Feb | Bn remained in billets at BAILLEUL. | |

15th Bde.
28th Div.

Joined 28th Div. with Bde. 3rd March 1915.

1st DORSETS

MARCH

1915

# WAR DIARY
## or
## INTELLIGENCE SUMMARY.
*(Erase heading not required.)*

Army Form C. 2118.

| Place | Date | Hour | Summary of Events and Information | Remarks and references to Appendices |
|---|---|---|---|---|
| | 1st March 2nd March 3rd March | | Bn remained in billets at BAILLEUL. | app 2 |
| VLAMERTINGHE | | 9 a.m. | Bn marched with 15th Bde [via LOCRE – LA CLYTTE – OUDERDOM] and occupied huts on OUDERDOM – VLAMERTINGHE Road. 15th Bde now joining 28th Division. | app 1 3/9 |
| | 4th March | 5 p.m. | Marched via VLAMERTINGHE – YPRES to trench relieving LINCOLNS in B Section. | |
| YPRES | | 11.40 p.m. | Relief completed. Relief much delayed by inaccuracy of guides, darkness, and works. | app |

Army Form C. 2118.

# WAR DIARY
## or
## INTELLIGENCE SUMMARY.
(Erase heading not required.)

Instructions regarding War Diaries and Intelligence Summaries are contained in F.S. Regs., Part II. and the Staff Manual respectively. Title pages will be prepared in manuscript.

| Hour, Date, Place | Summary of Events and Information | Remarks and references to Appendices |
|---|---|---|
| YPRES 1915 | | Reference OSTEND map. Squared maps 20,000 and 40,000 |
| 5th March 5.17 pm | Reported to Brigade - Quiet night, no change in situation. Intermittent rifle fire increasing in intensity between 1 am and 3 am. | |
| 11.30 am | Reported to Bde. Casualties to 12 noon. 8 wounded. | |
| 5.4 pm | Reported to Brigade - Situation unchanged. | |
| 11.10 pm | Reported to Brigade - Situation unchanged. 1.Company 6th Liverpools attached to 8th Brigade. | |
| 6th March 5.25 am | Reported to Bde - Situation unchanged - fairly quiet night. | |
| 11.6 am | Reported to Bde - Situation unchanged. Enemy firing continuously at parapets and loopholes of 32 a. (trench shared with Germans). Casualties to 12 noon. 3 killed, 17 wounded. | and |
| 5.25 pm | Reported to Bde - Situation unchanged - nothing to report. | |
| 10 pm | Relief of 1st R. Berks Bn. by Bedfords completed. Bn (less C.ffs Coy) withdrew to ROSENTAL Chateau C.ffs Coy being in LANKHOF Chateau with post on bridge where YPRES - ST ELOI Road crosses YPRES - COMINES Canal. | and |

(73989) W4141-463. 400,000. 9/14. H.& J. Ltd. Forms/C. 2118/10.

# WAR DIARY
## or
## INTELLIGENCE SUMMARY.
*(Erase heading not required.)*

Army Form C. 2118.

| Hour, Date, Place | Summary of Events and Information | Remarks and references to Appendices |
|---|---|---|
| YPRES 1915 7th March | Bn remained at ROSENTAL and LANKHOF Chateaux. A few shrapnel burst in Chateau grounds. Casualties to 12 noon 2 killed, 2 wounded. | Reference OSTEND map and Ypres Maps 1/20,000 and 1/40,000. AHB |
| 8th March | Casualties to 12 noon — Nil. | |
| 6.15 pm | Bn moved to relieve Bedfords. One Coy 6th L'verpools attached | |
| 11 pm | Relief completed. Report of completion delayed owing to telephone positions being changed. Disposition of Bn — A Coy, C Coy, D Coy front trenches and support dug outs — B Coy reserve at H.Q. farm. | |
| 11.55 pm | Reported to Brigade — Situation quiet. | AHB |
| 9th March 12pm 2 am | Small patrol of enemy — about 30 or 40 — attempted to crawl up to trench — occupied by 90 men of D Coy from German trench 40 yards away. When 20 yards they were seen & fired at, men and rapid fire and grenades were immediately used. Germans tried to their parapet and lay down. After half-hearted attempt to crawl forward again they climbed back into their trench. | |
| 5 am | Reported result of night attack to Brigade — Since attack all quiet. | AHB |

Army Form C. 2118.

# WAR DIARY
## or
## INTELLIGENCE SUMMARY.
*(Erase heading not required.)*

Instructions regarding War Diaries and Intelligence Summaries are contained in F. S. Regs., Part II. and the Staff Manual respectively. Title pages will be prepared in manuscript.

| Hour, Date, Place | Summary of Events and Information | Remarks and references to Appendices |
|---|---|---|
| YPRES 9th March 1915 (Cont.) | | Reference OSTEND map and Special maps 1/20,000 and 1/40,000 |
| 5.30am | Brigadier wired "Well done garrison of 32a". | |
| 11.30am | Reported to Bde. Situation quiet - ascertained that heavy rifle fire kept on my left at 10.35am was prepared by 13th Bde. - 2/Lieut G. WHEELER wounded - 2 killed, 3 wounded (other ranks) Casualties to 12 noon (Reported to Bde) | |
| 4.40 p.m. | Situation unchanged. (Reported to Bde.) | |
| 8 pm 10 pm | Were received that demonstration of artillery and rifle fire would take place tomorrow - every effort to be made to put the enemy to this formed | |
| 11 pm | Reported to Bde. Situation unchanged | |
| 10th March 4.45 am | Reported to Bde - Situation unchanged. Enemy active against parapet of 32a - We replied with rifle grenades with success. | |
| 8.5 am | Spies that Germans appear to be trying to flood 32 a. Pump asked for urgently. | |
| 11.15am | Reported to Bde. Situation unchanged - Germans pumping water into right end of 32a. Pump hire pump and R.E. assistance. Parapet of 32a badly damaged, but am now repairing it | |

# WAR DIARY or INTELLIGENCE SUMMARY.

Army Form C. 2118.

(Erase heading not required.)

| Place | Hour, Date, 1915 | Summary of Events and Information | Remarks and references to Appendices |
|---|---|---|---|
| YPRES. | 10th March | | Reference OSTEND sheet and Squires sheets 1/20,000 and 1/40,000 – |
| | 1.15 pm to 4.45 pm | Casualties to noon – 10 wounded. H.Q. Farm shelled incessantly. Reg. Reserve had to take to dug outs and has had two casualties. Farm buildings much damaged. | |
| | 4.55 pm | Reported to Bde. Situation unchanged – | |
| | 6 pm | Bedfords arrived to commence relief – | and |
| | 8.30 pm | Relief completed – Bn withdrew to ROSENTAL Chateau, less B Coy who reoccupied LANKHOF Chateau – No Casualties. | |
| | 11th March | Bn remained in billets at ROSENTAL and LANKHOF | |
| | 12th March 5.30 pm | Bn moved by companies to relieve Bedfords. | and |
| | 8.10 pm | Relief completed. | |
| | 11.10 pm | Reported to Bde – Situation unchanged – no yet repair of parapet in 32a. | |
| | 13th March | | |
| | 12.15 am | Asked urgently to push on in 32a. | and |
| | 4.55 am | Reported to Bde – Situation unchanged. Fire by Germans only leaving in reply to our own –  | |

Army Form C. 2118.

# WAR DIARY
## or
## INTELLIGENCE SUMMARY.
(Erase heading not required.)

Instructions regarding War Diaries and Intelligence Summaries are contained in F.S. Regs., Part II. and the Staff Manual respectively. Title pages will be prepared in manuscript.

| Hour, Date, Place | | Summary of Events and Information | Remarks and references to Appendices |
|---|---|---|---|
| YPRES | 1915 | | |
| | 13th March | | Reference OSTEND Map and Squared Map 1/20,000 and 1/40,000 - |
| | 11.15 am | Reported to Bde - Situation unchanged - Casualties to 12 noon - 3 killed, 5 wounded - | |
| | 2.30 pm | Germans used trench mortar against 32a. | |
| | 4.50 pm | Reported to Bde - Situation unchanged - Some damage to 29 by shell fire - | |
| | 11 pm | Reported to Bde - Situation unchanged - | |
| | 14th March | | |
| | 4.55 am | Situation unchanged - | |
| | | Casualties to 12 noon - 4 killed 13 wounded - | |
| | 5.10 pm | Reported to Bde - Situation unchanged - | |
| | 5.15 pm | Heavy bombardment & Nunny mine with explosion of mine began on our right and included 29 trench - also heavy rifle fire - | |
| | | Relief by Bedfords continued as usual - | |
| | 9.30 pm | Relief by Bedfords complete - | |

# WAR DIARY or INTELLIGENCE SUMMARY

Army Form C. 2118.

| Hour, Date, Place | Summary of Events and Information | Remarks and references to Appendices |
|---|---|---|
| YPRES | | Reference OSTEND map and revised maps 1/20000 and 1/40000 |
| **14th March 1915** | | |
| 9 pm to 10 pm | Owing to attack on 27th Division at ST ELOI, Brigade received following dispositions — D Coy with 2 machine guns to hold Canal bridge. While YPRES – ST ELOI road crosses YPRES – COMINES Canal – Other Coys to be in state of readiness. | |
| 10.30 pm | Adzvs sent to Captain Partridge commanding at Canal bridge to send officers patrol towards ST ELOI to gain touch of patrols with 27th Divn. It would appear this patrol reported that as he approached ST ELOI a machine gun opened fire on him from village. | |
| **15th March** | | |
| 1.20 am | Advs sent to Captain Partridge to continue patrolling YPRES – ST ELOI Road. | |
| 2.30 am | Reports received Germans reported advancing in both sides of road towards Canal bridge. | |
| 2.45 am | A Coy sent to support D Coy – and 2 platoons to Canal crossing I 28 e (squared map) | |
| 5.30 am | A Coy and one machine gun withdrawn to ROSENTAL | |

Army Form C. 2118.

# WAR DIARY
## or
## INTELLIGENCE SUMMARY.
(Erase heading not required.)

Instructions regarding War Diaries and Intelligence Summaries are contained in F.S. Regs, Part II. and the Staff Manual respectively. Title pages will be prepared in manuscript.

| Hour, Date, Place | Summary of Events and Information | Remarks and references to Appendices |
|---|---|---|
| YPRES 1915 15th February (cont) | and D Coy to LANKHOF having small post on Canal bridge. — Situation Quiet. | Reference OSTENDHOF and Ismail maps 1/20,000 and 1/40,000. |
| 7.55 pm | Quiet day except that 2 N.C.O.'s who were killed about 5pm and 2/Lieut CAVE killed. 2/Lieut W— also went to Captain Pashe by at LANKHOF to patrol in direction of ST ELOI and report result. Two machine guns placed to cover Canal bridge. | |
| 11 pm | Patrol reported that it reached a point 300 yds from ST ELOI and found all quiet — | and |
| 16th March | Remained in position of yesterday. Casualties to 12 noon — 2/Lieut W.H.C. CAVE killed — other ranks Nil — Advice received that our battalion Captain W— who is to go into Reserve. | |
| 12 noon | | |
| 6 pm | orders cancelled. 13th Bde to relieve 15th Bde. | |
| 9 pm | Bn moved via PORTE DE LILLE — VLAMERTINGHE to huts on VLAMERTINGHE — OUDEDOM Road | and |

# WAR DIARY
## INTELLIGENCE SUMMARY.
*(Erase heading not required.)*

Army Form C. 2118.

Instructions regarding War Diaries and Intelligence Summaries are contained in F.S. Regs., Part II. and the Staff Manual respectively. Title pages will be prepared in manuscript.

| Hour, Date, Place | Summary of Events and Information | Remarks and references to Appendices |
|---|---|---|
| YPRES. 1915 | | |
| 17th March 12.10am | Bn reached huts. | Reference OSTEND map and YPRES map 1/20,000 and 1/40,000 |
| 18th March 19th March 20th March | } Bn remains in huts. | and |
| 21st March 5pm | Bn marched via VLAMERTINGHE and YPRES and relieved A/R. Fusiliers in C Sector. | |
| 10.45pm | Relief completed. | |
| 11.35pm | Reported to Bde - Situation unchanged. - | and |
| 22nd March 4.50pm | Reported to Bde - Situation unchanged - Very quiet on left. - | |
| 16.47am | Reported to Bde - Situation unchanged. Casualties to 12 noon - 3 wounded - | |
| 5pm | Reported to Bde - Situation unchanged. Enemy active with | and |

Army Form C. 2118.

# WAR DIARY
## or
## INTELLIGENCE SUMMARY.
*(Erase heading not required.)*

| Place | Hour, Date | Summary of Events and Information | Remarks and references to Appendices |
|---|---|---|---|
| YPRES | 22nd March | Rifle and machine guns opened on aeroplanes - Parapet of 35 damaged by bomb - but with grenades checked bombing | Reference OSTEND map and trench map 1/20000 and 1/40000. |
| | 6.20 pm | Advice sent to C.O.y "35" to reconnoitre German sap in front of 35. | |
| | 11.20 pm | Reported to Bde - Situation normal - Mortar was from 34 - Germans reported very nervous and often shooting in air. | |
| | 23rd March | | |
| | 5.10 am | Reported to Bde - Situation unchanged. Patrol sent from 35 to reconnoitre German sap was fired on & has to return. | |
| | 11 am | Reported to Bde - Situation unchanged - Quiet along front - Casualties to 12 noon - 4 wounded. | |
| | 5 pm | Situation Reported to Bde - Situation unchanged - Quiet | |
| | 9.30 pm | Diary to Bde Relief Completed - Rn flrs A & RS Cays Wns were left behind when new Rn of AC Norfolks) move to hof Barracks YPRES | quiet |

# WAR DIARY or INTELLIGENCE SUMMARY.

Army Form C. 2118.

| Hour, Date, Place | Summary of Events and Information | Remarks and references to Appendices |
|---|---|---|
| YPRES 24th March 1915 | Bn. unmoved at YPRES. Casualties to 12 noon – 3 wounded. | Reference OSTEND map and DUNKERQUE map 1/200000 and 1/100000 – aug. |
| 25th March | Bn. marched to relieve Norfolks in C Sector | |
| 6.30pm | Relief completed. | |
| 9.30pm | | |
| 10.35pm | Reported to Bde. Situation unchanged – quiet along front | and |
| 26th March | Reported to Bde. | |
| 4.35am | Situation unchanged – quiet night | |
| 10.45am | Reported to Bde. Situation unchanged. All quiet along front. Casualties to 12 noon – 2 killed, 8 wounded. | |
| 4.45pm | Situation unchanged – parapet of 33 bodys damaged. | |
| 8.45pm | Reported to Bde. Situation unchanged. | |
| 10.45pm | Reported to Bde. Situation unchanged – now quiet | and |
| 27th March | | |
| 4.45am | Reported to Bde – Situation unchanged – quiet along front – knots of fire during night. | and |

Army Form C. 2118.

# WAR DIARY
## or
## INTELLIGENCE SUMMARY.
*(Erase heading not required.)*

Instructions regarding War Diaries and Intelligence Summaries are contained in F.S. Regs., Part II. and the Staff Manual respectively. Title pages will be prepared in manuscript.

| Hour, Date, Place | Summary of Events and Information | Remarks and references to Appendices |
|---|---|---|
| YPRES – 1915 | | Reference OSTEND map and Squared map 1/20000 and 1/40000 |
| 27th March 11 am | Reported to Bde. – Situation unchanged – | |
| 4.30 pm | Casualties to 12 noon – killed 9 wounded. Reported to Bde. – Situation unchanged. | And. |
| 10.50 pm | Situation unchanged. | |
| 28th March 4.35 am | Reported to Bde. – Situation unchanged. | |
| 10.55 am | Situation unchanged – | |
| 10.30 pm | Relief by Norfolks completed. Bn (2nd C.M.R. Corps) remaining with Norfolks returned to YPRES | And. |
| 29th March 30th March 31st March | Bn reviewed at YPRES. | and |
| 8 pm | Bn (2nd C.M.R. Corps) marched to huts on VLAMERTINGHE – OUDERDOM Road. C and D Coy rejoined later – | and |

(73989) W4141—463. 400,000. 9/14. H.&J.Ltd. Forms/C. 2118/10.

15th Bde.
5th Div.

Left 28th Div & returned with Bde to 5th Div. /4/15.

1st DORSETS.

APRIL

1 9 1 5

# WAR DIARY
## or
## INTELLIGENCE SUMMARY.
(Erase heading not required.)

Army Form C. 2118.

Instructions regarding War Diaries and Intelligence Summaries are contained in F.S. Regs., Part II. and the Staff Manual respectively. Title pages will be prepared in manuscript.

| Hour, Date, Place | Summary of Events and Information | Remarks and references to Appendices |
|---|---|---|
| YPRES 1915 | | |
| 1st April | } Bn remained in huts | Ref. # OSTEND Squared maps 1/40,000 and 1/20,000 |
| 2nd April | | |
| 3rd April | | |
| 4th April | | |
| 5th April – 5pm | Bn marched via VLAMERTINGHE and YPRES and relieved R. Fusiliers (60th Bde) in B. Sector. Casualties – 2 killed 3 wounded. | |
| 6th April | Quiet day | |
| 5pm | Reported to Bde – Situation unchanged. | |
| 10.50pm | Reported to Bde – Situation unchanged – Very wet night – Casualties 1 killed, 2 wounded. | |
| 7th April | | |
| 8.20am | Reported to Bde – Situation unchanged. | |
| 4.30pm | C and D Coys relieved by 2 Coys K.O.Y.L.I. and D Coy then went into support/reserve. | |
| 6.55pm | Reported to Bde – Situation unchanged. | |
| 8pm to 12 m/n | B, C, D Coys relieved by K.O.Y.L.I. and A Coy by Manchesters. Casualties. 1 killed 7 wounded | |

Army Form C. 2118.

# WAR DIARY
## or
## INTELLIGENCE SUMMARY.

(Erase heading not required.)

Instructions regarding War Diaries and Intelligence Summaries are contained in F.S. Regs., Part II. and the Staff Manual respectively. Title pages will be prepared in manuscript.

| Hour, Date, Place | Summary of Events and Information | Remarks and references to Appendices |
|---|---|---|
| 1915 | | |
| YPRES. 9th April | | Ref. OSTEND and surround maps 1/200,000 and 1/40,000 |
| 9th April 12mdft to 5am | Bn moved by Companies to huts in H.32.a. | |
| 10th April | Bn remained in huts. | |
| | Bn marched via DICKEBUSCH and PORTE DE LILLE, YPRES and relieved R.C.Y.L.I. in 31, 32 b, 32 a and 33 trenches. Casualties - 2 wounded. | |
| 11th April 12.45am | Relief completed. Situation unchanged. | |
| 6.10am | Reported to Bde - Situation unchanged. | |
| 6.15pm | Reported to Bde - Situation unchanged. Casualties. one wounded. | |
| 12th April 6am. | Reported to Bde - Situation unchanged. 2/Lt Wood killed when in charge of a patrol. Situation unchanged. | |
| 6.20 pm | Casualties. 2/Lt T.H.H. WOOD killed - other ranks - 2 wounded. | |
| 13th April | Reports to Bde - Situation unchanged. Some rifle fire from usual m.both sides during night. | |
| 6pm | Reported to Bde - Situation unchanged. - 3 wounded | |

Army Form C. 2118.

# WAR DIARY
## or
## INTELLIGENCE SUMMARY.
*(Erase heading not required.)*

Instructions regarding War Diaries and Intelligence Summaries are contained in F.S. Regs., Part II. and the Staff Manual respectively. Title pages will be prepared in manuscript.

| Hour, Date, Place | Summary of Events and Information | Remarks and references to Appendices |
|---|---|---|
| YPRES 1915 | | Ry. OSTEND map and sheet maps 1/20,000 and 1/40,000 — out |
| 14th April 8.25 am | Reported to Bde - Situation unchanged | |
| 6.15 pm | Reported to Bde - Situation unchanged. Casualties - One killed, one wounded. | |
| 15th April 5.15 am | Reported to Bde - Situation unchanged. Exploded trench of rifle and machine gun fire, accompanied by grenades from – | out |
| 6.25 pm | Reported to Bde - Situation unchanged. Casualties - One killed, 2 wounded. | |
| 16th April 8 am | Reported to Bde - Situation unchanged | |
| 6.10 pm | Reported to Bde - Situation unchanged. Casualties - 2 killed 4 wounded. | out |
| 17th April 8.20 am | Reported to Bde - Situation unchanged. 3 trench occupied by Coy shelled during night and parapets damaged. | |
| 6.5 pm | Reported to Bde - Situation unchanged - | |
| 6.45 pm | All men issued to cover to be prepared for Explosion of mine at Hill 60. | out |
| 7 pm | Mine exploded. Heavy artillery bombardment by our guns. German Guns Replied. | |

Head Quarters
3rd Echelon

Reference War Diary, for April, of
1st Bn Dorsetshire Regiment:-

Under April 30th 1.15 a.m. kindly
delete "Bn remained in support through
out day" and add "3 pm "Bn relieved
Devons in trenches"

A. Ransome
Captain
20. 5. 1915    Comdg 1st Dorset Regt

Army Form C. 2118.

# WAR DIARY
## or
## INTELLIGENCE SUMMARY.
*(Erase heading not required.)*

| Hour, Date, Place | Summary of Events and Information | Remarks and references to Appendices |
|---|---|---|
| YPRES | 1915 | |
| 17th April | | Ref OSTEND map sheet 5 & new maps 1/20,000 and 1/40,000 |
| 10.25 p.m. | Telephone wires to Capranes broken – about one repaired – Signal Sergeant and one man under artillery fire – Heavy shelling Potyze Storpe – Reported to Bde – Satisfactory reports from all Coys. Casualties – one killed, 4 wounded – | AW3 |
| 18th April | | |
| 8.20 am | Reported to Bde – Situation normal in my front – Little damage done by last night's shelling – | |
| 4 pm | Wire received that 13th hf side would assault Hill 60 at 6 pm and that 15th was to demonstrate against trenches in front – Casualties – one killed, 11 wounded. | AW3 |
| 19th April | | |
| 8.20 am | Reported to Bde – Situation unchanged. | |
| 7 pm | Reported to Bde – Situation unchanged – Quiet in front – Casualties – 2 killed, 2 wounded | AW3 |
| 20th April | | |
| 8.15 am | Reported to Bde – Situation unchanged. Quiet day in Dorset front – Heavy shelling South of Broodseinde – Casualties – Captain H.D. THWAYTES, C Coy in 31 Field suffering heavily from shelling – 2/Lieut E.D. LE SAUVAGE, 2/Lieut R.J. CORBALLIS (3rd Dorset) wounded, other ranks 2 wounded | AW3 |

**Army Form C. 2118.**

# WAR DIARY
## or
## INTELLIGENCE SUMMARY.
*(Erase heading not required.)*

Instructions regarding War Diaries and Intelligence Summaries are contained in F.S. Regs., Part II. and the Staff Manual respectively. Title pages will be prepared in manuscript.

| Hour, Date, Place | Summary of Events and Information | Remarks and references to Appendices |
|---|---|---|
| YPRES 1915 21st April | | Ref. OSTEND map and Special maps 1/20000 and 1/40 000. |
| 8.30 a.m. | Reported to Bde – Situation quiet in my front – 31 French heavy shells during yesterday evening – and throughout night – | |
| 6.20 p.m. | Reported to Bde – Situation unchanged – Casualties – one killed, 6 wounded – | Au/3 |
| 22nd April 8.20 a.m. | Reported to Bde – Situation normal. 31 French shelled continuously throughout night – | |
| 6.15 p.m. 6.30 p.m. 7 p.m. | Reported to Bde – Situation unchanged – Heavy shelling of YPRES and approaches. Received message from O.C. 1st S.Batch, 13th Bde would not take place as arranged. Casualties 4 wounded – | Au/2 |
| 23rd April 8.20 a.m. 6 p.m. | Reported to Bde – Situation normal. Adens received to reconnoitre route to 2nd line of trenches in event of it becoming necessary for troops in trenches to withdraw – 31 French again shelling Wytschaete night – | |
| 6.25 p.m. | Reported to Bde – Situation normal. Casualties – 7 wounded. | Au/2 |

**Army Form C. 2118.**

# WAR DIARY
## or
## INTELLIGENCE SUMMARY.
(Erase heading not required.)

Instructions regarding War Diaries and Intelligence Summaries are contained in F.S. Regs., Part II. and the Staff Manual respectively. Title pages will be prepared in manuscript.

| Hour, Date, Place | Summary of Events and Information | Remarks and references to Appendices |
|---|---|---|
| YPRES. 24th April 1915 | | Ref OSTEND map and Ypres map 1/20,000 and 1/40,000. |
| 6.20 am | Reported to Bde. Situation normal | |
| 2 pm. | Orders received that if situation permitted Bn would be relieved by D.C.L.I. and go to Camp F at OUDERDOM. | |
| 4 pm. | Orders received that relief could not take place. | |
| 6.40 pm | Reported to Bde – Situation normal. Casualties – 2 killed 17 wounded – | and |
| 25th April | | |
| 8.25 am | Reported to Bde. Situation unchanged. | |
| 6 pm. | Orders received that Bn would be relieved by D.C.L.I. | |
| 6.30 pm | Reported to Bde – Situation unchanged | |
| From 10 pm | Relief by 1st Bn D.C.L.I. carried out. Germans open heavy artillery and rifle fire during relief – but few casualties resulted | and |
| | Casualties | |
| 26th April | Bn moved across country to Companies to billets at KRUISSTRAAT | mg |
| | Casualties 4 wounded | |

# WAR DIARY
## or
## INTELLIGENCE SUMMARY.
*(Erase heading not required.)*

Army Form C. 2118.

| Place | Hour, Date | Summary of Events and Information | Remarks and references to Appendices |
|---|---|---|---|
| YPRES | 27th April 1915 | Bn remained in billets in KRUISSTRAAT. | Ref. OSTEND maps and Squared maps 1/20,000, and 1/40,000 |
|  | 6 p.m. | Billets shelled. |  |
|  | 7 p.m. | C and D Coys marched to ZILLEBEKE and thence to Squared 1.24.d where they were employed at digging new line known as "HOOGE Switch". Casualties - 2/Lieut D.I.P. STAYNER. other ranks 6 wounded. | AuB |
|  | 28th April | A+B Coys marched to Square 1.24.d for digging |  |
|  | 7.30 p.m. | Battalion - B Coy and H.Q. section moved into bivouac in H.24.a and H.23.d. |  |
|  | 8 p.m. | Casualties Lieut C.V. Bartlett + 10 O.R. wounded | AuB |
|  | 29th April 6 a.m. | A+B Coys came into bivouac on return from digging. |  |
|  | 11 a.m. | Orders received that Bn was to relieve Cameron Highlanders in support of Hill 60 during the present repose about 8 p.m. then relieved Duke of Wellingtons. |  |
|  |  | Bn moved by Companies to Hill 60 - |  |
|  |  | Enemy were shelling all roads, ridge etc and railway cutting approaching hill. |  |
|  | 8.30 p.m. | Casualties One killed, 12 wounded | AuB |

Army Form C. 2118.

# WAR DIARY
## or
## INTELLIGENCE SUMMARY.
(Erase heading not required.)

Instructions regarding War Diaries and Intelligence Summaries are contained in F.S. Regs., Part II. and the Staff Manual respectively. Title pages will be prepared in manuscript.

| Hour, Date, Place | Summary of Events and Information | Remarks and references to Appendices |
|---|---|---|
| YPRES 30th April 1915 | Bn. was disposed in dugouts in close support to Devons who were holding the line and trenches on either flank of it. | Ref. OSTEND map and squares maps 1/20,000, and 1/40,000 |
| 1.15 am | Relief by Camerons complete. Arrived in support at (front line?). All quiet except for shelling & railway cutting at intervals. Casualties 8 wounded | See arrangement maps M.G.T. 20/4/15 attached. ans'd K.1+12. W.5+128 |

15th Bde.
5th Div.

1st DORSETS

MAY

1915

**Army Form C. 2118.**

# WAR DIARY
## or
## INTELLIGENCE SUMMARY
*(Erase heading not required.)*

Instructions regarding War Diaries and Intelligence Summaries are contained in F.S. Regs., Part II and the Staff Manual respectively. Title pages will be prepared in manuscript.

| Hour, Date, Place | Summary of Events and Information | Remarks and references to Appendices |
|---|---|---|
| YPRES. HILL 60.<br>1915<br>1st May<br><br>7 p.m.<br><br>7.15 p.m. | Bn. remained in trenches on Hill 60 - with Devons in close support.<br>Enemy commenced bombardment of supporting area of Hill 60.<br>Enemy fired an asphyxiating gas from 3 posts in front of 38 trench and from 2 in front of 43 & 45 trenches and also probably from others in front of 60.<br>The direction of the wind caused the fumes of 38, but the garrisons of 60, 43, 45 and 46 got the full benefit of the gas.<br>The situation became critical but was saved by the prompt action of Captain Bolton - Seven Officers on the spot, and by the equally prompt despatch of reinforcements from A & B Coys. Devons.<br>The telephones were not working well, but a report of a message that an attack on 60 was taking place, having come through, Devons went into trenches and took up his position on Hill 60 as being the key of the position.<br>Trenches 43, 45, 46 were suffering severely from the gas.<br>The enemy, in addition to using gas and shelling supporting area heavily with different types of guns, opens heavy rifle and machine gun fire on Hill 60 and endeavoured to bomb the trenches of this trench | Reference OSTENDURG and ZANDVOORDE Map 20,000<br>— 40,000<br><br><br><br><br><br><br><br><br><br><br><br><br><br>Note: The trench on Hill 60 is known as "60" trench and is referred to as 60. |

WAR DIARY
INTELLIGENCE SUMMARY.
(Erase heading not required.)

Army Form C. 2118.

| Hour, Date, Place | Summary of Events and Information | Remarks and references to Appendices |
|---|---|---|
| YPRES – HILL 60. 1st May (cont.) | Beyond sending some bombs thrown up a communication trench the enemy apparently made no attempt to cross the open. | Ref OSTEND map 1/20,000 and 1/40,000 — |
| 10 p.m. | The situation had now become practically normal and the firing had much abated. | |
| | Casualties – one killed, one wounded – killed by gas poisoning – Lieut C.G. Butcher. 52 other ranks. Admitted to Field Ambulance Suffering from gas poisoning Capt. A.E. Hawkins, 2/Lt J.H.C. R. Ludo (since died) 2/Lt J. Hodgson, 2/Lt J. Sampson. 39 O.ranks. 2/Lt J.R. Weston-Stevens. 3rd O. ranks and 200 other ranks. Missing – 32 other ranks. | aur |
| 2nd May 5 a.m. | B and C Coy relieved on Hill 60 by Devons, and withdrew to 39 and 40 trenches. | |
| 4.30 p.m. | D. ranks relieved in trenches h'Devons – Angels withdrew to dug outs. Casualties – 2 killed 2 wounded | aud |

Army Form C. 2118.

# WAR DIARY
## or
## INTELLIGENCE SUMMARY.
*(Erase heading not required.)*

Instructions regarding War Diaries and Intelligence Summaries are contained in F.S. Regs., Part II. and the Staff Manual respectively. Title pages will be prepared in manuscript.

| Hour, Date, Place | Summary of Events and Information | Remarks and references to Appendices |
|---|---|---|
| YPRES. HILL 60. 3rd May 1915 | Bn remained in dugouts in close support of Devons. Casualties - One killed, 5 wounded. | Reference OSTEND map and Zillebeke map 1/20,000 and 1/40,000 and 1/10,000 map |
| 4th May | Bn remained in dugouts in close support of Devons. Casualties. 5 wounded | |
| 5th May | Duke of Wellingtons relieved Devons on Hill 60 and trenches. Maxim Pmts. assumed command of Sectr. | |
| 5.45am | Major Crane wounded. | |
| 9am | Report received from 38 trench - "Gas coming over." Places by message asking for reinforcements. C and D Coys (with one piquet [advance] to 38 to Knutsfree - OC Duke of Wellingtons appeared to the relieving of A & B Coys moved to trenches - | |
| 9.15am | Telephone communication with trenches and 15th Bde and also supporting artillery cut by bombardment. Gas very thick and men overcome at support dugout. Telephone communication to 38 trench repaired. From reports received it appeared that situation was as follows :- Trenches holding 60 also part of 39, 40, 43-45 (known as ZWARTELEEN salient. Duke of Wellingtons had forced A, B, C & the remnant of D Coy holding to 38 and most of 39. | |

# WAR DIARY or INTELLIGENCE SUMMARY.

Army Form C. 2118.

| Hour, Date, Place | Summary of Events and Information | Remarks and references to Appendices |
|---|---|---|
| YPRES. HILL 60. 5th May 1915 (cont.) | | Ref. OSTEND map and Square map 1/20,000 and 1/40,000 |
| About 11 am onwards | Germans reported to have broken through at a point between H.8 and collected in places in position to cover gap above mentioned. There arrived 6 relieves and been already... Frequent messages that our Blythe was falling, that our B.H. [line unworkable], that Cheshires were reinforced, that Colonel Scott, Comdg Cheshires, would take over command. Cheshires arrived. Colonel Scott mortally wounded. Cheshires advance against Germans in ZWARTELEEN Salient. Small party of Germans who had advanced nearly to ZILLEBEKE wiped out. | |
| Afternoon | Duosts reinforced by parties of Cheshires retake 39 and by bombing reoccupy nearly all 40. Situation at dusk — Duosts and Cheshires holding 38, 39 and nearly all 40. Germans holding 60 and 43 to 45 forced by Cheshires. Two patrols digging in opposite. | |
| 10 p.m. | Counter attack by 2 Bns. 13th K.L.Isle. | |

**WAR DIARY**
or
**INTELLIGENCE SUMMARY.**
(Erase heading not required.)

Army Form C. 2118.

Instructions regarding War Diaries and Intelligence Summaries are contained in F.S. Regs., Part II and the Staff Manual respectively. Title pages will be prepared in manuscript.

| Hour, Date, Place | Summary of Events and Information | Remarks and references to Appendices |
|---|---|---|
| YPRES. HILL 60  1915. 6th May 2am. | Bn relieved by K.O.S.B's and withdrew to bivouac in Square H24a — Bn billeted from tawdrie about 200 strong. Casualties 2/Lt G.S. Skeaping killed. Major R.M.P. Gore, Capt Collin, 2/Lt Lyster & Graham wounded. Major Harrison successfully thro' attack, but 25 Officers present. Bn reports 45 or cent as being sick. | OSTEND map and Square maps 1/20,000, 1/40,000 Square Poperinge. 36 near Reningh -st [?] |
| 8pm | Bn marched to E. Camp OUDERDOM. — H.Qrs. be ar came as | |
| 7th May 8th May 9th May 10th May 11th May 12th May 13th May 14th May 15th May 16th May 17th May 18th May 19th May 20th May | Bn remained in E. Camp OUDERDOM | and |

# WAR DIARY or INTELLIGENCE SUMMARY.

Army Form C. 2118.

(Erase heading not required.)

| Hour, Date, Place | | Summary of Events and Information | Remarks and references to Appendices |
|---|---|---|---|
| YPRES HILL 60 | 20th May 21st May 1 a.m. | B'n relieved 1st Gordons in trenches in HILL 60 Sector. B'n a Bow 1100 strong. R/F OSTEND MAP aug 36J and maps 1/200,000 1/40,000 | RAMC RAMC |
| | About 11 pm onwards | Reinf Completed. Situation. Bosces holding 38, 39, 41, 41A (new frontline) in front of (41) 42 and 47 Support. | RAMC |
| | | Two patrols went out – one flogged Communication Trench towards 43 Trench (was in possession) (fearless) (in about 2 spots – There were signs of Germans on position – the other patrol examined Communication Trench from end of 41 to 46 Support (was held by Germans) and advanced 50 yards beyond and obtained info. No opposition. | |
| | | Casualties killed 2/Lt C. RAWLINSON 3rd Batal Regt – Other ranks killed 1, wounded 2. | |
| | 22nd May About 10 pm onwards | Barricade erected 70 yards from 41 & 41 in communication Trench leading to 46 Support and manned. | RAMC |
| | | Casualties one killed four wounded | |
| | 23rd May about 9.30 pm | German Barricade pulled down. Party observed down True 40, encountering Germans, whom they bombed – Germans replied, so party retired – was repeated. Were out 35 yards to Trench. Germans were nervous. | RAMC |
| | | Casualties 2/Lt G.O.'s CREE wounded. 2 killed 3 wounded | RAMC |
| | 24th May | Casualties 2/Lt C.J. MASSY killed. 2/Lt R.A. SMELLIE wounded. 1 Sm Allen wounded | RAMC |
| | | 2 wounded, 1 missing | |
| | 25th May | Casualties 1 O/R Burwinded 1 Sm Allan wounded & aired. | RAMC |
| | 26th May | Casualties 2/Lt A. AGELASTO wounded. 1 killed 9 wounded | RAMC |
| | | 5/Lt Allan wounded 38 | |

Army Form C. 2118.

# WAR DIARY
## or
## INTELLIGENCE SUMMARY.
*(Erase heading not required.)*

Instructions regarding War Diaries and Intelligence Summaries are contained in F. S. Regs., Part II. and the Staff Manual respectively. Title pages will be prepared in manuscript.

| Hour, Date, Place | Summary of Events and Information | Remarks and references to Appendices |
|---|---|---|
| YPRES HILL 60 | | Ref OSTEND MAP and |
| 27th May | Casualties 1 killed, 6 wounded. | Situation unchanged. Sq. Sheet maps 1/20000 / 1/40000 |
| 28th May | Casualties 1 killed, 3 wounded | Situation unchanged |
| 29th May | Casualties 1 killed, 1 wounded | Situation unchanged |
| 30th May | Casualties 1 killed, 2 wounded | Situation unchanged |
| 31st May | Casualties 1 killed, 1 wounded | Situation unchanged |

15th Bde.
5th Div.

1st DORSETS

JUNE

1915

# WAR DIARY
## or
## INTELLIGENCE SUMMARY.

Army Form 18.

| Place | Date | Hour | Summary of Events and Information | Remarks and references to Appendices |
|---|---|---|---|---|
| Albert | 1st June | 11.30 pm | Battalion in relieve of by 1st Beaufort distribution as follows:— Ord'd Company in square T.20.b. and T.21.c., 2 Platoons being posted in supporting points T.28.b. and T.58.a. Casualties 2/Lt A M EARLE slightly wounded, 1 killed, 1 wounded. | [illegible] Capmcca 20" K.2+15. W4+30 |

# WAR DIARY
## or
## INTELLIGENCE SUMMARY.
*(Erase heading not required.)*

Army Form C. 2118.

| Hour, Date, Place | Summary of Events and Information | Remarks and references to Appendices |
|---|---|---|
| YPRES - HILL 60 - June 2nd | | Reference OSTENDMAP Sheet 28 1/20000 & 1/40000 |
| " 3rd | | |
| " 4th | | |
| " 5th | | |
| " 6th | Battalion remained in closing dug-outs along Railway in I.20 and I.21.c | |
| " 7th | | |
| " 8th | | |
| " 9th | | |
| " 10th | | |
| " 11th | | |
| " 12th | | |
| June 13th 11.5 pm | Bn relieved 1st BEDFORDS in HILL 60 Sector. | |
| June 14th | Situation Quiet. 2/Lt. H.C. BUTCHER wounded. | |
| " 15th 6 | Bombing parties went out. Two parties went out in front of 38 and 39 about Manor House met one another without being spotted. Each party erected a O (barricade) but position was undecisive by daylight. 2 other parties went forward some yards and bombed the enemy barricades. Casualties 2 killed 23 wounded. | |
| June 16th | Situation quiet. | |
| June 17th 10.45 pm | Bn relieved by 1st BEDFORDS, withdrawn to Dugouts along Railway in I.20 and I.21.c | |

Army Form C. 2118.

# WAR DIARY
## or
## INTELLIGENCE SUMMARY.

(Erase heading not required.)

Instructions regarding War Diaries and Intelligence Summaries are contained in F.S. Regs., Part II. and the Staff Manual respectively. Title pages will be prepared in manuscript.

| Hour, Date, Place | | Summary of Events and Information | Remarks and references to Appendices |
|---|---|---|---|
| YPRES HILL 60 | June 18th } June 19th } June 20 | Battn. remained in Dugouts near the Railway I 20 d I 21 c | Re OSTEND TRAP June 28 1600 d 4000 |
| | June 21st | Capt RANSOME transferred to HQ 15th Infantry Brigade as Brigade Major and Major CANTAN D.C.L.I. assumed command of the Battn. | |
| | 11.30pm | Battn. relieved 1st BEDFORDS in HILL 60 sector. | |
| | June 22nd | Situation Quiet during day. Wire Bombing ammunitions were carried out during the night. | |
| | June 23rd | Situation Quiet | |
| | June 24th | Situation Quiet | |
| | June 25th | Situation Quiet | |
| | June 26th | Situation Quiet | |
| | June 27th 11.30pm | Battalion relieved by 1st BEDFORDS. Withdrew to Dugouts along the Railway I 20 d I 21 c. | |
| | June 28th } June 29th } June 30th | June 30th. Major CANTAN transferred to D.C.L.I and Major RADCLIFFE D.S.O. R.Dublin & assumed command of Bn. Battalion remained in Dugouts near the Railway I 20 , I 21 c. | |
| July | July 1st 3.0pm July 3rd 11.30pm | Battalion relieved 1st BEDFORDS in HILL 60 sector | |

5th Division

15th Infantry Bde

1st Dorsets

July to December

1915

To 14 Bde
32 Div

15th Bde.
5th Div.

1st D O R S E T S

J U L Y

1 9 1 5

Army Form C. 2118.

# WAR DIARY
## or
## INTELLIGENCE SUMMARY.
*(Erase heading not required.)*

Instructions regarding War Diaries and Intelligence Summaries are contained in F.S. Regs., Part II. and the Staff Manual respectively. Title pages will be prepared in manuscript.

| Place | Date | Hour | Summary of Events and Information | Remarks and references to Appendices |
|---|---|---|---|---|
| | | | Copied from previous months diary. | |
| July | 1st | | | |
| | 2nd | | Battalion remained in dugouts near the Railway I 20 & I 21c. | |
| | 3rd | | Battalion relieved 1st Bedfords in Hill 60 Sector. | |

Army Form C. 2118.

# WAR DIARY
## or
## INTELLIGENCE SUMMARY.
(Erase heading not required.)

Instructions regarding War Diaries and Intelligence Summaries are contained in F.S. Regs., Part II. and the Staff Manual respectively. Title pages will be prepared in manuscript.

| Hour, Date, Place | Summary of Events and Information | Remarks and references to Appendices |
|---|---|---|
| YPRES HILL 60 Sector July 4th | Situation quiet. | See OSTEND MAP Sheet 28 1/100000 & 1/20000 |
| July 5th 3 p.m. | 38 Trench was violently bombarded. This was followed by three minnenwerfer bombs just behind 39. Soon after this the Germans | |
| 5.15 | bombarded 38, 38 C.T. also 38 support, very heavily with | |
| 6 p.m. | minnenwerfer, eventual shelling was very accurate. Each minnenwerfer was followed by 4 smaller shells. Two machine gun emplacements were destroyed & other important portions of trenches – such as the junction of two trenches. The bombardt. was lasted for 2 hours and minnie lifts & craters & dugouts were driven in to ruin the dugouts – which were quickly complete. | |
| | Casualties A Coy Wounded 2. suffering from Search 8. | |
| | B Coy Wounded 3. | Killed 1 Missing |
| | C Coy Wounded 27. | Killed 15 Missing 4 |
| | D Coy Wounded 2. | Wounded 2. |
| | CAPT ALGEO Wounded. | * 7150 Pte TASKER F. Rifles |
| July 6th | Situation quiet. | |
| July 7th | Two or three minnenwerfer fell in 38 Trench. One man was killed in trying to throw the shell from the trench. One man slightly wounded, before it exploded. In leaving his Bombs. | N.W.K. |
| July 8th | Situation quiet. | N.W.K. |
| July 9th | Situation quiet. 2/Lt WEBSTER accidentally wounded. Battalion relieved by 1st BEDFORDS & withdrew to August along the Railway in I 20 and I 21 c | N.W.K. |

W Reilly
(73989) W4141—463. 400,000. 9/14. H. & J. Ltd. Forms/C. 2118/10.

Army Form C. 2118.

# WAR DIARY
## or
## INTELLIGENCE SUMMARY.
*(Erase heading not required.)*

Instructions regarding War Diaries and Intelligence Summaries are contained in F.S. Regs., Part II. and the Staff Manual respectively. Title pages will be prepared in manuscript.

| Hour, Date, Place | Summary of Events and Information | Remarks and references to Appendices |
|---|---|---|
| YPRES. July 10th, July 11th, July 12th | Battalion remained in Dugouts by the Railway in I.20.D & I.21.c | Ref Ostend Map + squared maps sheets 28 1/40000 . 1/20000 |
| July 13th | Battalion relieved by 1st LEICESTERS withdrew to RENINGHELST. Bn H.Q. A & B Coys were placed in hutments in square M.6.a. C & D Coys in G.34.c. | |
| RENINGHELST 11.30 pm | | |
| July 14th, July 15th, July 16th, July 17th, July 18th, July 19th, July 20th | Battalion remained in hutments in square M.5.a and G.34.c. 5th Division has been temporarily attached to 5th Corps. | |
| July 21st 9 pm | Battalion marched to fresh billeting area in squares L.19, 25 and 31. Bns being billeted in farms. Bn. H.Q. in L.19.c. | Refs Squared Map Sheet 27 1/40000 + 1/20000 |
| WATOU July 22nd, July 23rd, July 24th, July 25th, July 26th, July 27th, July 28th, July 29th | Battalion remained in farms in squares L.19, 25 and 31 | |

Army Form C. 2118.

# WAR DIARY
## or
## INTELLIGENCE SUMMARY.
*(Erase heading not required.)*

Instructions regarding War Diaries and Intelligence Summaries are contained in F.S. Regs., Part II. and the Staff Manual respectively. Title pages will be prepared in manuscript.

| Hour, Date, Place | Summary of Events and Information | Remarks and references to Appendices |
|---|---|---|
| PONT NOYELLE July 30th 6.33am | Battalion entrained at GODEWAERSVELDE and proceeded by train to CORBIE [AMIENS Sheet 12]. Two halts of 1 hour's duration were made. The first at CALAIS TRIAGE at 9.45am. The second at | Reference AMIENS Sheet 12 and Sheet 27 1/20000, 1/40000 maps of France. |
| 9.45am | | |
| 3.15pm | ABBEVILLE at 3.15pm. The Battalion found itself in AMIENS at | |
| 6.20pm | | |
| 6.45pm | Battalion detrained at CORBIE. During the journey the Advance Officer came for down and broke his leg in a tunnel. His was shot by the Transport Officer. MMC | |
| 10.5pm | The Battalion in billets at PONT NOYELLE | |
| July 31st Aug 1st | Remained in billets at PONT NOYELLE | |

15th Bde.
5th Division

1st D O R S E T S

A U G U S T

1 9 1 5

Army Form C. 2118.

# WAR DIARY
## or
## INTELLIGENCE SUMMARY.

(Erase heading not required.)

Instructions regarding War Diaries and Intelligence Summaries are contained in F.S. Regs., Part II. and the Staff Manual respectively. Title pages will be prepared in manuscript.

| Hour, Date, Aug. 1st. | Remained in billets at PONT NOYELLES and Information | Remarks and references to Appendices |
|---|---|---|
| PONT NOYELLE Aug 2nd 6.0.30 p.m. | Battalion marched to DERNANCOURT. | Ref AMIENS Sheet 12 Scale 1/20000 Inch = 1¼ miles and ALBERT Map Scale 1/40000 |
| DERNANCOURT 10.40 p.m. Aug 3rd 8 p.m. | Battalion in billets at DERNANCOURT. Battalion marched to MEAULTE. From there A Company proceeded to point 107. B Company to BECORDEL. Bn H.Q and A and B Coys remained in MEAULTE. | Printed by 2nd Printing Coy RE 3rd Army NYHA NYHA |
| MEAULTE Aug 4th Aug 5th Aug 6th Aug 7th Aug 8th | Battalion remained in MEAULTE, BECORDEL and Point 107 | See Appendix for weekly state measures up Aug 7th NYHA |
| Aug 9th 9.30 p.m. | Battalion relieved the CHESHIRES in sub-sector C.I. [the sector which includes PETIT BOIS FRANCAIS] Trenches 76-83 inclusive | NYHA |
| Aug 10th Aug 11th | Casualties one killed two wounded (one accidentally). A German was shot by C Coy when leaving our trenches by WEST RIDING S-situation normal | NYHA NYHA |
| Aug 12th | Casualties one killed no wounded S-situation normal | NYHA |
| Aug 13th | Casualties 2 wounded S-situation normal | NYHA |
| Aug 14th | Casualties Nil - S-situation Normal | NYHA |
| Aug 15th | Casualties Nil - Situation Normal | NYHA |
| | | See Appendix for weekly state measures up Aug 14th NYHA |

Army Form C. 2118.

# WAR DIARY
## or
## INTELLIGENCE SUMMARY.
*(Erase heading not required.)*

Instructions regarding War Diaries and Intelligence Summaries are contained in F. S. Regs. Part II. and the Staff Manual respectively. Title pages will be prepared in manuscript.

| Place | Date | Hour | Summary of Events and Information | Remarks and references to Appendices |
|---|---|---|---|---|
| Trenches 76-83 | Aug 15th | | 6 men were accidentally wounded by one of our own bombs out of wounds. | Refers to AMIENS Sheet 12 Scale 1/20000 |
| NofMoFRICOURT | 12 | 10pm | Battalion relieved by 1st CHESHIRES. Withdrew to MEAULTE - BECORDEL, A.B.D Companies to MEAULTE, C Coy BECORDEL. | MM |
| MEAULTE and | Aug 16th | | Battalion resting in billets in MEAULTE - BECORDEL. C.O. called on O.C. 1st WARWICKS to arrange party | Routine party |
| BECORDEL | Aug 17th | | Major J.F. RADCLIFFE D.S.O. being posted to 1st DEVONS, Major L.N. JONES-BATEMAN, O.C. 1st NORFOLK Regt. assumed command of the Battalion. Battn. found working party | Routine party |
| | Aug 18th | | Casualties at work 1 wounded on working party | Routine |
| | Aug 19th | | | Routine |
| | Aug 20th | | | Routine |
| | Aug 21st | | Casualties on march: Missing Sergt. found lying fatigue, 1 case of wound of shrapnel wire | Routine Southampton |
| | Aug 22nd | | | work for week |
| | | | C Coy withdrew to MEAULTE on relief by 7th BUFFS. (in a mine shaft from five days) | |
| MEAULTE | Aug 23rd | | | (illegible) |
| | Aug 24th | | | |
| | Aug 25th | | Battalion resting in billets in MEAULTE | |
| | Aug 26th | | | |

Army Form C. 2118.

# WAR DIARY
## or
## INTELLIGENCE SUMMARY.

(Erase heading not required.)

Instructions regarding War Diaries and Intelligence Summaries are contained in F. S. Regs., Part II. and the Staff Manual respectively. Title pages will be prepared in manuscript.

| Place | Date | Hour | Summary of Events and Information | Remarks and references to Appendices |
|---|---|---|---|---|
| MEAULTE | Aug 27 | 7.30pm | Battalion moved from MEAULTE to billets in ETINEHEM and CHIPILLY | Sept of brigade Infantry instr. |
| ETINEHEM & CHIPILLY | Aug 28 | | B Coy's at ETINEHEM, HQ, C and D at CHIPILLY | Gp. of AMIENS Sheet 12 20000 |
| | Aug 29 | | | |
| | Aug 30 | | Battalion remained in billets in ETINEHEM and CHIPILLY. | |
| | Aug 31 | | | |

**Army Form B. 213.**

# FIELD RETURN.

No. of Report _____

(To be furnished by all arms, services, and departments to the A.G.'s Office at the Base in accordance with Field Service Regulations, Part II.) Date _____

RETURN showing numbers RATIONED by, and Transport on charge of, 1/5th Devonshire Regiment on the Field 1.5.1915

| DETAIL | Personnel | | | Animals | | | | | | | Guns, carriages, and limbers and transport vehicles | | | | Horsed | | Mechanical | | | | REMARKS |
|---|---|---|---|---|---|---|---|---|---|---|---|---|---|---|---|---|---|---|---|---|---|
| | Officers | Other ranks | Natives | Horses Riding | Horses Draught | Horses Heavy Draught | Pack | Mules Large | Mules Small | Camels | Oxen | Guns, carriages and limbers, showing description | Ammunition wagons and limbers | Machine Guns | Aircraft, showing description | 4 Wheeled | 2 Wheeled | Motor Cars | Tractors | Lorries | Trucks | Trailers | Motor Bicycles | Bicycles |
| Effective Strength of Unit | 25 | 1030 | | 10 | 34 | 15 | 6 | | 3 | | | | | 4 | | 14 | 9 | | | | | | | 5 |
| Details, by *Arms* attached to unit as in War Establishment:— R.A.M.C. | 1 | 5 | | | | | | | | | | | | | | | | | | | | | | |
| A.O.C. | | 1 | | | | | | | | | | | | | | | | | | | | | | |
| Total | 26 | 1036 | | 10 | 34 | 15 | 6 | | 3 | | | | | 4 | | 14 | 9 | | | | | | | 5 |
| War Establishment | 30 | 995 | | 12 | 35 | 16 | 6 | | 3 | | | | | 4 | | 14 | 9 | | | | | | | 9 |
| Wanting to complete | 4 | | | 2 | 1 | 1 | | | | | | | | | | | | | | | | | | 1 |
| Surplus | | 41 | | | | | | | | | | | | | | | | | | | | | | |
| *Attached (not to include the details shown above) | | | | | | | | | | | | | | | | | | | | | | | | |
| Civilians:— Employed with the Unit Accompanying the Unit | | | 1 | | | | | | | | | | | | | | | | | | | | | |
| TOTAL RATIONED ... | 26 | 1036 | 1 | 10 | 34 | 15 | 6 | | 3 | | | | | 4 | | 14 | 9 | | | | | | | 5 |

Signature of Commander _____

Date of Despatch 1.5.1915

* In the case of field ambulances, hospitals or depots, the number of patients are to be included here, the names being shown in A.F.A. 36.

Wt.-W. 6005-894 (35047) U. B. Ltd. 500,000 10/14 Forms B. 213

*For information of the A.G.'s Office at the Base.*

Officers and men who have become casuals, been transferred or joined since last report.

Place *In the Field*  Date *1-8-1915*

| Regtl. Number | Rank | Name | Corps | Nature of casualty, or name of unit from or to which transferred | Date of being struck off or coming on the ration return | Remarks* |
|---|---|---|---|---|---|---|
| | | | | | | |
| | | | | | | |
| | | | | | | |
| | | | | | | |
| | | | | | | |
| | | | | | | |
| | | | | | | |
| | | | | | | |
| | | | | | | |
| | | | | | | |
| | | | | | | |
| | | | | | | |
| | | | | | | |
| | | | | | | |
| | | | | | | |
| | | | | | | |
| | | | | | | |
| | | | | | | |
| | | | | | | |
| | | | | | | |

\* State whether absence is of a permanent or temporary nature, adding, in the case of casuals from wounds or disease, any available information for communication to the relatives.

Army Form B. 213.

# FIELD RETURN.

No. of Report _____

(To be furnished by all arms, services, and departments to the A.G.'s Office at the Base in accordance with Field Service Regulations, Part II.)

Date _____

RETURN showing numbers RATIONED by, and Transport on charge of, John Donaldson Byrne at _____ Date 7th August 1915.

| DETAIL. | Personnel | | | Animals | | | | | | | Guns, carriages, and limbers and transport vehicles | | | | | | | | | REMARKS |
|---|---|---|---|---|---|---|---|---|---|---|---|---|---|---|---|---|---|---|---|---|
| | Officers | Other ranks | Natives | Horses Riding | Draught | Heavy Draught | Pack | Mules Large | Mules Small | Camels | Oxen | Guns, carriages and limbers, showing description | Ammunition wagons and limbers | Machine Guns | Aircraft, showing description | Horsed 4 Wheeled | Horsed 2 Wheeled | Motor Cars | Tractors | Mechanical Lorries / Trucks / Trailers / Motor Bicycles / Bicycles |
| Effective Strength of Unit Details, by Arms attached to unit as in War Establishment:— | 26 | 1060 | | 10 | 34 | 15 | 6 | | 3 | | | | | 4 | | 14 | 9 | | | 7 |
| R.A.M.C. | 1 | 3 | | | | 1 | | | | | | | | | | | | | | |
| A.C.C. | | 1 | | | | | | | | | | | | | | | | | | |
| Total | 27 | 1066 | | 10 | 34 | 15 | 6 | | 3 | | | | | 4 | | 14 | 9 | | | |
| War Establishment | 30 | 944 | | 12 | 35 | 16 | 9 | | 3 | | | | | 4 | | 14 | 9 | | | 9 |
| Wanting to complete | 3 | | | 2 | 1 | 1 | | | | | | | | | | | | | | |
| Surplus | | 29 | | | | | | | | | | | | | | | | | | |
| *Attached (not to include the details shown above) | | | | | | | | | | | | | | | | | | | | |
| Civilians:— Employed with the Unit Accompanying the Unit | | 1 | | | | | | | | | | | | | | | | | | |
| TOTAL RATIONED … | 27 | 1066 | 1 | 10 | 34 | 15 | 6 | | 3 | | | | | 4 | | 14 | 9 | | | 8 |

* In the case of field ambulances, hospitals or depots, the number of patients are to be included here, the names being shown in A.F.A. 36.

Signature of Commander _____

Date of Despatch _____

*For information of the A.G.'s Office at the Base.*

Officers and men who have become casuals, been transferred or joined since last report.

Place _In the Field_   Date _8-8-1915_

| Regtl. Number | Rank | Name | Corps | Nature of casualty, or name of unit from or to which transferred | Date of being struck off or coming on the ration return | Remarks* |
|---|---|---|---|---|---|---|
| | Lieut | C.K.C. Bartlett | 3/Dorsets | To F. Amb | 2.8.1915 | |
| | Lieut | C.H. Morris | 1/Dorsets | To F. Amb | 2.8.1915 | |
| | Lieut | C.P.B. Sawyer | 3/Dorsets | From M.G. Course | 4.8.1915 | |
| | Lieut | E.J. Smith | 1/Dorsets | From F. Amb | 5.8.1915 | |
| | Lieut | J.G. Hunt | 1/Dorsets | Joined Bn | 1.8.1915 | |
| | Lieut | R.B. Webster | 3/Dorsets | Rejoined Bn | 6.8.1915 | |

* State whether absence is of a permanent or temporary nature, adding, in the case of casuals from wounds or disease, any available information for communication to the relatives.

Army Form B. 213.

# FIELD RETURN.

No. of Report _____

(To be furnished by all arms, services, and departments to the A.G.'s Office at the Base in accordance with Field Service Regulations, Part II.)

RETURN showing numbers RATIONED by, and Transport on charge of, *1st Devonshire Regt* at *In the Field*   Date. *15th August 1915*

| DETAIL. | Personnel | | | Animals | | | | | | | Guns, carriages, and limbers and transport vehicles | | | | | | | | | REMARKS |
|---|---|---|---|---|---|---|---|---|---|---|---|---|---|---|---|---|---|---|---|---|
| | Officers | Other ranks | Natives | Horses Riding | Horses Draught | Horses Heavy Draught | Pack | Mules Large | Mules Small | Camels | Oxen | Guns, carriages and limbers, showing description | Ammunition wagons and limbers | Machine guns | Aircraft, showing description | Horsed 4 Wheeled | Horsed 2 Wheeled | Motor Cars | Tractors | Mechanical Lorries | Mechanical Trucks | Trailers | Motor Bicycles | Bicycles | |
| Effective Strength of Unit | 24 | 966 | | 11 | 34 | 15 | 6 | | 3 | | | | | 4 | | 14 | 9 | | | | | | | 6 | |
| Details, *by Arms* attached to unit as in War Establishment:— | | | | | | | | | | | | | | | | | | | | | | | | | |
| R.A.M.C. | 1 | 5 | | 1 | 1 | 1 | | | | | | | | | | | | | | | | | | | |
| A.O.C. | | 1 | | | | | | | | | | | | | | | | | | | | | | | |
| Total | 25 | 972 | | 12 | 35 | 16 | 6 | | 3 | | | | | 4 | | 14 | 9 | | | | | | | 6 | |
| War Establishment | 30 | 993 | | 12 | 35 | 16 | 6 | | 3 | | | | | 4 | | 14 | 9 | | | | | | | 6 | |
| Wanting to complete | 5 | 21 | | 1 | 1 | 1 | | | | | | | | | | | | | | | | | | | |
| Surplus | | | | | | | | | | | | | | | | | | | | | | | | | |
| *Attached (not to include the details shown above) | | | | | | | | | | | | | | | | | | | | | | | | | |
| Civilians:— | | | | | | | | | | | | | | | | | | | | | | | | | |
| Employed with the Unit | | | 1 | | | | | | | | | | | | | | | | | | | | | | |
| Accompanying the Unit | | | | | | | | | | | | | | | | | | | | | | | | | |
| TOTAL RATIONED ... | 24 | 966 | 1 | 11 | 34 | 15 | 6 | | 3 | | | | | 4 | | 14 | 9 | | | | | | | 6 | |

* In the case of field ambulances, hospitals or depôts, the number of patients are to be included here, the names being shown in A.F.A. 36.

Forms B. 213.

Signature of Commander _____

Date of Despatch. *15.8.1915*

*For information of the A.G.'s Office at the Base.*

Officers and men who have become casuals, been transferred or joined since last report.

Place **In the Field**　　　　Date **15.8.1915**

| Regtl. Number | Rank | Name | Corps | Nature of casualty, or name of unit from or to which transferred | Date of being struck off or coming on the ration return | Remarks* |
|---|---|---|---|---|---|---|
| | Lieut | A.B. Lindsay | RAMC | vacated appt of MO | 5.8.15 | |
| | Lieut | R.J. English | RAMC | Joined B'n as MO | 5.8.15 | |
| | Lieut | H.A.E. Mathews | 1/Dorset | To leave | 9.8.15 | Temporary |

\* State whether absence is of a permanent or temporary nature, adding, in the case of casuals from wounds or disease, any available information for communication to the relatives.

**Army Form B. 213.**

# FIELD RETURN.

No. of Report _____

(To be furnished by all arms, services, and departments to the A.G.'s Office at the Base in accordance with Field Service Regulations, Part II.)

Date. 22nd August 1915.

RETURN showing numbers RATIONED by, and Transport on charge of, /6/A Dorsetshire Regiment at In the field

| DETAIL | Personnel | | | Animals — Horses | | | Mules | | Camels | Oxen | Guns, carriages, limbers, showing description | Ammunition wagons and limbers | Machine guns | Aircraft, showing description | Horsed 4 Wheeled | Horsed 2 Wheeled | Motor Cars | Tractors | Mechanical Lorries, showing description | Mechanical Trucks, showing description | Trailers | Motor Bicycles | Bicycles | REMARKS |
|---|---|---|---|---|---|---|---|---|---|---|---|---|---|---|---|---|---|---|---|---|---|---|---|---|
| | Officers | Other ranks | Natives | Riding | Draught | Heavy Draught | Pack | Large | Small | | | | | | | | | | | | | | | |
| Actually with the Effective Strength of Unit | 23 | 935 | | 11 | 34 | 15 | 6 | | 3 | | | | | 4 | | 14 | 9 | | | | | | 3 | |
| Details, by Arms attached to unit as in War Establishment:— R.A.M.C. | 5 | 52 | | | | | | | | | | | | | | | | | | | | | | |
| A.O.C. | 1 | 5 | | | | | | | | | | | | | | | | | | | | | | |
| | | 1 | | | | | | | | | | | | | | | | | | | | | | |
| Total | 24 | 939 | | 11 | 34 | 15 | 6 | | 3 | | | | | 4 | | 14 | 9 | | | | | | 6 | *Officer 1 O.R. /Norfolks |
| War Establishment | 30 | 995 | | 12 | 35 | 16 | 9 | | | | | | | 4 | | 14 | 9 | | | | | | 2 | |
| Wanting to complete | 6 | 56 | | 1 | 1 | 1 | | | | | | | | | | | | | | | | | | |
| Surplus | | | | | | | | | 3 | | | | | | | | | | | | | | | |
| *Attached (not to include the details shown above) | 1 | 1 | | | | | | | | | | | | | | | | | | | | | | |
| Civilians:— Employed with the Unit Accompanying the Unit | | | | | | | | | | | | | | | | | | | | | | | | |
| TOTAL RATIONED | 24 | 944 | 1 | 11 | 34 | 15 | 6 | | 3 | | | | | 4 | | 14 | 9 | | | | | | 3 | |

* In the case of field ambulances, hospitals or depots, the number of patients are to be included here, the names being shown in A.F.A. 36.

Wt.-W. 6005-894 (33047) U.B. Ltd. 500,000 10/14 Forms B. 213

_____ Signature of Commander.

28.8.1915 Date of Despatch.

*For information of the A.G.'s Office at the Base.*

Officers and men who have become casuals, been transferred or joined since last report.

Place  In the Field            Date  22.8.1915

| Regtl. Number | Rank | Name | Corps | Nature of casualty, or name of unit from or to which transferred | Date of being struck off or coming on the ration return | Remarks* |
|---|---|---|---|---|---|---|
| | Major | J.F. Radcliffe DSO | 2/Devons | To 1/Devons | 17.8.15 | |
| | Major | L.N. Jones-Bateman CMG | Norfolks | assumes Command | 17.8.15 | |
| | Lieut | S Lancaster | 1/Dorsets | Rejoined Battn | 17.8.1915 | |
| | Lieut | H.C. Butcher | 3/Dorsets | Rejoined Battn | 14.8.1915 | |
| | Lieut | C.P.S. Sawyer | 3/Dorsets | To Field Amb | 19.8.15 | |
| | Lieut | P.L.C. Walker | 3/Dorsets | To Field Amb | 20.8.15 | |
| | Lieut | S.B. Gomez | 3/Dorsets | Joined Bn | 21.8.15 | |
| | Lt & QM | W Alderman | 1/Dorsets | To F Amb | 15.8.15 | |
| | Lt | H.A.C. Mathews | 1/Dorsets | From Leave | 18.8.1915 | |
| | Lieut | H.J. Green | 1/Dorsets | To Leave | 18.8.1915 | Temporary |
| | Lieut | O.R. Tulles | 3/Dorsets | To Leave | 18.8.1915 | Temporary |

* State whether absence is of a permanent or temporary nature, adding, in the case of casuals from wounds or disease, any available information for communication to the relatives.

Army Form B. 213.

# FIELD RETURN.

No. of Report _____     Date. 29.5.1915

(To be furnished by all arms, services, and departments to the A.G.'s Office at the Base in accordance with Field Service Regulations, Part II.)

RETURN showing numbers RATIONED by, and Transport on charge of, 10th Devonshire Regiment at In the field

| DETAIL. | Personnel | | | Animals | | | | | | | Guns, carriages, and limbers and transport vehicles | | | Horsed | | Mechanical | | | | REMARKS |
|---|---|---|---|---|---|---|---|---|---|---|---|---|---|---|---|---|---|---|---|---|
| | Officers | Other ranks | Natives | Horses Riding | Horses Draught | Horses Heavy Draught | Pack | Mules Large | Mules Small | Camels | Oxen | Guns, carriages and limbers, showing description | Ammunition wagons and limbers | Machine guns | Aircraft, showing description | 4 Wheeled | 2 Wheeled | Motor Cars | Tractors | Lorries, showing description | Trucks, showing description | Trailers | Motor Bicycles | Bicycles |
| Effective Strength of Unit | 30 | 1084 | | 11 | 34 | 15 | 6 | | 3 | | | | | 4 | | 14 | 9 | | | | | | | 12 |
| Details, by Arms attached to unit as in War Establishment:— | | | | | | | | | | | | | | | | | | | | | | | | |
| R.A.M.C. | 1 | 5 | | | | 1 | | | | | | | | | | | | | | | | | | |
| A.O.C. | | 1 | | | | | | | | | | | | | | | | | | | | | | |
| Total | 31 | 1090 | | 11 | 34 | 15 | 6 | | 3 | | | | | 4 | | 14 | 9 | | | | | | | 1 |
| War Establishment | 30 | 995 | | 12 | 35 | 16 | 9 | | | | | | | 4 | | 14 | 9 | | | | | | | 9 |
| Wanting to complete | | | | 1 | 1 | 1 | | | | | | | | | | | | | | | | | | |
| Surplus | 1 | 99 | | | | | | | 3 | | | | | | | | | | | | | | | |
| * Attached (not to include the details shown above) | | | | | | | | | | | | | | | | | | | | | | | | |
| Civilians:— Employed with the Unit Accompanying the Unit | | | 1 | | | | | | | | | | | | | | | | | | | | | |
| TOTAL RATIONED ... | 31 | 1090 | 1 | 11 | 34 | 15 | 6 | | 3 | | | | | 4 | | 14 | 9 | | | | | | | 3 |

Wt.-W. 6005-894 (35047) U. B. Ltd. 500,000 10/14     Forms B. 213

* In the case of field ambulances, hospitals or depots, the number of patients are to be included here, the names being shown in A.F.A. 36.

Signature of Commander _____

Date of Despatch 29.5.1915

*For information of the A.G.'s Office at the Base.*

Officers and men who have become casuals, been transferred or joined since last report.

Place _In the Field_    Date _29.5.1915_

| Regtl. Number | Rank | Name | Corps | Nature of casualty, or name of unit from or to which transferred | Date of being struck off or coming on the ration return | Remarks* |
|---|---|---|---|---|---|---|
| | Lieut | A. Lancaster | 1/Dorset | To leave | 25.5.1915 | Temporary |
| | Lieut | R.B. Webster | 3/Dorsets | To F.Amb. | 27.5.1915 | |
| | Lieut | A. Preedy | 3/Devons | From F.Amb. | 22.5.1915 | |
| | Lieut | W.R. Fuller | 3/Dorsets | From leave | 25.5.1915 | |
| | Lieut | H.J. Green | 1/Dorset | From leave | 25.5.1915 | |

* State whether absence is of a permanent or temporary nature, adding, in the case of casuals from wounds or disease, any available information for communication to the relatives.

15th Bde.
5th Div.

1st DORSETS

SEPTEMBER

1 9 1 5

**Army Form C. 2118.**

# WAR DIARY
## or
## INTELLIGENCE SUMMARY.
*(Erase heading not required.)*

Instructions regarding War Diaries and Intelligence Summaries are contained in F. S. Regs., Part II. and the Staff Manual respectively. Title pages will be prepared in manuscript.

| Place | Date | Hour | Summary of Events and Information | Remarks and references to Appendices |
|---|---|---|---|---|
| ETINEHEM | Sept 1st | 3pm | HQ, Coys & Companies marched to ETINEHEM | |
| | | 7pm | Battalion moved from ETINEHEM to trenches 19-27 at MARICOURT, where | |
| MARICOURT | Sept 2nd | 12.25am | Battalion relieved 2nd D.C.L.I. Relief completed 12.25am. | See Appendix a "Casualty State" |
| | Sept 3rd | | | |
| | Sept 4th | | Battalion remained in trenches 19-27 at MARICOURT. Patrols went | |
| | Sept 5th | | out nearly every night. Patrols had nothing to report saw that | |
| | Sept 6th | | the sides lay was exceptionally quiet. Only two casualties occurred | |
| | Sept 7th | | during the Battalion tour of duty in the trenches. One man slightly wounded on 7th | |
| | Sept 8th | | | |
| | Sept 9th | | One man wounded on 9th | OWMC |

Army Form C. 2118.

# WAR DIARY
## or
## INTELLIGENCE SUMMARY.
*(Erase heading not required.)*

Instructions regarding War Diaries and Intelligence Summaries are contained in F. S. Regs., Part II. and the Staff Manual respectively. Title pages will be prepared in manuscript.

| Place | Date | Hour | Summary of Events and Information | Remarks and references to Appendices |
|---|---|---|---|---|
| MARCOURT | Sept 10 | 11.15pm | The Battalion being relieved by 12th DCLI were withdrawn to Bivouacs in CHIPILLY | [illegible] Feb 1918 Map Sheet AMIENS 2 62d NE 1/20000 |
| | Sept 11 | 4.45am | Battalion in Billets in CHIPILLY | Map Sheet 2 1/20000 |
| | Sept 12 | | Battalion at CHIPILLY | NOVA |
| | Sept 13 | | " | |
| | Sept 14 | 9pm | Battalion was exercised in Raid marching. Route CHIPILLY – CERISY – Gots Roads Jn – N.W. of Point 66 – Road Junction in N.W. of ABANCOURT – HAMEL – Ontlesant Jnct North of HAMEL – CERISY – CHIPILLY. | NOVA |
| | Sept 15 | | Battalion remained at CHIPILLY | NOVA |
| | Sept 16 | | " | NOVA |
| | Sept 17 | 5.45pm | Battalion moved from CHIPILLY to BRAY | See Appendix forwarded with this MVC |
| | | 8pm | Battalion in billets in BRAY | MVC |
| | Sept 18 | | Battalion remained in BRAY in Brigade Reserve | MVC |
| | Sept 19 | | " " " " . One man killed working for R.E. near CITADEL | MVC |
| | Sept 20 | | " " " " | |
| | Sept 21 | | " " " " | |
| | Sept 22 | | " " " " | MVC |

Army Form C. 2118.

# WAR DIARY
## or
## INTELLIGENCE SUMMARY.
*(Erase heading not required.)*

Instructions regarding War Diaries and Intelligence Summaries are contained in F. S. Regs., Part II. and the Staff Manual respectively. Title pages will be prepared in manuscript.

| Place | Date | Hour | Summary of Events and Information | Remarks and references to Appendices |
|---|---|---|---|---|
| CARNOY Support Sector Trenches 36 to 48 inclusive | Sept 23rd | 10.30pm | Battalion relieves 2nd K.O.Y.L.I. and 2 Companies Q.V.R. in trenches. Relief completed 10.35pm | |
| | Sept 24th | | Quiet Day. No casualties | |
| | Sept 25th | | One man wounded. | |
| | Sept 26th | | One man wounded (Self inflicted wound) | |
| | Sept 27th | | Quiet Day. | |
| | Sept 28th | | Quiet Day - One L.Cpl. accidentally wounded by WEST BOMB THROWER | |
| | Sept 29th | | One man killed. Quiet Day. | |
| | Sept 30th | | German Artillery very active all day in registering on the Trenches and the approaches to them. Casualties Nil. | |

Army Form B. 213.

# FIELD RETURN.

No. of Report _____

(To be furnished by all arms, services, and departments to the A.G.'s Office at the Base in accordance with Field Service Regulations, Part II.)

Date. 5th September 1915.

RETURN showing numbers RATIONED by, and Transport on charge of, 1/5th Devonshire Regiment at the Field.

| DETAIL. | Personnel | | | Animals | | | | | | | Guns, carriages, and limbers and transport vehicles | | | | | | | | | REMARKS |
|---|---|---|---|---|---|---|---|---|---|---|---|---|---|---|---|---|---|---|---|---|
| | Officers | Other ranks | Natives | Horses Riding | Horses Draught | Horses Heavy Draught | Pack | Mules Large | Mules Small | Camels | Oxen | Guns, carriages and limbers, showing description | Ammunition wagons and limbers | Machine guns | Aircraft, showing description | Horsed 4 Wheeled | Horsed 2 Wheeled | Motor Cars | Tractors | Mechanical Lorries, showing description | Mechanical Trucks, showing description | Trailers | Motor Bicycles | Bicycles | |
| Actually Present with Unit Effective Strength of Unit Details, by Arms attached to unit as in War Establishment:— | 25 | 964 | | 12 | 35 | 16 | 6 | | 3 | | | | | 4 | | 14 | 9 | | | | | | | 4 | |
| R.A.M.C. | 6 | 91 | | | | | | | | | | | | | | | | | | | | | | | |
| A.O.C. | 1 | 5 | | 1 | | | | | | | | | | | | | | | | | | | | | |
| | | 1 | | | | | | | | | | | | | | | | | | | | | | | |
| Total | 26 | 970 | | 12 | 35 | 16 | 6 | | 3 | | | | | 4 | | 14 | 9 | | | | | | | 4 | officers 108 rifles etc. |
| War Establishment | 30 | 995 | | 12 | 35 | 16 | 9 | | | | | | | 4 | | 14 | 9 | | | | | | | 9 | |
| Wanting to complete | 4 | 25 | | | | | | | | | | | | | | | | | | | | | | 2 | |
| Surplus | | | | | | | | | | | | | | | | | | | | | | | | | |
| *Attached (not to include the details shown above) | 1 | 1 | | | | | | | | | | | | | | | | | | | | | | | |
| Civilians:— Employed with the Unit Accompanying the Unit | | | | | | | | | | | | | | | | | | | | | | | | | |
| TOTAL RATIONED ... | 26 | 970 | 1 | 12 | 35 | 16 | 6 | | 3 | | | | | 4 | | 14 | 9 | | | | | | | 4 | |

* In the case of field ambulances, hospitals or depots, the number of patients are to be included here, the names being shown in A. F. A. 36.

_____ Signature of Commander.

5.9.1915 Date of Despatch.

Wt.-W. 6005-894 (35047) U. B. Ltd. 500,000 10/14 Forms B. 213

*For information of the A.G.'s Office at the Base.*

Officers and men who have become casuals, been transferred or joined since last report.

Place __In the Field__  Date __5th September 1915__

| Regtl. Number | Rank | Name | Corps | Nature of casualty, or name of unit from or to which transferred | Date of being struck off or coming on the ration return | Remarks* |
|---|---|---|---|---|---|---|
| | Lieut | A Lancaster | 1/Dorsets | From Leave | 2.9.1915 | |
| | Lieut | C E Green | 3/Dorsets | To Field Amb | 31.8.1915 | |
| | Lieut | C P B Sawyer | 3/Dorsets | From F Amb | 28.8.1915 | |
| | Lieut | C E Young | 3/Dorsets | To Field Amb | 31.8.1915 | |
| | Lieut | J H Butler | 3/Dorsets | Joined Batt'n | 1.9.1915 | |

* State whether absence is of a permanent or temporary nature, adding, in the case of casuals from wounds or disease, any available information for communication to the relatives.

**Army Form B. 213.**

# FIELD RETURN.

No. of Report _____

(To be furnished by all arms, services, and departments to the A.G.'s Office at the Base in accordance with Field Service Regulations, Part II.)

RETURN showing numbers RATIONED by, and Transport on charge of _Lt Col Donaldson Bequest_ at _In the Field_  Date _12th September 1915_

| Detail | Personnel | | | Animals | | | | | | | Guns, carriages, and limbers and transport vehicles | | | | Mechanical | | | | Remarks |
|---|---|---|---|---|---|---|---|---|---|---|---|---|---|---|---|---|---|---|---|
| | Officers | Other ranks | Natives | Horses Riding | Horses Draught | Horses Heavy Draught | Pack | Mules Large | Mules Small | Camels | Oxen | Guns, carriages and limbers, showing description | Ammunition wagons and limbers | Machine guns | Aircraft, showing description | Horsed 4 Wheeled | Horsed 2 Wheeled | Motor Cars | Tractors | Lorries | Trucks | Trailers | Motor Bicycles | Bicycles | |
| *Actually Present with Battn* Effective Strength of Unit | 25 | 949 | | 12 | 35 | 16 | 6 | | 3 | | | | | 4 | | 14 | 9 | | | | | | | 8 | |
| Details, by Arms attached to unit as in War Establishment:— R.A.M.C. A.O.C. | 1 1 | 5 1 | | | | | | | | | | | | | | | | | | | | | | | |
| Total | 26 | 955 | | 12 | 35 | 16 | 6 | | 3 | | | | | 4 | | 14 | 9 | | | | | | | 6 | |
| War Establishment | 30 | 995 | | 12 | 35 | 16 | 9 | | 3 | | | | | 4 | | 14 | 9 | | | | | | | 9 | |
| Wanting to complete | 4 | 40 | | | | | 3 | | | | | | | | | | | | | | | | | 1 | |
| Surplus | | | | | | | | | | | | | | | | | | | | | | | | | |
| *Attached (not to include the details shown above) | 1 | 2 | 1 | | | | | | | | | | | | | | | | | | | | | | Officer 1st Norfolks & 2 Interpreters |
| Civilians:— Employed with the Unit Accompanying the Unit | | | | | | | | | | | | | | | | | | | | | | | | | |
| Total Rationed ... | 26 | 957 | 1 | 12 | 35 | 16 | 6 | | 3 | | | | | 4 | | 14 | 9 | | | | | | | 7 | |

\* In the case of field ambulances, hospitals or depots, the number of patients are to be included here, the names being shown in A.F.A. 36.

Signature of Commander _____

Date of Despatch _12.9.1915_

Wt.W.6005-894 (34047) U.B. Ltd. 500,000 10/14 Forms B. 213

For information of the A.G.'s Office at the Base.

Officers and men who have become casuals, been transferred or joined since last report.

Place: In the Field        Date: 12th September 1915

| Regtl. Number | Rank | Name | Corps | Nature of casualty, or name of unit from or to which transferred | Date of being struck off or coming on the ration return | Remarks* |
|---|---|---|---|---|---|---|
| | Capt | J.K. Shute | 1/Dorset | Joined Batt<sup>n</sup> | 10.9.1915 | |
| | Lieut | G.A. Turner | 3/Dorsets | To R.F.C. | 11.9.1915 | |

* State whether absence is of a permanent or temporary nature, adding, in the case of casuals from wounds or disease, any available information for communication to the relatives.

Army Form B. 213.

# FIELD RETURN.

No. of Report _____

(To be furnished by all arms, services, and departments to the A.G.'s Office at the Base in accordance with Field Service Regulations, Part II.) Date _____

RETURN showing numbers RATIONED by, and Transport on charge of, _1st Dorsetshire Regiment_ at _in the field_. Date _19th September 1915_

| DETAIL. | Personnel | | | Animals | | | | | | | Guns, carriages, and limbers and transport vehicles | | | | Horsed | | Mechanical | | | | | REMARKS |
| --- | --- | --- | --- | --- | --- | --- | --- | --- | --- | --- | --- | --- | --- | --- | --- | --- | --- | --- | --- | --- | --- | --- |
| | Officers | Other ranks | Natives | Horses Riding | Horses Draught | Horses Heavy Draught | Pack | Mules Large | Mules Small | Camels | Oxen | Guns, carriages and limbers, showing description | Ammunition wagons and limbers | Machine guns | Aircraft, showing description | 4 Wheeled | 2 Wheeled | Motor Cars | Tractors | Lorries, showing description | Trucks, showing description | Trailers | Motor Bicycles | Bicycles |
| Effective Strength of Unit _Actually present with Batln_ | 25 | 956 | | 12 | 35 | 15 | 6 | | 3 | | | | | 4 | | 14 | 9 | | | | | | | 9 |
| Details of Arms attached to unit as in War Establishment:— R.A.M.C. | 4 | 100 | | | | | | | | | | | | | | | | | | | | | | |
| A.O.C. | 1 | 5 | | | | | | | | | | | | | | | | | | | | | | |
| | | 1 | | | | | | | | | | | | | | | | | | | | | | |
| Total | 26 | 962 | | 12 | 35 | 15 | 6 | | 3 | | | | | 4 | | 14 | 9 | | | | | | | 9 |
| War Establishment | 30 | 995 | | 12 | 35 | 16 | 6 | | 3 | | | | | 4 | | 14 | 9 | | | | | | | 9 |
| Wanting to complete | 4 | 23 | | | | 1 | | | | | | | | | | | | | | | | | | |
| Surplus | | | | | | | | | | | | | | | | | | | | | | | | |
| *Attached (not to include the details shown above) | | | | | | | | | | | | | | | | | | | | | | | | |
| Civilians:— Employed with the Unit Accompanying the Unit | | 2 | 1 | | | | | | | | | | | | | | | | | | | | | |
| TOTAL RATIONED | 26 | 962 | 1 | 12 | 35 | 15 | 3 | | 6 | | | | | 4 | | 14 | 9 | | | | | | | 9 |

*Officer 1/R/Norfolks 1/B.R. yet being dispersed

* In the case of field ambulances, hospitals or depots, the number of patients are to be included here, the names being shown in A.F.A. 36.

Forms B. 213.

Signature of Commander _____

Date of Despatch _____

*For information of the A.G.'s Office at the Base.*

Officers and men who have become casuals, been transferred or joined since last report.

Place _In the Field_   Date _19th September 1915_

| Regtl. Number | Rank | Name | Corps | Nature of casualty, or name of unit from or to which transferred | Date of being struck off or coming on the ration return | Remarks* |
|---|---|---|---|---|---|---|
|  | Lieut | W.E. Young | 5 Dorsets | rejoined Bn | 11.9.1915 |  |
|  | Lieut | H.A.E. Mathews | 5 Dorsets | To F Amb | 15.9.1915 |  |

* State whether absence is of a permanent or temporary nature, adding, in the case of casuals from wounds or disease, any available information for communication to the relatives.

Army Form B. 213.

# FIELD RETURN

No. of Report _____

(To be furnished by all arms, services, and departments to the A.G.'s Office at the Base in accordance with Field Service Regulations, Part II.)

RETURN showing numbers RATIONED by, and Transport on charge of, *1st Br. Dowsetin Regt. In the Field* at _____ Date. 26.9.1915.

| DETAIL. | Personnel | | | Animals | | | | | | | Guns, carriages, and limbers and transport vehicles | | | | Horsed | | Mechanical | | | | Motor Bicycles | Bicycles | REMARKS. |
|---|---|---|---|---|---|---|---|---|---|---|---|---|---|---|---|---|---|---|---|---|---|---|---|
| | Officers | Other ranks | Natives | Horses Riding | Horses Draught | Horses Heavy Draught | Pack | Mules Large | Mules Small | Camels | Oxen | Guns, carriages and limbers, showing description | Ammunition wagons and limbers | Machine guns | Aircraft, showing description | 4 Wheeled | 2 Wheeled | Motor Cars | Tractors | Lorries, showing description | Trucks, showing description | Trailers | | | |
| Effective Strength of Unit | 29 | 1034 | | 12 | 35 | 15 | 6 | | 3 | | | | | 4 | | 14 9 | | | | | | | | 8 | attached 3 Officers 96 O.R. |
| Details, by Arms attached to unit as in War Establishment:— R.A.M.E. 1 5 A.O.E. | | | | | | | | | | | | | | | | | | | | | | | | | | |
| Total | 30 | 1040 | | 12 | 35 | 15 | 6 | | 3 | | | | | 4 | | 14 9 | | | | | | | | | | |
| War Establishment | 30 | 995 | | 12 | 35 | 16 | 9 | | | | | | | 4 | | 14 9 | | | | | | | | 9 | | |
| Wanting to complete | | | | | | 1 | | | | | | | | | | | | | | | | | | 1 | | |
| Surplus | | 2 | | | | | | | 3 | | | | | | | | | | | | | | | | | |
| * Attached (not to include the details shown above) | 1 | 2 | | | | | | | | | | | | | | | | | | | | | | | | |
| Civilians:— Employed with the Unit Accompanying the Unit | | | | | | | | | | | | | | | | | | | | | | | | | | |
| TOTAL RATIONED ... | 27 | 944 | | 12 | 35 | 15 | 6 | | 3 | | | | | 4 | | 14 9 | | | | | | | | 8 | | |

* Attached (not to include the details shown above)

* In the case of field ambulances, hospitals or depots, the number of patients are to be included here, the names being shown in A.F.A. 36.

W. McBullan Lt. Col. Major Signature of Commander.
26.9.1915. Date of Despatch.

Wt.W. 6005-894 (35047) U.B. Ltd. 500,000 10/14 Forms B. 213.

For information of the A.G.'s Office at the Base.

Officers and men who have become casuals, been transferred or joined since last report.

Place _In the Field_  Date _26.9.15._

| Regtl. Number | Rank | Name | Corps | Nature of casualty, or name of unit from or to which transferred | Date of being struck off or coming on the ration return | Remarks* |
|---|---|---|---|---|---|---|
| | Lieut | W. E. Green | 2/Dorsets | rejoined from Field Amb | 29.9.15 | |

* State whether absence is of a permanent or temporary nature, adding, in the case of casuals from wounds or disease, any available information for communication to the relatives.

15th Bde.
5th Div.

1st DORSETS

OCTOBER

1915

# WAR DIARY
## INTELLIGENCE SUMMARY.
*(Erase heading not required.)*

Army Form C. 2118.

| Place | Date | Hour | Summary of Events and Information | Remarks and references to Appendices |
|---|---|---|---|---|
| CARNOY Trenches 36 & 48 | Oct 2nd | 3.30am | Very heavy burst of rifle fire about 70 yards N.W. of 48 Trench. Otherwise quiet day. Enemy artillery still fairly active. No casualties. | Ref AMIENS Sheet 12 & 57000 |
| | Oct 2nd | 3 pm | The shelters at B.N.H.Q. caught on fire and the HQ offices were no effect to slow the flames. Inspite of columns of dense smoke the Germans were no effect to slow the flames. | |
| | | 9.30pm | Battalion withdrew to BRAY on relief by 2nd KOSB – Casualties on this day nil. | |
| BRAY | | 11.45pm | Battalion in billets in BRAY – During the same tour of duty in trenches the trenches active patrolling was carried out every night and are preparations were made for an advance. | |
| | Oct 3rd | | Battalion remained in billets in BRAY. | |
| | Oct 4th | 1.15pm | According to information received that Army Commander wished the Battalion at ETINEHEM, Battalion marched to ETINEHEM by road running close to the SOMME. Passing the Brigadier General on leaving BRAY. On arrival ETINEHEM was informed by Brigade Major that owing to withdrawal Army Commander would not inspect Battalion. Battalion returned to BRAY. | |
| | Oct 5th | | Battalion remained in billets in BRAY. 3 nos O.R. rolled on a running footage by the explosion of a BEDFORD Rod. | |
| BARNOY Somewhere in | Oct 6th | 6pm | Battalion left BRAY to relieve 1st BEDFORD Reg in Trenches 67 & 69. Summer C1 | |

# WAR DIARY or INTELLIGENCE SUMMARY.

Army Form C. 2118.

(Erase heading not required.)

| Place | Date | Hour | Summary of Events and Information | Remarks and references to Appendices |
|---|---|---|---|---|
| CARNOY | Oct 6th | 10pm | Battalion relieved 1st BEDFORD Regt in Trenches 62 to 69. Bn HQ at MINDEN POST. | Nil By A.M.F.E. NS? Map Sheet 72 F poooo |
| Subsector C1 | Oct 7th | | | Nil |
| | Oct 8th | | | |
| | Oct 9th | | One man slightly wounded whilst on wiring Duty | Nil |
| | Oct 10th | | One man wounded | |
| | Oct 11th | | | Nil |
| | Oct 12th | | | |
| | Oct 13th | | One man killed by German rifle grenade (one man wounded) (rifle wound) | Nil |
| | Oct 14th | 8pm | 3 men wounded. A & B Coy Rapid burst of fire was opened by the Germans, who were starting on our left and spreading across all the whole of our front. | Nil |
| | | 8.11pm | The explosion of 10 mines were heard and three trench mortars were heard to fire in the Centre on our left. | Nil |
| | | 8.30pm | Rapid firing began. Our Situation became normal | |
| | Oct 15th | | One man wounded | Nil |
| | Oct 16th | | | Nil |
| | Oct 17th | 9pm | One man wounded. A & 9 Coy Battalion was relieved by 2nd ROYAL SCOTS FUSILIERS | Nil |

Army Form C. 2118.

# WAR DIARY
or
## INTELLIGENCE SUMMARY.
(Erase heading not required.)

Instructions regarding War Diaries and Intelligence Summaries are contained in F. S. Regs., Part II. and the Staff Manual respectively. Title pages will be prepared in manuscript.

| Place | Date | Hour | Summary of Events and Information | Remarks and references to Appendices |
|---|---|---|---|---|
| CARNOY Subsector C.1. | Oct 17 | | During this tour of duty in the trenches (Oct 16 to 17th inclusive) active patrolling was carried out nightly by ourselves and the Germans. One of our patrols saw a German patrol of about 4 men accompanied by a dog. The Germans were active with their light fees guns and especially with rifle grenades and it was very difficult to obtain adequate retaliation from our own Artillery | Ref AMIENS map sheet 12 F9000 |
| BRAY | Oct 18 | 10.30pm | Battalion in billets in BRAY | Nil |
| | Oct 19 | 5.45pm | Battalion relieved in BRAY | Nil |
| | | | Battalion entrained on subsidiary line to Subrecves (on right and left of when Railway crosses road in Square F 28 b) | |
| | | 7.30pm | Battalion in position – 2 Companies came up by train from BRAY. This was a feat. | Nil Nil Nil |
| | Oct 20 | 7.50pm | Battalion proceeded to billets in BRAY | |
| | | 6pm | Battalion left BRAY for SAILLY LAURETTE | |
| SAILLY LAURETTE | Oct 21st | 8.40pm | Battalion in billets in SAILLY LAURETTE | Nil |
| | Oct 22 | | Battalion remained in billets in SAILLY LAURETTE | Nil |

# WAR DIARY or INTELLIGENCE SUMMARY

Army Form C. 2118.

| Place | Date | Hour | Summary of Events and Information | Remarks and references to Appendices |
|---|---|---|---|---|
| SAILLY LAURETTE | Oct 23rd | | Battalion remained in billets in SAILLY LAURETTE. | |
| | Oct 24th | | | |
| | Oct 25th | 7.30am | Battalion marched via SAILLY & SEC - MERICOURT - RIBEMONT & Square 21 | |
| | | 11am 12.15pm | Battalion was formed up in Mass formation in D21, representing (together with 1st NORFOLK Regt) the 15th Bde. There were also present 2 Battalions of 19th Division and 2 Bn of 18th Division. The parade received His Majesty the KING accompanied by President POINCARÉ with the Royal Salute. The Parade then marched past in close column of platoons. | |
| | Oct 26th Oct 27th Oct 28th | | Battalion remained in billets in SAILLY LAURETTE | |
| | Oct 29th | 4pm 6.20pm | Battalion moved to BRAY with Brigade Reserve. Battalion in billets in BRAY | |
| | Oct 30th Oct 31st | | Battalion remained in billets in BRAY | |

**Army Form B. 213.**

# FIELD RETURN.

No. of Report _____

(To be furnished by all arms, services, and departments to the A.G.'s Office at the Base in accordance with Field Service Regulations, Part II.) Date. 1st October 1915

RETURN showing numbers RATIONED by, and Transport on charge of, 10th Barilshire Regiment at In the Field

| DETAIL. | Personnel | | | Animals | | | | | | | Guns, carriages, and limbers and transport vehicles | | | | | | | | | REMARKS |
|---|---|---|---|---|---|---|---|---|---|---|---|---|---|---|---|---|---|---|---|---|
| | Officers | Other ranks | Natives | Horses Riding | Horses Draught | Horses Heavy Draught | Pack | Mules Large | Mules Small | Camels | Oxen | Guns, carriages and limbers, showing description | Ammunition wagons and limbers | Machine guns | Aircraft, showing description | Horsed 4 Wheeled | Horsed 2 Wheeled | Motor Cars | Tractors | Mechanical Lorries, showing description | Mechanical Trucks, showing description | Trailers | Motor Bicycles | Bicycles | |
| Effective Strength of Unit | 29 | 1023 | | 12 | 35 | 8 | 6 | | 3 | | | | | 4 | | 10 | 9 | | | | | | | 6 | 4 officers 97 O.R. attached from 8th Bn. |
| Details, by Arms attached to unit as in War Establishment:— R.A.M.C. A.O.C. | 1 | 3 1 | | | | | | | | | | | | | | | | | | | | | | | |
| Total | 30 | 1031 | | 12 | 35 | 8 | 6 | | 3 | | | | | 4 | | 10 | 9 | | | | | | | 6 | |
| War Establishment | 30 | 995 | | 12 | 35 | 8 | 9 | | | | | | | 4 | | 10 | 9 | | | | | | | 8 | |
| Wanting to complete | | | | | | 1 | 3 | | | | | | | | | | | | | | | | | | |
| Surplus | | 36 | | | | | | | | | | | | | | | | | | | | | | | |
| *Attached (not to include the details shown above) | 1 | 2 | | | | | | | | | | | | | | | | | | | | | | 1 | 1 officer v.c.R. 1 Major 1 O.R. 7 Kings Royal. |
| Civilians:— Employed with the Unit Accompanying the Unit | | | | | | | | | | | | | | | | | | | | | | | | | |
| TOTAL RATIONED ... | 26956 | | | 12 | 35 | 8 | 6 | | 3 | | | | | 4 | | 10 | 9 | | | | | | | 6 | |

* In the case of field ambulances, hospitals or depots, the number of patients are to be included here, the names being shown in A. F. A. 36.

Wt.W. 6005-894 (35047) U. B. Ltd. 500000. 10/14 Forms B. 213

_____ Signature of Commander.

1st Oct. 1915 Date of Despatch.

*For information of the A.G.'s Office at the Base.*

Officers and men who have become casuals, been transferred or joined since last report.

Place_____     Date_____

| Regtl. Number | Rank | | Name | Corps | Nature of casualty, or name of unit from or to which transferred | Date of being struck off or coming on the ration return | Remarks* |
|---|---|---|---|---|---|---|---|
| | | | | | | | |
| | | | | | | | |
| | | | | | | | |
| | | | | | | | |
| | | | | | | | |
| | | | | | | | |
| | | | | | | | |
| | | | | | | | |
| | | | | | | | |
| | | | | | | | |
| | | | | | | | |
| | | | | | | | |
| | | | | | | | |
| | | | | | | | |
| | | | | | | | |
| | | | | | | | |
| | | | | | | | |
| | | | | | | | |
| | | | | | | | |
| | | | | | | | |
| | | | | | | | |
| | | | | | | | |
| | | | | | | | |
| | | | | | | | |

\* State whether absence is of a permanent or temporary nature, adding, in the case of casuals from wounds or disease, any available information for communication to the relatives.

Army Form B. 213.

# FIELD RETURN.

No. of Report _____

(To be furnished by all arms, services, and departments to the A.G.'s Office at the Base in accordance with Field Service Regulations, Part II.)

Date _____

RETURN showing numbers RATIONED by, and Transport on charge of, *John Dualesbury Regt* at *on the march* 

| DETAIL. | Personnel | | | Animals | | | | | | | | Guns, carriages, and limbers and transport vehicles | | | | | | | | | REMARKS |
|---|---|---|---|---|---|---|---|---|---|---|---|---|---|---|---|---|---|---|---|---|---|
| | Officers | Other ranks | Natives | Horses Riding | Horses Draught | Horses Heavy Draught | Pack | Mules Large | Mules Small | Camels | Oxen | Guns, carriages and limbers, showing description | Ammunition wagons and limbers | Machine guns | Aircraft, showing description | Horsed 4 Wheeled | Horsed 2 Wheeled | Motor Cars | Tractors | Mechanical Lorries, showing description | Mechanical Trucks, showing description | Trailers | Motor Bicycles | Bicycles | |
| Effective Strength of Unit Details, by *Arms* attached to unit as in War Establishment:— | 24 | 1012 | | 12 | 35 | 8 | 6 | | 3 | | | | | 4 | | 10 | 9 | | | | | | | 9 | 9 Officers and 9 O.R. detached from B6 |
| R.A.M.C. | 1 | 5 | | | | | | | | | | | | | | | | | | | | | | | |
| A.O.C. | | 1 | | | | | | | | | | | | | | | | | | | | | | | |
| Total | 25 | 1018 | | 12 | 35 | 8 | 6 | | 3 | | | | | 4 | | 10 | 9 | | | | | | | 9 | |
| War Establishment | 29 | 990 | | 12 | 35 | 8 | 19 | | 3 | | | | | 4 | | 10 | 9 | | | | | | | 9 | |
| Wanting to complete | | 24 | | | | | | | | | | | | | | | | | | | | | | | |
| Surplus | 1 | 2 | | | | | | | | | | | | | | | | | | | | | | | |
| *Attached (not to include the details shown above) | | | | | | | | | | | | | | | | | | | | | | | | | 1 Officer 1st K.Y.L.I. attd. 1st R. Irish Fusiliers |
| Civilians:— Employed with the Unit Accompanying the Unit | | | | | | | | | | | | | | | | | | | | | | | | | |
| TOTAL RATIONED ... | 26 | 996 | | 12 | 35 | 8 | 6 | | 3 | | | | | 4 | | 10 | 9 | | | | | | | 9 | |

* In the case of field ambulances, hospitals or depots, the number of patients are to be included here, the names being shown in A. F. A. 36.

(Sd) _____ Capt/Maj. Signature of Commander.

5. 10. 15. Date of Despatch.

Wt.W. 6005-894 (3547) U. B. Ltd. 500,000 10/14   Forms B. 213

*For information of the A.G.'s Office at the Base.*

Officers and men who have become casuals, been transferred or joined since last report.

Place_____  Date_____

| Regtl. Number | Rank | Name | Corps | Nature of casualty, or name of unit from or to which transferred | Date of being struck off or coming on the ration return | Remarks* |
|---|---|---|---|---|---|---|
| | | | | | | |
| | | | | | | |
| | | | | | | |
| | | | | | | |
| | | | | | | |
| | | | | | | |
| | | | | | | |
| | | | | | | |
| | | | | | | |
| | | | | | | |
| | | | | | | |
| | | | | | | |
| | | | | | | |
| | | | | | | |
| | | | | | | |
| | | | | | | |
| | | | | | | |
| | | | | | | |
| | | | | | | |
| | | | | | | |
| | | | | | | |
| | | | | | | |
| | | | | | | |

* State whether absence is of a permanent or temporary nature, adding, in the case of casuals from wounds or disease, any available information for communication to the relatives.

Army Form B. 213.

# FIELD RETURN.

No. of Report _____

(To be furnished by all arms, services, and departments to the A.G.'s Office at the Base in accordance with Field Service Regulations, Part II.)

Date. 15 - 10 - 15

RETURN showing numbers RATIONED by, and Transport on charge of, *1/5th Essex Regt* at *in the field*

| DETAIL. | Personnel | | | Animals | | | | | | | Guns, carriages, and limbers and transport vehicles | | | | Horsed | | Mechanical | | | | | REMARKS |
|---|---|---|---|---|---|---|---|---|---|---|---|---|---|---|---|---|---|---|---|---|---|---|
| | Officers | Other ranks | Natives | Horses Riding | Horses Draught | Horses Heavy Draught | Pack | Mules Large | Mules Small | Camels | Oxen | Guns, carriages and limbers, showing description | Ammunition wagons and limbers | Machine guns | Aircraft, showing description | 4 Wheeled | 2 Wheeled | Motor Cars | Tractors | Lorries, showing description | Trucks, showing description | Trailers | Motor Bicycles | Bicycles | |
| Effective Strength of Unit | 29 | 1001 | | 11 | 34 | 7 | 6 | | 3 | | | | | 4 | | 10 | 9 | | | | | | | 9 | Officers no R/ detached |
| Details, by *Arms* attached to unit as in War Establishment:— R.A.M.C. | 1 | 5 | | 1 | | | | | | | | | | | | | | | | | | | | | |
| A.O.C | | 1 | | | | | | | | | | | | | | | | | | | | | | | |
| Total | 30 | 1007 | | 12 | 34 | 7 | 6 | | 3 | | | | | 4 | | 10 | 9 | | | | | | | 9 | Officer R/Norfolks |
| War Establishment | 29 | 995 | | 11 | 35 | 8 | 9 | | | | | | | 4 | | 10 | 9 | | | | | | | 9 | Officer 1/7 extra |
| Wanting to complete | | | | | 1 | | | | | | | | | | | | | | | | | | | | 1/5 R/ Inverness |
| Surplus | 2 | 2 | | | | | | | | | | | | | | | | | | | | | | | |
| Civilians:— | | | | | | | | | | | | | | | | | | | | | | | | | |
| * Employed with the Unit | | | | | | | | | | | | | | | | | | | | | | | | | |
| Accompanying the Unit | | | | | | | | | | | | | | | | | | | | | | | | | |
| TOTAL RATIONED ... | 26 | 900 | | 12 | 34 | 5 | 6 | | 3 | | | | | 4 | | 10 | 9 | | | | | | | 9 | |

* In the case of field ambulances, hospitals or depots, the number of patients are to be included here, the names being shown in A.F.A. 36.

Forms B. 213

(Sd) E.H. Jones Bateman *Maj* Signature of Commander.

13 - 10 - 15 Date of Despatch.

For information of the A.G.'s Office at the Base.

Officers and men who have become casuals, been transferred or joined since last report.

Place_____    Date_____

| Regtl. Number | Rank | Name | Corps | Nature of casualty, or name of unit from or to which transferred | Date of being struck off or coming on the ration return | Remarks* |
|---|---|---|---|---|---|---|
| | 2d | G E R Witt | 3/Dorset | w/ Batt | 13.10.15 | |
| | Lieut | R D Taylor | -"- | On Leave | 12.10.15 | Temporary |
| | Lieut | W C Blakeway | -"- | -"- | 12.10.15 | -"- |
| | Lieut | J K Nethercote | -"- | To F. Amb. | 13.10.15 | |
| | Lieut | J B Hunt | 1/Dorset | From F Amb | 11.10.15 | |

\* State whether absence is of a permanent or temporary nature, adding, in the case of casuals from wounds or disease, any available information for communication to the relatives.

Army Form B. 213.

# FIELD RETURN.

No. of Report. _____

(To be furnished by all arms, services, and departments to the A.G.'s Office at the Base in accordance with Field Service Regulations, Part II.)

Date. _____

RETURN showing numbers RATIONED by, and Transport on charge of, *John Donaldson* at *in the field* 22.10.15.

| DETAIL. | Personnel | | | Animals | | | | | | | | Guns, carriages, and limbers and transport vehicles | | | | | | | | | |
|---|---|---|---|---|---|---|---|---|---|---|---|---|---|---|---|---|---|---|---|---|---|
| | Officers | Other ranks | Natives | Horses | | | | Mules | | Camels | Oxen | Guns, carriages and limbers, showing description | Ammunition wagons and limbers | Machine guns | Aircraft, showing description | Horsed | | Motor Cars | Tractors | Mechanical | | | Motor Bicycles | Bicycles | REMARKS |
| | | | | Riding | Draught | Heavy Draught | Pack | Large | Small | | | | | | | 4 Wheeled | 2 Wheeled | | | Lorries, showing description | Trucks, showing description | Trailers | | | |
| Effective Strength of Unit | 29 | 953 | | 11 | 35 | 6 | 6 | | 3 | | | Maxim 2 Vickers 2 | | 4 | | 10 | 9 | | | | | | | 9 | 3 officers 10.R. detached from Bn |
| Details, by Arms attached to unit as in War Establishment:— | | | | | | | | | | | | | | | | | | | | | | | | | |
| R.A.M.C. | 1 | 5 | | 1 | | | | | | | | | | | | | | | | | | | | | |
| A.O.C. | | 1 | | | | | 2 | | | | | | | | | | | | | | | | | | |
| Total | 30 | 959 | | 12 | 35 | 6 | 9 | | 3 | | | | | 4 | | 10 | 9 | | | | | | | 9 | |
| War Establishment | 29 | 956 | | 11 | 35 | 6 | 9 | | | | | | | 4 | | 10 | 9 | | | | | | | 9 | |
| Wanting to complete | | | | | | | 2 | | | | | | | | | | | | | | | | | | |
| Surplus | 2 | 2 | | | | | | | | | | | | | | | | | | | | | | | 1 officer 10.R. y Norfolks 1 officer 6 Devon 1 O.R. y R Warwickshire |
| *Attached (not to include the details shown above) | | | | | | | | | | | | | | | | | | | | | | | | | |
| Civilians :— Employed with the Unit Accompanying the Unit | | | | | | | | | | | | | | | | | | | | | | | | | |
| TOTAL RATIONED ... | 27 | 963 | | 12 | 35 | 6 | 6 | | 3 | | | | | 4 | | 10 | 9 | | | | | | | 9 | |

\* In the case of field ambulances, hospitals or depots, the number of patients are to be included here, the names being shown in A. F. A. 36.

Forms B. 213.

(Sd) *Tot. Jones Bateman Lt Col* Signature of Commander.

22.10.15. Date of Despatch.

*For information of the A.G.'s Office at the Base.*

Officers and men who have become casuals, been transferred or joined since last report.

Place_____     Date_____

| Regtl. Number | Rank | Name | Corps | Nature of casualty, or name of unit from or to which transferred | Date of being struck off or coming on the ration return | Remarks* |
|---|---|---|---|---|---|---|
| | Lt & QM | W Alderman | 1/Dorset | Rejoined Bn | 19.10.15 | |
| | Lt | H.J. Green | 1/Dorset | To 7 Amb. | 14.10.15 | |
| | Lt | C.F.B Sawyer | 1/Dorset | To Leave | 17.10.15 | Temporary |
| | Lt | R. Drayton | 1/Dorset | From Leave | 19.10.15 | |
| | Lt | H.C. Stakeway | 1/Dorset | — | — | |

* State whether absence is of a permanent or temporary nature, adding, in the case of casuals from wounds or disease, any available information for communication to the relatives.

Army Form B. 213.

# FIELD RETURN.

(To be furnished by all arms, services, and departments to the Base Record Office in accordance with Field Service Regulations, Part II.)

No. of Report _____ Date. 29.10.15

RETURN showing numbers RATIONED by, and Transport on charge of, 1th Battalion "A" at 7th the Field

| DETAIL. | Personnel | | | Animals | | | | | | | Transport Vehicles | | Guns, carriages, and limbers, showing description | Ammunition wagons and limbers | Machine guns | REMARKS |
|---|---|---|---|---|---|---|---|---|---|---|---|---|---|---|---|---|
| | Officers | Other ranks | Natives | Horses Riding | Draught | Pack | Mules Large | Small | Camels | Oxen | 4 Wheeled | 2 Wheeled | | | | |
| Effective Strength of Unit | 29 | 995 | | 11 | 43 | 6 | | 3 | | | 10 | 9 | 2 Maxims 2 Vickers | 4 | 4 | Effective 1360 R attached from 2nd |
| Details, by Arms attached to Unit as in War Establishment:— R.A.M.C. A.O.C. | 1 1 | 3 1 | | 1 | | | | | | | | | | | | |
| Total | 30 | 1004 | | 12 | 43 | 6 | | 3 | | | 10 | 9 | | 4 | 4 | |
| War Establishment | 29 | 908 | | 11 | 43 | 9 | | | | | 10 | 9 | | | | |
| Wanting to complete | | | | | | | | | | | | | | | | |
| Surplus | | 10 | | | | | | | | | | | | | | |
| *Attached (not to include the details shown above) | 1 | 2 | | | | | | | | | | | | | | 1 Officer 10R 1/Norfolks 16R 4/K Liverpool Regt |
| Civilians:— Employed with the Unit Accompanying the Unit | | | | | | | | | | | | | | | | |
| TOTAL RATIONED | 24 | 970 | 1 | 12 | 43 | 6 | | 3 | | | 10 | 9 | | 4 | 4 | |

Forms B. 213

(Sd) R.H. Jones Lieutenant Colonel. Signature of Commander.
R.G. 10.15. Date of Despatch.

* In the case of field ambulances, hospitals or depôts, the number of patients are to be included here, the names being shown in A.F.A. 36.

*For information of the Officer i/c of a Base Record Office.*

Officers and men who have left or joined since last report.

Place **In the Field**    Date **29.10.15**

| Regtl. Number | Rank | Name | Corps | Name of unit from or to which transferred | Date of being struck off or coming on the ration return | Remarks * |
|---|---|---|---|---|---|---|
| | Capt | J.V. Shute | 1/Dorsets | On Leave | 27.10.15 | Temporary |
| | Lt | H.G.M. Mansel Pleydell | —"— | —"— | 27.10.15 | —"— |
| | Lt | H.C. Butcher | 3/Dorsets | —"— | 22.10.15 | —"— |
| | Lt | H.K. Latham | 3/Dorsets | —"— | 22.10.15 | —"— |
| | | 21 O.R. Joined Bn | | | 27.10.15 | |

* State whether absence is of a permanent or temporary nature.

15th Bde.
5th Div.

1st DORSETS

NOVEMBER

1 9 1 5

Army Form C. 2118.

# WAR DIARY
## or
## INTELLIGENCE SUMMARY.
(Erase heading not required.)

Instructions regarding War Diaries and Intelligence Summaries are contained in F.S. Regs., Part II. and the Staff Manual respectively. Title pages will be prepared in manuscript.

| Place | Date 1915. | Hour | Summary of Events and Information | Remarks and references to Appendices |
|---|---|---|---|---|
| BRAY | Nov. 1st | | Battalion in billets in BRAY in Bde. Reserve. | Trench Map. Sheet 62 N.E. 1/10,000 F.11.2 and D. Bn. H.R. F.17.3.4.6. |
| " | " 2nd | | Do Do | |
| " | " 3rd | | Do Do | |
| Sub-sector | " 4th | | Battalion left BRAY 4.55 pm and relieved 1/Bedfords in Trenches (Subsector E.1.) Bn. H.Q. MINDEN POST. | |
| " | " 5 | | Situation quiet. Trenches in wet and muddy condition. 13th Bde. on our right, 1/Wiltshires on our left. | |
| | | | do Bombs thrown by NEST bomb-thrower at enemy working-party in trench opposite | |
| " | " 6 | | our 62 trench | |
| " | " 7 | | Our artillery successfully ranged on point opposite 63 trench where enemy trench-mortar was located. | |
| " | " 8 | 5.30 pm | Enemy fired trench mortar and within 15 seconds our artillery fired at point previously located. | |
| " | " 9 | 7.40 pm | Machine was relieved & have moved. | |
| | | 10 pm | 1st Bedfords relieved Battalion. No casualties during this tour in trenches. | |
| BRAY | " 10 | | Battalion in billets in BRAY. | |
| " | " 11 | | Do | |
| " | " 12 | | Do | |

# WAR DIARY or INTELLIGENCE SUMMARY.

Army Form C. 2118.

| Place | Date 1915 | Hour | Summary of Events and Information | Remarks and references to Appendices |
|---|---|---|---|---|
| BRAY | Nov 13 | | Battalion in billets in BRAY. | |
| " | " 14 | | Do | |
| " | " 15 | 4.50 pm | Battalion left BRAY to relieve 1/Bedfords in subsector. C.1. | |
| Sub-sector C.1 | | 1.20 pm | Battalion in trenches. 13th Bde. on our right; 1st Cheshires on our left. | |
| " | " 16 | | After a sharp frost on 15th inst. a thaw set in and trenches became very muddy & collapsed in several places | |
| " | " 17 | | | |
| " | " 18 | | | |
| " | " 19 | | One man killed, one wounded. | |
| " | " 20 | | | |
| " | " 21 | 6.50 pm | 1/Bedfords relieved Battalion. | |
| BRAY | " 22 | 9.10 pm | Battalion in billets in BRAY. | |
| " | " 23 | | Do | |
| " | " 24 | | Do | |
| " | " 25 | | Do | |

Army Form C. 2118.

# WAR DIARY
## or
## INTELLIGENCE SUMMARY.

(Erase heading not required.)

Instructions regarding War Diaries and Intelligence Summaries are contained in F. S. Regs., Part II. and the Staff Manual respectively. Title pages will be prepared in manuscript.

| Place | Date 1915 | Hour | Summary of Events and Information | Remarks and references to Appendices |
|---|---|---|---|---|
| BRAY Sub-Sector C.1 | Nov 26 | | Battalion in BRAY. | |
| " | " 27 | 4.50pm | Battalion left BRAY and relieved 1/Bedfords in Trenches (Subsector C1). Situation quiet | |
| " | " 28 | | C.S.M. SHEPTON died of wounds. Hit in head by sniper. | |
| " | " 29 | | | |
| " | " 30 | | One man wounded | |

# FIELD RETURN.

**Army Form B. 213.**

No. of Report _____

(To be furnished by all arms, services, and departments to the Base Record Office in accordance with Field Service Regulations, Part II.)

Date. 5.11.1915

RETURN showing numbers RATIONED by, and Transport on charge of, _1st Yorkshire Regiment in the Field_

| DETAIL. | Personnel | | | Animals | | | | | | Transport Vehicles | | Guns, carriages, and limbers, showing description | Ammunition wagons and limbers | Machine guns | REMARKS |
|---|---|---|---|---|---|---|---|---|---|---|---|---|---|---|---|
| | Officers | Other ranks | Natives | Horses Riding | Horses Draught | Horses Pack | Mules Large | Mules Small | Camels | Oxen | 4 Wheeled | 2 Wheeled | | | | |
| Effective Strength of Unit | 28 | 956 | | 11 | 43 | 6 | | 3 | | | 10 | 9 | 2 Maxims 2 Vickers | | 4 | 6 Officers 996.R. attached for Battalion |
| Details, by Arms attached to Unit as in War Establishment:— | | | | | | | | | | | | | | | | |
| R.A.M.C. | 1 | 5 | | 1 | | | | | | | | | | | | |
| A.O.C. Corps | | 1 | | | | | | | | | | | | | | |
| Total | 29 | 994 | | 12 | 43 | 6 | | 3 | | | 10 | 9 | | | 4 | |
| War Establishment | 29 | 996 | | 11 | 43 | 9 | | 3 | | | 10 | 9 | | | 4 | |
| Wanting to complete | | | | | | | | | | | | | | | | |
| Surplus | | | | | | | | | | | | | | | | |
| *Attached (not to include the details shown above) | 6 | 2* | | | | | | | | | | | | | | *Officers & O.R. thought of theirs not attached for duty & names 16.R. 1st King's Liverpool |
| Civilians:— Employed with the Unit | | | | | | | | | | | | | | | | |
| Accompanying the Unit | | | | | | | | | | | | | | | | |
| TOTAL RATIONED | 35 | 896 | | 12 | 43 | 6 | | 3 | | | 10 | 9 | | | 4 | |

\* In the case of field ambulances, hospitals or depôts, the number of patients are to be included here, the names being shown in A.F.A. 36.

(Sd) W. Ackerman Lt Col. Bt Lt Col Signature of Commander. 5.11.1915 Date of Despatch.

*For information of the Officer i/c of a Base Record Office.*

Officers and men who have left or joined since last report.

Place _____  Date _____

| Regtl. Number | Rank | Name | Corps | Name of unit from or to which transferred | Date of being struck off or coming on the ration return | Remarks* |
|---|---|---|---|---|---|---|
| | Captain | J C Shute | 1/Dorsets | From Leave | 4.11.15 | |
| | Lt | H G M Mansel Pleydell | " | " | 4.11.15 | |
| | Lt | R B Webster | " | To Leave | 1.11.15 | Temporary |
| | Lt | A J Smith | 1/Dorsets | " | 1.11.15 | Temporary |
| | Lt | A Preedy | 1/Devon | To 1/Devons | 1.11.15 | |
| | Lt | R J English | R.A.M.C. | To Leave | 2.11.15 | Temporary |
| | Capt | E McCormick | R.A.M.C. | Joined B | 2.11.15 | Temporary |

* State whether absence is of a permanent or temporary nature.

**Army Form B. 213.**

# FIELD RETURN.

No. of Report _____  Typed _____  Nature _____

(To be furnished by all arms, services, and departments to the Base Record Office in accordance with Field Service Regulations, Part II.)

Date. 12.11.12.

RETURN showing numbers RATIONED by, and Transport on charge of, 1 Bn Devonshire Regt. at In the Field

| DETAIL. Name | Personnel | | | Animals | | | | | | Transport Vehicles | | Guns, carriages, and limbers, showing description | Ammunition wagons and limbers | Machine guns | REMARKS |
|---|---|---|---|---|---|---|---|---|---|---|---|---|---|---|---|
| | Officers | Other ranks | Natives | Horses Riding | Horses Draught | Horses Pack | Mules Large | Mules Small | Camels | Oxen | 4 Wheeled | 2 Wheeled | | | | |
| Effective Strength of Unit | 24 | 950 | | 11 | 43 | 6 | | 3 | | | 10 | 9 | 2 Maxims 2 Vickers | | 4 | * 5 officers 114 O.R. attached |
| Details by Arms attached to Unit as in War Establishment:— | | | | | | | | | | | | | | | | |
| R.A.M.C. | 1 | 5 | | 1 | | | | | | | | | | | | |
| A.O.C. | | 1 | | | | | | | | | | | | | | |
| Corps | | | | | | | | | | | | | | | | |
| Total | 25 | 956 | | 12 | 43 | 6 | | 3 | | | 10 | 9 | | | 4 | |
| War Establishment | 29 | 958 | | 11 | 43 | 6 | | 3 | | | 10 | 9 | | | 4 | |
| Wanting to complete | | 8 | | | | | | | | | | | | | | |
| Surplus | | | | | | | | | | | | | | | | |
| *Attached (not to include the details shown above) | *2 | *2 | | | | | | | | | | | | | | * 1 officer 1 O.R. 1 Norfolks 1 officer R.A. home/Army/ 1 O.R. 4 Kings Own R.Regt |
| Civilians:— Employed with the Unit Accompanying the Unit | | | | | | | | | | | | | | | | |
| TOTAL RATIONED | 22 | 841 | | 12 | 43 | 6 | | 3 | | | 10 | 9 | | | 4 | |

Remarks. _____

*In the case of field ambulances, hospitals or depôts, the number of patients are to be included here, the names being shown in A.F.A. 36.

Forms B. 213

(Sd.) L.R. Jones-Bateman Lt.Col. Signature of Commander.
12.11.12. Date of Despatch.

*For information of the Officer i/c of a Base Record Office.*

Officers and men who have left or joined since last report.

Place  In the Field                    Date  12-11-15

| Regtl. Number | Rank | Name | Corps | Name of unit from or to which transferred | Date of being struck off or coming on the ration return | Remarks * |
|---|---|---|---|---|---|---|
| | Capt | R.C. Partridge | 1/Dorsets | To H.Q. 5th Div. | 9.11.15 | |
| | Capt | V.S. Morley | —"— | To 3rd Army School | 10.11.15 | |
| | Lt | G.C.R. Webb | 3/Dorsets | To Leave | 6.11.15 | Temporary |
| | Lt | J.H. Butler | 3/Dorsets | —"— | 6.11.15 | —"— |
| | Lt | W.J. Smith | 1/Dorsets | From Leave | 9.11.15 | |

* State whether absence is of a permanent or temporary nature.

# FIELD RETURN.

**Army Form B. 213.**

No. of Report _____

Number _____ Rank _____

(To be furnished by all arms, services, and departments to the Base Record Office in accordance with Field Service Regulations, Part II.)

RETURN showing numbers RATIONED by, and Transport on charge of, *Mr Expeditionary* at *Onitsha* Date. *19.11.12*

| DETAIL. | Personnel | | | Horses | | | Animals | | | | Transport Vehicles | | Guns, carriages, and limbers, showing description | Ammunition wagons and limbers | Machine guns | REMARKS |
|---|---|---|---|---|---|---|---|---|---|---|---|---|---|---|---|---|
| | Officers | Other ranks | Natives | Riding | Draught | Pack | Mules Large | Mules Small | Camels | Oxen | 4 Wheeled | 2 Wheeled | | | | |
| Effective Strength of Unit | 24 | 94 | | 11 | 43 | 6 | | 3 | | | 10 | 9 | 2 | 2 Maxims 2 Vickers | | 5 Officers 143 Other ranks detached for duty at |
| Details, by Arms attached to Units in War Establishment:— | | | | | | | | | | | | | | | | |
| R.A.M.C. | 1 | 3 | | | | | | | | | | | | | | |
| A.O.D. | 1 | 1 | | 1 | | | | | | | | | | | | |
| D'do | | | | | | | | | | | | | | | | |
| Total | 25 | 98 | | 12 | 43 | 6 | | 3 | | | 10 | 9 | 2 | | | |
| War Establishment | 29 | 95 | | 11 | 43 | 9 | | | | | 10 | 9 | | | | |
| Wanting to complete | 5 | 17 | | | | | | | | | | | | | | |
| Surplus | | | | 1 | | | | | | | | | | | | |
| *Attached (not to include the details shown above) | 2 | 0 | | | | | | | | | | | | | | |
| Civilians:— | | | | | | | | | | | | | | | | |
| Employed with the Unit | | | | | | | | | | | | | | | | |
| Accompanying the Unit | | | | | | | | | | | | | | | | |
| D'do | | | | | | | | | | | | | | | | |
| **TOTAL RATIONED** | 19 | 140 | | 12 | 43 | 6 | | 3 | | | 10 | 9 | | | | |

* In the case of field ambulances, hospitals or depôts, the number of patients are to be included here, the names being shown in A.F.A. 36.

Forms B. 213

Signature of Commander. _____

Date of Despatch. *19.11.12*

*For information of the Officer i/c of a Base Record Office.*

## Officers and men who have left or joined since last report.

Place: In the Field     Date: 19.11.15

| Regtl. Number | Rank | Name | Corps | Name of unit from or to which transferred | Date of being struck off or coming on the ration return | Remarks* |
|---|---|---|---|---|---|---|
| | Lt Col | L.J. Jones-Bateman C.M.G. | 5/Dorsets | To leave | 15.11.15 | Temporary |
| | Capt | R.L. Crankshaw | 5/Dorsets | " | 14.11.15 | " |
| | Capt | C. Rogers | 5/Dorsets | " | 19.11.15 | " |
| | Lt | R.H. Kesteven | 5/Dorsets | " | 14.11.15 | " |
| | Lt | R.H. Webb | 5/Dorsets | from leave | 16.11.15 | |
| | Lt | W.F. Smith | 5/Dorsets | To F. Amb. | 16.11.15 | |
| | 2/Lt | J.H. Butler | 5/Dorsets | from leave | 16.11.15 | |
| | 2/Lt | S.A. Gorey | 5/Dorsets | To 3rd Army School | 14.11.15 | " |

*State whether absence is of a permanent or temporary nature.

Army Form B. 213.

# FIELD RETURN.

(To be furnished by all arms, services, and departments to the Base Record Office in accordance with Field Service Regulations, Part II.)

No. of Report _____  Date _____

RETURN showing numbers RATIONED by, and Transport on charge of, 1/4th Devonshire Regt. at in the field. Date 26.11.15

| DETAIL. | Personnel | | | Animals | | | | | | Transport Vehicles | | Guns, carriages, and limbers, showing description | Ammunition wagons and limbers | Machine guns | REMARKS |
|---|---|---|---|---|---|---|---|---|---|---|---|---|---|---|---|
| | Officers | Other ranks | Natives | Horses Riding | Horses Draught | Horses Pack | Mules Large | Mules Small | Camels | Oxen | 4 Wheeled | 2 Wheeled | | | | |
| Effective Strength of Unit | 26 | 963 | | 11 | 43 | 6 | | 3 | | | 10 | 9 | | 2 Maxims } 2 Vickers } | 4 | 10 Officers & 2 other ranks detached from Bn. |
| Details, by Arms attached to Unit as in War Establishment:— | | | | | | | | | | | | | | | | |
| R.A.M.C. | 1 | 5 | | 1 | | | | | | | | | | | | |
| A.V.C. | | 1 | | | | | | | | | | | | | | |
| Total | 27 | 969 | | 12 | 43 | 6 | | 3 | | | 10 | 9 | | | 4 | |
| War Establishment | 29 | 965 | | 12 | 43 | 9 | | | | | 10 | 9 | | | | |
| Wanting to complete | 3 | 25 | | | | 3 | | | | | | | | | | |
| Surplus | | | | | | | | | | | | | | | | |
| *Attached (not to include the details shown above) | 2 | 2 | | | | | | | | | | | | | | |
| Civilians:— Employed with the Unit | | | | | | | | | | | | | | | | |
| Accompanying the Unit | | | | | | | | | | | | | | | | |
| TOTAL RATIONED | 29 | 974 | | 12 | 43 | 6 | | 3 | | | 10 | 9 | | | 4 | |

* Attached personnel and animals, to state the Officer in charge of whom they are to be shown and to state for what purpose attached.

* In the case of field ambulances, hospitals or depôts, the number of patients are to be included here, the names being shown in A. F. A. 36.

_____ Captain Signature of Commander.

26.11.15 Date of Despatch.

Forms B. 213

*For information of the Officer i/c of a Base Record Office.*

Officers and men who have left or joined since last report.

Place _In the field_  Date _26.11.15_

| Regtl. Number | Rank | Name | Corps | Name of unit from or to which transferred | Date of being struck off or coming on the ration return | Remarks * |
|---|---|---|---|---|---|---|
| | Capt | H.B. Algeo | Dorset | To Leave | 24.11.15 | Temporary |
| | Lt | W.E. Green | " | " | 24.11.15 | " |
| | Lt | R.G. Kestell Cornish | Dorset | From Leave | 22.11.15 | |
| | Lt | W.A. Smellie | " | Rejoined | 24.11.15 | |
| | Lt | Lindsay | K.R.Lanc R. | Rejoined on unit | 23.11.15 | |

* State whether absence is of a permanent or temporary nature.

15th Bde.
5th Div.

Left to join 95th Bde, 32nd Div. 31.12.15.

1st DORSETS

DECEMBER

1 9 1 5

Army Form C. 2118.

# WAR DIARY
## or
## INTELLIGENCE SUMMARY.
(Erase heading not required.)

Instructions regarding War Diaries and Intelligence Summaries are contained in F. S. Regs., Part II. and the Staff Manual respectively. Title pages will be prepared in manuscript.

| Place | Date | Hour | Summary of Events and Information | Remarks and references to Appendices |
|---|---|---|---|---|
| | Dec 1 | 3 pm | A mine was blown by 183rd Tunneling Co. R.E. opposite trenches on our left. | |
| " | " 2 | 7 pm | Six inch guns fired between our 65 trench and German lines in order to make craters required for proposed bombing attack. | |
| " | " 3 | | One man killed by collapsing trench. Trenches in very bad state. | |
| | | 8.15 pm | 1/Bedfords relieved Battalion in trenches A. B. & D. Companies withdrew to billets in BRAY, "C" Coy to billets in ÉTENEHEM (ETINEHEM) | |
| BRAY | " 4 | | Battalion in billets in BRAY and ETINEHEM. | |
| " | " 5 | | | |
| " | " 6 | 11 am | Lieut YOUNG went up to trenches to examine gaps in German wire (opposite 67 trench) through which bombing parties are to attack tonight. Gaps reported repaired; artillery failed to open them again. | |

… C. 2118.

# WAR DIARY
## or
## INTELLIGENCE SUMMARY.
*(Erase heading not required.)*

Instructions regarding War Diaries and Intelligence Summaries are contained in F.S. Regs., Part II. and the Staff Manual respectively. Title pages will be prepared in manuscript.

| Hour, Date, Place | Summary of Events and Information | Remarks and references to Appendices |
|---|---|---|
| 7 Dec. 1916. BRAY | Party of 110 O.R. under 2/Lieut. Fuller, 2/Lieut. Young, & 2/Lieut. Manuel. Played up BRAY for 9.1. subsector. Object: enter German trench through 2 gaps in enemy wire made by artillery and capture or kill any German in trench or dugouts. Returns by signal as soon as object accomplished. Regiments on right & left carried out similar enterprise at same hour (2 a.m.). Platoons arriving at German wire party found it repaired + wire powerfully, unable to enter trench; all the grenades (about 300) were thrown + party withdrew. Our artillery cooperated & enemy artillery retaliated. 2/Lieut. Fuller and 6 other ranks slightly wounded. As no rifle fire came from enemy trench attacked it is presumed German was put out of action. | Ref. Amiens map. Sheet 17. 1/80,000. & Trench map 6? N.E. & 1/10000 F.11. C & d. |
| 8 Dec. | BRAY & ÉTINEHEM  Battn. in billets. | |
| 9 Dec. 6.30 p.m. (approx) Gr. InTheGz | Battn. relieved 1st Bedford Regt. in G.1. subsector. Trenches very muddy. | Bn. HQ. F.17.d.9/6. |
| 10 Dec. do. | One man killed by collapse of a dugout. Two men wounded. Situation normal. Continued to neutralise sniping on front of the enemy. | |
| 11 Dec. do. | Situation quiet. No man wounded (G.I.W.) | |

Army Form C. 2118.

# WAR DIARY
## or
## INTELLIGENCE SUMMARY.
(Erase heading not required.)

Instructions regarding War Diaries and Intelligence Summaries are contained in F.S. Regs., Part II. and the Staff Manual respectively. Title pages will be prepared in manuscript.

| Hour, Date, Place | Summary of Events and Information | Remarks and references to Appendices |
|---|---|---|
| 1915. | | Refer: Amiens Map. Sheet 5Y. |
| 12th Dec. G.1 Subsector. | Situation quiet. | 1/20,000 & Trench map. 62. |
| 13th Dec. do | do  Enemy aeroplane dropped bombs near 69 trench | N.E.2. 1/10000 F.11.c.9.d. |
| " | without doing any damage. | B.M.A. F.17.d.4/6. |
| " 7.45 p.m. | Battalion relieved by 1st Bedford Rgt. | WSt |
| " 9.35 p.m. | B.C. & D. Coys in billets in BRAY. | WSt |
| " 10.40 p.m. | A. Coy in billets in ETINEHEM. | WSt |
| 14th Dec. BRAY & ETINEHEM | Battalion in billets. | WSt |
| 15. Dec. " | " | WSt |
| 16. Dec. " | " | |
| 17. Dec. " | " | |
| 6 p.m. 18th Dec. G.1 Subsector. | Battalion relieved 1st Bedford Rgt. in Trenches. The Coy 16th Rgl. Warwicks attached for instruction | WSt |
| 19th Dec. | Reinforcement draft of 150 o.R. arrived. | |
| " | Situation quiet. Enemy fired a few heavy shells at 68 trench | |
| " | without doing any damage.  Capt Rogers, O.C. A Coy's wounded | |
| " | by bullet in shoulder. | WSt |
| 20th Dec. " | Nothing to report | WSt |
| 21st Dec. " | One man 16th Royal Warwicks killed | WSt |
| 22nd Dec. " | In the early part of the evening enemy artillery & trench mortars | |
| " | were very active. Our artillery replied with excellent shooting & | |
| " | eventually silenced all opposition. | WSt |
| " 9.20 p.m. BRAY & ETINEHEM | Battalion relieved by 1st Bedford Rgt. A.B. & C Coys in billets in | |
| | BRAY, D Coy in billets in ETINEHEM. | |

# WAR DIARY or INTELLIGENCE SUMMARY.

Army Form C. 2118.

| Hour, Date, Place | Summary of Events and Information | Remarks and references to Appendices |
|---|---|---|
| 1915 | | Ref. Amiens map Sheet 1x. 1/40000 |
| 23rd Dec. | Battalion in Billets in Bray & Etinehem. | & trench map 62.N.E.2 1/20000 |
| 24th Dec. | " | |
| 25th Dec. | " | |
| 26th Dec. 8 p.m. C.I.S. Sector | Battalion relieved 1st Bedfords in trenches. (With the exception of a few small mining features, observed as at Noticing) | 1st Bn. relieves on our left and 1st Royal Warwicks on our rt. H.S.T. |
| 27th Dec. " | Battalion in trenches. Situation quiet; Trenches very wet and muddy. | H.S.T. |
| 28th Dec. " | do. do. | H.S.T. |
| 29th Dec. " | Between 11am & noon enemy artillery rather active. Considerable artillery fire on both sides. One man wounded. Our 9.2 guns shelled MAMETZ. 1st Norfolks relieved Battalion in Trenches. A.C. & D. Coys. with H.Q. to billets in BRAY, B. Coy to billets in ETINEHEM. | H.S.T. |
| 8.20 p.m. | | |
| 30th Dec. " | Battalion in billets in BRAY and ETINEHEM. | H.S.T. |
| 31st Dec. | Battalion marched to billets in SAILLY LORETTE and became part of 95th Infantry Bde., 32nd Division. | H.S.T. |

Army Form B 231.

# FIELD STATE.

To be rendered in accordance with Field Service Regulations, Part II.

Unit  1/4th Devonshire Regt
Place  in the field
Date  10.12.15

## FIGHTING STRENGTH

This should *not* include details attached to unit, or personnel detailed to march with the Train, or any men unfit to go into action with unit

## RATION STRENGTH

To include Fighting Strength, Personnel detailed to march with the Train, and all Personnel and animals attached for Rations and Forage

| UNIT | Personnel | | Horses and Mules | | Other Animals | Guns and Ammunition Wagons (stating nature) | Machine Guns | Ambulances | Tool Carts, Technical Carts (stating nature) | Remarks | Personnel Total, all Ranks entitled to Rations. | Horses and Mules | | Other Animals | Mechanically Propelled Vehicles | | | | | Remarks |
|---|---|---|---|---|---|---|---|---|---|---|---|---|---|---|---|---|---|---|---|---|
| | Officers | Other Ranks | Riding | Draught and Pack | | | | | | | | Heavy Horses | Other Horses and Mules | | Motor Cars | Motor Bicycles | Lorries 3 Ton | Lorries 30 Cwt. | Tractors | |
| (1) | (2) | (3) | (4) | (5) | (6) | (7) | (8) | (9) | (10) | (11) | (12) | (13) | (14) | (15) | (16) | (17) | (18) | (19) | (20) | (21) | (22) | (23) |
| 1/4 Battalion Th Devonshire Regiment | 30 | 942 | 11 | 52 | | | | 4 | | 19 | | 709 | | 64 | | | | | | | | Details of Horses 142 Trucks attached from Tn. |
| TOTALS ... | 30 | 942 | 11 | 52 | | | | 4 | | 19 | | 709 | | 64 | | | | | | | | |

Ammunition with Unit :—
 .303 inch ; approximate number of rounds per Man _____
 .303 inch ;  ,,   ,,   ,,   ,,  per Machine Gun _____
 Gun or Howitzer ; approximate number of rounds per Gun or Howitzer _____

Supplies with Unit :—
Approximate number of days' rations for men of ration strength _____
  ,,   ,,   ,,   ,,  forage for Animals _____
  ,,   ,,   ,,   ,,  fuel and lubricants for Mechanically Propelled Vehicles _____

Signature of Commander Lt Col H Newman
Comdg 1/4th Devonshire Regt

2Lt C.A. Steele / Dorset / Joined Batt. 4. 12. 15.
" A.E. Mainwood " " " " 4. 12. 15.
" M.A. Fraser 3/ " " " 9. 12. 15.
" R Brodie " " " " 9. 12. 15.
" W.D.P. Cousins " " " " 9. 12. 15.
" W.H. Clarke " " " " 9. 12. 15.
" C.P.B. Sawyer 1/ " To M.G. Course 6. 12. 15.
" H.D. Thwaytes " " To Leave 4. 12. 15.
" J.R. Hunt " " " " 10. 12. 15.
Lt W.J. Smith " " To England 29. 11. 15.

Army Form B 231.

# FIELD STATE.

Unit _1st Th. Royalshire Regt_
Place _H.Th. field_
Date _31.12.15_

To be rendered in accordance with Field Service Regulations, Part II.

## FIGHTING STRENGTH

This should not include details attached to unit, or personnel detailed to march with the Train, or any men unfit to go into action with unit

## RATION STRENGTH

To include Fighting Strength, Personnel detailed to march with the Train, and all Personnel and animals attached for Rations and Forage

| UNIT | Personnel | | Horses and Mules | | Other Animals | Guns and Ammunition Wagons (stating nature) | Machine Guns | Ambulances | Tool Carts, Technical Carts (stating nature) | Remarks | Personnel | Horses and Mules | | Other Animals | Mechanically Propelled Vehicles | | | | | Remarks |
|---|---|---|---|---|---|---|---|---|---|---|---|---|---|---|---|---|---|---|---|---|
| | Officers | Other Ranks | Riding | Draught and Pack | | | | | | | Total, all Ranks entitled to Rations. | Heavy Horses | Other Horses and Mules | | Motor Cars | Motor Bicycles. | Lorries 3 Ton | Lorries 30 Cwt. | Tractors | |
| (1) | (2) | (3) | (4) | (5) | (6) | (7) | (8) | (9) | (10) | (11) | (12) | (13) | (14) | (15) | (16) | (17) | (18) | (19) | (20) | (21) | (22) | (23) |
| 1st Battalion 1st Royalshire Regiment | 24 | 916 | 11 | 43 | | | | 4 | | 14 | | 649 | | 33 | | | | | | | | 10 officers 61 O.ranks detachment from Scotia |
| TOTALS ... | 21 | 916 | 11 | 43 | | | | 4 | | 14 | | 649 | | 33 | | | | | | | | |

Ammunition with Unit:—
.303 inch; approximate number of rounds per Man _____
.303 inch; " " " per Machine Gun _____
Gun or Howitzer; approximate number of rounds per Gun or Howitzer _____

Supplies with Unit:—
Approximate number of days' rations for men of ration strength _____
" " " forage for Animals _____
" " " fuel and lubricants for Mechanically Propelled Vehicles _____

Signature of Commander _[signature]_
Comdg 1st Th. Royalshire Regiment

| | | | |
|---|---|---|---|
| Lt Col L.H. Jones Bateman C.M.G. | Came to be attd 10 Wils | 31.12.15 |
| Lieut. C.P.B. Sawyer | to 15th Bde M.G. Coy. | 23.12.15 |
| 3/ " S.A. Smellie s/Dorsets | to leave | 25.12.15 |
| " L.A. Somes | " " | 31.12.15 |

**Army Form B 231.**

# FIELD STATE.

To be rendered in accordance with Field Service Regulations, Part II.

Unit _1/4th Dorsetshire Regt_
Place _In the Field_
Date _24.12.15_

| UNIT | FIGHTING STRENGTH | | | | | | | | | | | RATION STRENGTH | | | | | | | | | | |
|---|---|---|---|---|---|---|---|---|---|---|---|---|---|---|---|---|---|---|---|---|---|---|
| | Personnel | | Horses and Mules | | Other Animals | | Guns and Ammunition Wagons (stating nature) | Machine Guns | Ambulances | Tool Carts, Technical Carts (stating nature) | Remarks | Personnel | Horses and Mules | | Other Animals | Mechanically Propelled Vehicles | | | | | Remarks |
| | Officers | Other Ranks | Riding | Draught and Pack | | | | | | | | Total, all Ranks entitled to Rations. | Heavy Horses | Other Horses and Mules | | Motor Cars | Motor Bicycles | Lorries 3 Ton | Lorries 30 Cwt. | Tractors | |
| (1) | (2) | (3) | (4) | (5) | (6) | (7) | (8) | (9) | (10) | (11) | (12) | (13) | (14) | (15) | (16) | (17) | (18) | (19) | (20) | (21) | (22) | (23) |
| Battalion 1/4th Dorsetshire Regiment | 28 | 932 | 11 | 44 | | | | 4 | | 14 | | 849 | | 56 | | | | | | | | 19 officers 868 attached |
| TOTALS | 28 | 932 | 11 | 44 | | | | 4 | | 14 | | 849 | | 56 | | | | | | | | |

Ammunition with Unit:—
.303 inch; approximate number of rounds per Man _____
.303 inch; " " " per Machine Gun _____
Gun or Howitzer; approximate number of rounds per Gun or Howitzer _____

Supplies with Unit:—
Approximate number of days' rations for men of ration strength _____
" " " forage for Animals _____
" " " fuel and lubricants for Mechanically Propelled Vehicles _____

Signature of Commander _P.K.O._ _Lt. Col. & Captain Comdg. 1/4th Dorsetshire_

| | | |
|---|---|---|
| Capt. C. Rogers /Dorsets | Wounded | 19.12.15. |
| Lt Col J.R. Jones-Bateman C.M.G. | To 15th Bde. H.Q. | 20.12.15. |
| Lt R.J. English R.A.M.C. | To 15th F. Amb. | 17.12.15. |
| Lt A.J. Turner " | Joined Bn. | 17.12.15. |
| 2t W.H. Clarke /Dorsets. | To Grenade Sch. | 19.12.15. |
| " C.A. Steele " | From " | 19.12.15 |
| " J.M. Hunt " | From Leave | 19.12.15. |

Army Form B 231.

# FIELD STATE.

Unit  1st Bn. the Dorsetshire Regt.
Place  En Tr. Billet
Date  19.12.15

To be rendered in accordance with Field Service Regulations, Part II.

## FIGHTING STRENGTH

This should not include details attached to unit, or personnel detailed to march with the Train, or any men unfit to go into action with unit

| UNIT | Personnel | | Horses and Mules | | Other Animals | Guns and Ammunition Wagons (stating nature) | Machine Guns | Ambulances | Tool Carts, Technical Carts (stating nature) | Remarks |
|---|---|---|---|---|---|---|---|---|---|---|
| | Officers | Other Ranks | Riding | Draught and Pack | | | | | | |
| (1) | (2) | (3) | (4) | (5) | (6) | (7) | (8) | (9) | (10) | (11) | (12) |
| 1st Battalion the Dorsetshire Regiment | 30 | 933 | 11 | 52 | | | | 4 | | | |
| TOTALS ... | 30 | 933 | 11 | 52 | | | | 4 | | | |

## RATION STRENGTH

To include Fighting Strength, Personnel detailed to march with the Train, and all Personnel and animals attached for Rations and Forage

| Personnel | Horses and Mules | | Other Animals | Mechanically Propelled Vehicles | | | | | Remarks |
|---|---|---|---|---|---|---|---|---|---|
| Total, all Ranks entitled to Rations. | Heavy Horses | Other Horses and Mules | | Motor Cars | Motor Bicycles. | Lorries. 3 Ton | Lorries. 30 Cwt. | Tractors | |
| (13) | (14) | (15) | (16) | (17) | (18) | (19) | (20) | (21) | (22) | (23) |
| 805 | | 64 | | | | | | | | 30 officers 165 horses attached 1st Bn |
| 805 | | 64 | | | | | | | | |

Ammunition with Unit:—
.303 inch; approximate number of rounds per Man _____
.303 inch;      "       "       "       per Machine Gun _____
Gun or Howitzer; approximate number of rounds per Gun or Howitzer _____

Supplies with Unit:—
Approximate number of days' rations for men of ration strength _____
         "       "       "       forage for Animals       " _____
         "       "       "       fuel and lubricants for Mechanically Propelled Vehicles _____

Signature of Commander  Lt Col K. Cowie
1st Bn. the Dorsetshire Regiment

| | | | | |
|---|---|---|---|---|
| Capt | H.M. Carpentale | 36th Jacobs Horse | ceased to be att'd Bn | 14.12.15 |
| Capt | H.D. Thwaytes | /Dorsets | To 15th Bde H.Q. | 14.12.15 |
| 2/Lt | H.K.J. Statham | " " | from Grenade School | 9.12.15 |
| 2/Lt | S.R. Fuller | 3/ " | Wounded | 10.12.15 |
| 2/Lt | W.E. Young | " " | To R.F.C. | 14.12.15 |
| 2/Lt | C.A. Steele | / " | To Grenade School | 12.12.15 |
| 2/Lt | C.P.B. Sawyer | " " | From M.G. Course | 12.12.15 |
| 2/Lt | W.G. Ball | " " | To 3rd Army school | 12.12.15 |
| 2/Lt | A.A. Gomez | 3/ " | From " " | 14.12.15 |

Army Form B. 213.

# FIELD RETURN.

No. of Report _____

(To be furnished by all arms, services, and departments to the Base Record Office in accordance with Field Service Regulations, Part II.)

Date. 3.12.15

RETURN showing numbers RATIONED by, and Transport on charge of, 4th Gurkha Rifles at In the Field

| DETAIL | Personnel | | | Animals | | | | | | Transport Vehicles | | Guns, carriages, and limbers, showing description | Ammunition wagons and limbers | Machine guns | REMARKS |
|---|---|---|---|---|---|---|---|---|---|---|---|---|---|---|---|
| | Officers | Other ranks | Natives | Horses Riding | Horses Draught | Horses Pack | Mules Large | Mules Small | Camels | Oxen | 4 Wheeled | 2 Wheeled | | | | |
| Effective Strength of Unit | 24 | 944 | | 11 | 43 | 6 | | 3 | | | 10 | 9 | Maxims 2 Vickers & I | | 4 | Officers 12 at attacks Wounded from 9th |
| Details, by Arms attached to Unit as in War Establishment:— | | | | | | | | | | | | | | | | |
| R.A.M.C. | 1 | 5 | | 1 | | | | | | | | | | | | |
| A.S.C. | | 1 | | | | | | | | | | | | | | |
| Total | 25 | 950 | | 12 | 43 | 6 | | 3 | | | 10 | 9 | | | 4 | |
| War Establishment | 29 | 964 | | 11 | 43 | 9 | | | | | 10 | 9 | | | 4 | |
| Wanting to complete | 4 | 14 | | | | 3 | | | | | | | | | | |
| Surplus | | | | 1 | | | | 3 | | | | | | | | |
| *Attached (not to include the details shown above) Civilians:— | 2 | 2 | | | | | | | | | | | | | | |
| Employed with the Unit | | | | | | | | | | | | | | | | |
| Accompanying the Unit | | | | | | | | | | | | | | | | |
| TOTAL RATIONED | 22 | 955 | | 12 | 43 | 6 | | 3 | | | 10 | 9 | | | 4 | |

Remarks

* In the case of field ambulances, hospitals or depôts, the number of patients are to be included here, the names being shown in A.F.A. 36.

Forms B. 213

(Sd.) _____ Signature of Commander.

3.12.15 Date of Despatch.

*For information of the Officer i/c of a Base Record Office.*

Officers and men who have left or joined since last report.

Place _____  Date _____

| Regtl. Number | Rank | Name | Corps | Name of unit from or to which transferred | Date of being struck off or coming on the ration return | Remarks * |
|---|---|---|---|---|---|---|
| | Lt | W.G. Ball | Dorsets | Joined from | 25.11.15 | |
| | Capt | B.B. Wyso | " | Rejoined | 28.12.15 | |
| | Capt | E Rogers | " | from | 27.11.15 | |
| | Lt | W.E. Green | " | Leave | 2.12.15 | |
| | Lt | W.N. Webb | " | To F. Amb. | 28.11.15 | |

\* State whether absence is of a permanent or temporary nature.

WO 95/15723

5th Division

15th Infantry Bde

1/6 Liverpools

Feb to June
1915

~~Dec 1915~~

15th Bde.
5th Div.

Disembarked from U.K. 25.2.15.

1/6th LIVERPOOL REGIMENT.

FEBRUARY & MARCH.

1 9 1 5

Army Form C. 2118.

# WAR DIARY
## or
## INTELLIGENCE SUMMARY

(Erase heading not required.)

Instructions regarding War Diaries and Intelligence Summaries are contained in F. S. Regs., Part II. and the Staff Manual respectively. Title pages will be prepared in manuscript.

| Hour, Date, Place | Summary of Events and Information | Remarks and references to Appendices |
|---|---|---|
| Canterbury 1-2-15 | Battn: at Canterbury. Nothing unusual to report. | |
| Canterbury 2-2-15 | Battn. at Canterbury. Nothing to Report. | |
| Canterbury 3-2-15 | Battn: at Canterbury. 1 officer & N.C.O & 117 Recruits proceeded to Sandwich to join Main Return. E Coy returned from East. | |

N. Onyx Major
Comdg. 1/6 Kings Liverpool Regt.

**Army Form C. 2118.**

# WAR DIARY
## *or*
## INTELLIGENCE SUMMARY

*(Erase heading not required.)*

Instructions regarding War Diaries and Intelligence Summaries are contained in F. S. Regs., Part II. and the Staff Manual respectively. Title pages will be prepared in manuscript.

| Hour, Date, Place | Summary of Events and Information | Remarks and references to Appendices |
|---|---|---|
| Canterbury 4. 2. 15 | Battn: At Canterbury. Nothing to Report | |
| Canterbury 5. 2. 15 | Battn at Canterbury. Nothing to Report. Equipment arrived for Battn | |
| Canterbury 6. 2. 15 | Battn: at Canterbury. Nothing to Report. | |

Signed,
Major.
Comdg. 1/6 Kings (Liverpool) Regt.

**Army Form C. 2118.**

# WAR DIARY
## or
## INTELLIGENCE SUMMARY

*(Erase heading not required.)*

Instructions regarding War Diaries and Intelligence Summaries are contained in F. S. Regs., Part II. and the Staff Manual respectively. Title pages will be prepared in manuscript.

| Hour, Date, Place | Summary of Events and Information | Remarks and references to Appendices |
|---|---|---|
| Canterbury 7.2.15 | Battn: at Canterbury. Bn. Parade at Cathedral for Divine Service. B. Coy. Proceeded to Sandwich for Musketry. Officers 2 Other Ranks 80. "D" Coy returned from musketry 7 officers 4+6 other ranks | |
| Canterbury 8.2.15 | Battn at Canterbury. 1 Officer 9 other Ranks proceeded to Hythe for Course Machine Gun. 2 Officer 65 other Rank returned from Ashford (musketry) "A" returned off. Leave. | |

Morris Major
Comdg. 1/6. King's Liverpool Rgt.

# WAR DIARY
## INTELLIGENCE SUMMARY
(Erase heading not required.)

Army Form C. 2118.

| Hour, Date, Place | Summary of Events and Information | Remarks and references to Appendices |
|---|---|---|
| Canterbury. 9.2.15 | Batt'n at Canterbury 1 Officer 982 O.R. 2/6 Lpool Regt. arrived in Canterbury & take over transport from 1/6 Br. K. Lpool Rgt. 1 Officer & 20 O.R. proceeded to Bottisham & take over transport. details of "a"&"b" & Coy. proceeded on leave. | |
| Canterbury. 10.2.15 | Batt'n at Canterbury. Nothing unusual to report. | |

Rainer Major
Comdg. 1/6. Kings Lpool Rgt.

**Army Form C. 2118.**

# WAR DIARY
## or
## INTELLIGENCE SUMMARY
*(Erase heading not required.)*

Instructions regarding War Diaries and Intelligence Summaries are contained in F. S. Regs., Part II. and the Staff Manual respectively. Title pages will be prepared in manuscript.

| Hour, Date, Place | Summary of Events and Information | Remarks and references to Appendices |
|---|---|---|
| Canterbury 11.2.15 | Bath at Canterbury. Nothing unusual to Report. "B" Coy: reviewed with Boots and Equipment. | |
| Canterbury 12.2.15 | Bath at Canterbury. Transport inspection by dept: Director of Transport. | |
| Canterbury 13.2.15 | Bath: at Canterbury. 2 Officers & 198 other Ranks returned from Sandwich. 2 Officers & 110 other Ranks arrived from 6 Kings Shoot Rgt. | |

Comdg 16 (Rifle) Bn Kings Shoot Rgt.
Major

**Army Form C. 2118.**

# WAR DIARY
## or
## INTELLIGENCE SUMMARY
*(Erase heading not required.)*

Instructions regarding War Diaries and Intelligence Summaries are contained in F. S. Regs., Part II. and the Staff Manual respectively. Title pages will be prepared in manuscript.

| Hour, Date, Place | Summary of Events and Information | Remarks and references to Appendices |
|---|---|---|
| Canterbury 14-2-15 | Baths at Canterbury. 1 officer & 95 other Ranks returned from Sandwich. Detail of Bn:- Paraded for service at Cathedral. "B" & "E" Coys fitted with Boots & Equipment. | |
| Canterbury 15-2-15 | Baths at Canterbury - Nothing of any importance to report. 2 officers & Sandwich "A" Coy fitted with Boots & Equipment. | |
| Canterbury 16-2-15 | Baths at Canterbury - Nothing to report | |

H. Fenn Major
Comdg:- 16 (Rifle) Bn:- King's Royal Rifle Corps

Army Form C. 2118.

# WAR DIARY
## of
## INTELLIGENCE SUMMARY
(Erase heading not required.)

Instructions regarding War Diaries and Intelligence Summaries are contained in F. S. Regs., Part II. and the Staff Manual respectively. Title pages will be prepared in manuscript.

| Hour, Date, Place | Summary of Events and Information | Remarks and references to Appendices |
|---|---|---|
| Canterbury 14.2.15. | Bath at Canterbury. Nothing unusual to Report. | |
| Canterbury 18.2.15. | Bath at Canterbury. Forcing Service men Paraded for fitting new Equipment. | |

A. Trower
Major
Comdg. 16 Kings Liverpool Regt.

**Army Form C. 2118.**

# WAR DIARY
## or
## INTELLIGENCE SUMMARY
*(Erase heading not required.)*

Instructions regarding War Diaries and Intelligence Summaries are contained in F.S. Regs., Part II. and the Staff Manual respectively. Title pages will be prepared in manuscript.

| Hour, Date, Place | Summary of Events and Information | Remarks and references to Appendices |
|---|---|---|
| Canterbury 19-2-15 | Baths at Canterbury - all MK VI ammunition withdrawn from Companies - all old Equipment returned to Depot Liverpool | |
| Canterbury 20-2-15 | Baths at Canterbury. Reorg'a balance of Contractors - Inspection by General Officer Comdg: Shool. Inf. Bde. Clothing &c. Strength 29 officers 1009 other Ranks. | |

T.W. [signature]
Major
Comdg. 1/6 King's L'pool R/L

Army Form C. 2118.

# WAR DIARY
## INTELLIGENCE SUMMARY
*(Erase heading not required.)*

Instructions regarding War Diaries and Intelligence Summaries are contained in F.S. Regs., Part II. and the Staff Manual respectively. Title pages will be prepared in manuscript.

| Hour, Date, Place | Summary of Events and Information | Remarks and references to Appendices |
|---|---|---|
| Canterbury 21-2-1915 | Both at Canterbury. Completed reclothing of Bath. | |
| Canterbury 22-2-1915 | Bath at Canterbury. Mark VII mmm issued to Bath. all surplus ordnance stores handed over to 7/6 Bn Kings Shot Regt. Bath inspected By Major General J.B Forsier. Strength 31 officers. 984 other Ranks. received orders to hold Bath in readiness to embark on Wednesday 24th - | |

A. Money Major
Comdg 1/6 Kings Shropl Regt.

Forms/C. 2118/11.

# WAR DIARY / INTELLIGENCE SUMMARY

Army Form C. 2118.

| Hour, Date, Place | Summary of Events and Information | Remarks and references to Appendices |
|---|---|---|
| Canterbury 23-2-15 | Batt'n: at Canterbury. Batt'n: Received orders to Embark. | |
| Canterbury 24-2-15 | Batt'n: left Canterbury in three Special trains for Southampton. 1st: train left Canterbury 6-40 am. arrived Southampton 12.o.c. 2nd train left Canterbury 8-15 am arrived Southampton 1-15. 3rd train left Canterbury 9-50 am arrived Southampton 3-4 oclock. Embraced on S.S. B'g. of Edinboro Embarked. On arrival Embarkah. Strength 31 Officers. | Comdg: 1/6 King's Liverpool Regt [signature] Major |

| Hour, Date, Place | Summary of Events and Information | Remarks and references to Appendices |
|---|---|---|
| 24-2-15<br>Columea | 1094 other ranks. 93 horses & mules, 19 four wheeled carts & 4 two wheeled carts. Entrainment completed at 4 pm. Sailed at 5 pm. | |
| Havre E<br>25-2-15 | Voyage completed without incident. Both devervented at 8 am. Proceeded to No 6 Rest Camp. Orders received. Ralle less first Reinforcement reserved. 9 tons Rylands Pierce engines at 9th Australia unknown. 9 am. Kostry completed as saran cloth & equipment with the exception of web only which was notified to the D.A.P.M.G. Baron Rose. | Major<br>Comdg. 1/6 Kings first Regt. |

Army Form C. 2118.

# WAR DIARY
## or
## INTELLIGENCE SUMMARY
*(Erase heading not required.)*

| Hour, Date, Place | Summary of Events and Information | Remarks and references to Appendices |
|---|---|---|
| Hans E. 26.2.1915 | Bath; Platoon 9 1st Reinforcements paraded at 4. a.m. and marched to Gare des Marchandises. Ambulations and entrained at 1 a.m. Train left at 1.6 p.m. and proceeded via: Rouen - Abeville - St. Omer - Hazebrouck to Bailleul. | Bangs: 1/c King's Shot 74 Major [signature] Bangs: 1/c King's Shot |
| Bailleul. 27.2.15 | Bath. arrived at Bailleul at 9.30. a.m. and marched to Bulto at L'École des jeunes filles, one Coy. Billeted at Lunatic Asylum. Strength of Battn. Officers 28. other Ranks 894 | |

# WAR DIARY or INTELLIGENCE SUMMARY

Army Form C. 2118.

*(Erase heading not required.)*

Instructions regarding War Diaries and Intelligence Summaries are contained in F.S. Regs., Part II. and the Staff Manual respectively. Title pages will be prepared in manuscript.

| Hour, Date, Place | Summary of Events and Information | Remarks and references to Appendices |
|---|---|---|
| Bailleul 26.2.1915 | Two platoons left at Havre, rejoined at 1. a.m. Casualties 3 Riflemen admitted to Hospital. Interpreter joined with the two platoons. Strength of Battn. 30 Officers 994 other Rks. | |
| Bailleul 1.3.1915 | Batn. inspected by Brigadier General Count Gleichen. Orders received 9.20am for the Bn to march at 9am via LOCRE – LA-CLYTTE – ZEVECOTTEN – OUDERDOM – to VLAMERTINGHE. Billeting party to proceed in advance. Necessary orders issued. Strength 30 officers 994 O.R. No Casualties. | |
| Bailleul 2.3.1915 | Batn. paraded at 9.am & left Bailleul at 10.am for Vlamertinghe. Billeting party 1 officer & 6 N.C.O's sent in advance. Batn. arrived at about 2.30pm. Billeted in farms about 1 mile West of Vlamertinghe. Very much scattered. Billeting completed. About 6.30pm Hd Qrs at Herding-Ca. Weys. C.O & Adjt proceeded to Poperinghe to report Arrival. | Lieut Colonel Commanding 1/8th (Irish) Battn. The King's (Liverpool Regt.) |

# WAR DIARY
## or
## INTELLIGENCE SUMMARY
*(Erase heading not required.)*

Army Form C. 2118.

| Hour, Date, Place | Summary of Events and Information | Remarks and references to Appendices |
|---|---|---|
| Calmeur 2. 3. 1915. | To H.Qrs 28th Div. | |
| Hanerlinghe 3. 3. 1915. | 1 Lieut. 3 Oprs. 920 other ranks sent to Div. H.Qrs Poperinghe Eye. Orderly also despatched. Orders received to test rifles with Mr VI ammn. 2 coys completed & info found satisfactory. Baths attached to 15th Brigade 28th Div. | |
| Hanerlinghe 4. 3. 1915. | C.O. & adjt attended Brigade H.Qrs at 9.30 am. Instructions received that the Battn to attach to 1st Cheshires for purpose of instruction in trench fighting. Coys parades at 6 time and move to YPRES with 15th Brigade. 2nd in Comd. H.Qrs & 2 Coys. Entrain at Belles D.M.C. Hinterfield. Proceeded to YPRES to arrange Billets. | |

[signature]
LIEUT. COLONEL,
Commanding 1/6th (Rifle) Battn. The L'pool Regt.

# WAR DIARY
## or
## INTELLIGENCE SUMMARY

Army Form C. 2118.

(Erase heading not required.)

| Hour, Date, Place | Summary of Events and Information | Remarks and references to Appendices |
|---|---|---|
| VLAMERTINGHE 5-3-15 | Commanding Officer & adjt. proceeded to YPRES to recit. the two Companys ["A" Coy] have been ordered to proceed to the trenches to be attached to the Dorsetshire Regt. | |

T Brown
LIEUT. COLONEL.
Commanding 1/8th (Rifle) Batt. "The King's"
(Liverpool Regt.)

# WAR DIARY
## or
## INTELLIGENCE SUMMARY

*(Erase heading not required.)*

Army Form C. 2118.

| Hour, Date, Place | Summary of Events and Information | Remarks and references to Appendices |
|---|---|---|
| VLAMERTINGHE 5-3-15- | Commanding Officer Jacqulains visited the two Coys. at YPRES. "A" Coy Paraded at 6 P.M. and which in the trenches and attd. to Cheshire Regt for instruction. | |
| VLAMERTINGHE 6-3-15- | H/qrs. & 2 Coys. Remain at Billets near VLAMERTINGHE running two Coys. at YPRES. "A" Coy. relieved from trenches at 9 P.M. Bivouetter. O.Rks. 3 wounded - | |
| VLAMERTINGHE 4-3-15- | "C" Coy. moved to YPRES. leaving at 6.20 p.m. overnight hours for "A" & "B" Coys. Remaining Coy to follow next day. | |
| YPRES. 8-3-15- | H/qrs. & "D" Coy moved from VLAMERTINGHE to YPRES. Paraded at 2 PM. Bn. quartered in Cavalry Barracks. Casualties in trenches "A" Coy - O.Rks. 2 killed 4 wounded. "B" Coy - | |

LIEUT. COLONEL
Commanding 1/8th (Rifle) Battn. ...
(L'pool Regt.)

# WAR DIARY
## or
## INTELLIGENCE SUMMARY

*(Erase heading not required.)*

Army Form C. 2118.

| Hour, Date, Place | Summary of Events and Information | Remarks and references to Appendices |
|---|---|---|
| YPRES. 9-3-15 | "D" Coy. in Trenches. "C" Coy. Casualties O.R. 3. "A" Coy. Casualties 1/2 wounded. O.R. Party of 100 men detailed for working party making R.E. near Canal. | |
| YPRES 10-3-15 | "A" Coy: in trenches. "D" Coy Relieved from Trenches. Casualties nil. "C" Coy. Casualties 2. O.R. Wounded. (Carrying Party) Strength of Batt.m. 30 Officers. 924 Other Ranks. (not including 25 Other R.K. on Divisional G.) | |
| YPRES. 11-3-15 | "B" Coy. in Trenches. "C" Coy. Carrying Party of 100 men. "A" Company Casualties 2 men wounded | |
| YPRES. 12-3-15 | "D" Coy. in Trenches. "B" Coy. Casualties 2 men Wounded. "A" Coy. 100 men Carrying Party | [signature] LIEUT. COLONEL. Commanding 1(0th) (Rifle) Battn. "The King's" (L'pool. Regt.) |

Army Form C. 2118.

# WAR DIARY
or
INTELLIGENCE SUMMARY
(Erase heading not required.)

Instructions regarding War Diaries and Intelligence Summaries are contained in F. S. Regs., Part II. and the Staff Manual respectively. Title pages will be prepared in manuscript.

| Hour, Date, Place | Summary of Events and Information | Remarks and references to Appendices |
|---|---|---|
| YPRES. 13-3-15 | Capt. W.S. Montgomery killed in trenches & died the same day. Other ranks 2 wounded (owed same day). "B" Coy. proceeded to trenches at 6 p.m. & carried up sandbags ammunition & rations. Trench stores for the Dorsets carried by 2 Platoons of "B" Coy. 2 Platoons of "D" Coy. employed as carrying party for Cheshires. Took up sandbags ammunition & trench stores | |
| YPRES 14-3-15 | Orders received 3.35 p.m. for 2 Platoons to act as carrying party for Bedfords and 2 Platoons for Dorsets. — Comdg. Officer & adjt. attached to H.Q. 2 Norfolk Regt. to see system of Bath Relief. — Telephone orders recd. by Major Warmington at 10 p.m. to send 160 men to ROSENTAL-CHATEAU to carry amm: to Dorset & Cheshires. Message recd 10.30 p.m. re S.A.A. carts, machine guns & Reserve amm: to be sent up to Brigade H.Q. | |

H.S. Poole(?)
LIEUT. COLONEL.
Commanding 1/8th (Rifle) Battn. "The King's" (L'pool. Regt.)

# WAR DIARY
## or
## INTELLIGENCE SUMMARY

| Hour, Date, Place | Summary of Events and Information | Remarks and references to Appendices |
|---|---|---|
| 15" 3. 15.<br>YPRES. | at 2.10 a.m. Message received that if any more ammunition required 500 to be sent at ROSENTHAL CHATEAU. 2.35 A.M. Message received keep S.A.A. carts from 31st Brigade ammunition column on HAMERTINGHE-OUDERDOM.R= 2 mile South of VLAMERTINGHE 4-10 A.M. Message received to send one company to be at Brigade H.Qrs. by daylight, to carry one days Rations & 200 Rounds per rifle. This Coy. delivered to Bullets at 6.30 A.M. "A" Coy. A Carrying Party of 2 Platoons + detachment to Brigade H.Qrs. 6.30 p.m. Had to be met by guide. at the Bedford - working party of 100 men with Shovels sent to Report at once Junction South of ROSENTHAL at 4.45 p.m. to be met by guide. of Norfolk Regiment Telephone message received by day at 6.15 p.m. Hd Qr march. Guns may return to billets at once. Limber waggon despatched together. | [signature]<br>LIEUT. COLONEL<br>Commanding 1/8th (Rifle) Battn. "The King's"<br>(Lpool Regt.) |

# WAR DIARY or INTELLIGENCE SUMMARY

Army Form C. 2118.

(Erase heading not required.)

| Hour, Date, Place | Summary of Events and Information | Remarks and references to Appendices |
|---|---|---|
| 16 - 3 - 15 Bosseboom | Battn. went into Rest Billets at BOSSEBOOM | |
| 17 - 3 - 15 Bosseboom | Battn. in Rest Billets at BOSSEBOOM nothing to Report | |
| 18 - 3 - 15 " | as above | |
| 20 - 3 - 15 | | |
| 21 - 3 - 15 Trenches YPRES | Brigade move up to YPRES and took over trenches from 9th Brigade. Battn. relieved 1st K.O.R. Scottish in trenches 38 - 39 - 40 - 41 - 9 & 2. D. Sector "B" & "D" Coy. in the trenches 2 in G. & 9 in Quarters. "A" & "C" Coys. in reserve at Infantry Barracks. YPRES. Ready for counter attack with S.a.a. carts cooks carts & Water Carts left Menin Gate at 4-30 pm. and marched | [signature] LIEUT. COLONEL Commanding 1/8th (Rifle) Battn. "The King's" (L'pool. Regt.) |

# WAR DIARY or INTELLIGENCE SUMMARY

Army Form C. 2118.

(Erase heading not required.)

Instructions regarding War Diaries and Intelligence Summaries are contained in F.S. Regs., Part II. and the Staff Manual respectively. Title pages will be prepared in manuscript.

| Hour, Date, Place | Summary of Events and Information | Remarks and references to Appendices |
|---|---|---|
| 21-3-15 | TUILERIES Square. 1.3.2.B. considered to trenches from than by guides from Ypres [illegible]. Trenches Garrisons as follows "B" Coy; 89 ¶ 40 trenches 51. men R.M. Guns. D.Coy 30 trench 62 men in support trench 41. 35 men Trench 42. 30 men | |
| 22.3.15 Trenches YPRES | All quiet. during night work done improving Head cover & traverses. Bngr; Parties trenches in the morning, casualties to noon 1 wounded. Support Coy 60 men move from 42 trench to dug out near Pt 2.5 in Railway cutting after dark. | |
| 23.3.16 Trenches YPRES | Heavy burst of firing from German lines about 4 am stood to arms until dawn on parapet. Parades in all trenches cancelled to hour 1 killed 4 W [illegible]. Mine work seen in progress by Germans on Hill 60 Citizen communication work. O fire exchange 2nd relieved "A" "B" C Coys relieved "B" "D" in trenches 9-30 pm. Trenches 9 A. Lrs Shellra by small arms about 9 pm. Trenches from Hill 60 | [signature] LIEUT. COLONEL. Commanding 1/6th (Rifle) Battn. "The King's" (L'pool Regt.) |

# WAR DIARY
## or
## INTELLIGENCE SUMMARY

Army Form C. 2118.

| Hour, Date, Place | Summary of Events and Information | Remarks and references to Appendices |
|---|---|---|
| 24. 3. 15<br>Trenches<br>YPRES | Work done as on previous days cancelled & men<br>1 Killed, 1 wounded. Part of parapet on 39 blown<br>down to floor in afternoon. | |
| 25. 3. 15<br>Trenches<br>YPRES | Knife rests put out in front of 38 trench in<br>parapet of 39 relines. Communication trench along<br>battn front. 38 & R's Coy Dug out commence.<br>Casualties 6 noon. 1 wounded. Communication<br>trench 41 & 39 & knees from trenches of 39 near<br>31 about 3pm our artillery replied shelling<br>ceased 4.30pm. "B" & "D" Coy. commenced TUILLERIE &<br>relieved trenches are quiet during my relief.<br>Capt Westby relinquishes duty adjt to Captn Herschell<br>work done on new communication trench along<br>embankment. First trenches improved. | |
| 26. 3. 15<br>Trenches<br>YPRES | Casualties 1 Killed 2 wounded. Captn Herschell<br>reported from Reserve Battn. | |
| 27. 3. 15<br>Trenches<br>YPRES | Work done as for 26th Casualties 6 noon.<br>2 Killed 4 wounded. Enemy's commenced firing<br>with artillery nearer from trench 39 - time<br>been for first to to trenches 9 minutes 40 secs.<br>"A" & "C" Coy's took over trenches at 5:20 pm | R. [signature]<br>LIEUT. COLONEL<br>Commanding 1/5th (Rifle) Battn. "The King's"<br>(Lpool. Regt.) |

# WAR DIARY or INTELLIGENCE SUMMARY

Army Form C. 2118.

| Hour, Date, Place | Summary of Events and Information | Remarks and references to Appendices |
|---|---|---|
| 28.3.15 Trenches YPRES | New communication trench opened up from 39 to 36. other work as before. new dug-outs constructed near A & B Trenches. Casualties 1 wounded. | |
| 29.3.15 Trenches YPRES | O.C. Trench 36 reports Loop hole were put out of action during night by German snipers. during night the communication trench 36-36 completed. Trenches Line 8 trenches sniping rapidly concealed 5 room. 1 killed. Q irrenches 13 "D" Boys took over trenches 7 Caps. shots at A-2os. Unnerving by one offer 9.85 mm. | |
| 30.3.15 YPres. | all quiet during night. work done on parapet. Knife rest hurdles out and new pieces in situ. under railway bridge. Casualties 6 men 1 killed. Report received from Brigade about 2 pm that a German R.E. was on the railway on the neighbour bridge ZILLEBEKE arid. A party consisting of 2210 Rfn Lloyd 2266 Bfn Clynch McConnell 1466 Bfn Saffe. 1933 J. Lancaster 2221 H. Shelton. 2350 T. Phillips 2061 Rfn Dowler. 1722 Rfn Wagstaff went to get him Shelton, Lancaster, wounded & great resource & courage in assisting Serjeant J. Brooks, in getting them in. | LIEUT. COLONEL Commanding 1/8th (Rifle) Battn. "The King's" (L'pool. Regt) |

# WAR DIARY or INTELLIGENCE SUMMARY

Army Form C. 2118.

| Hour, Date, Place | Summary of Events and Information | Remarks and references to Appendices |
|---|---|---|
| 31. 8. 16.<br>Lunch<br>YPRES. | The wounded Engineer was rescued under heavy fire & Phillips, Knight, Mason, &c photographed doing well: wounded & continues.<br>Heavy Artillery & our ammunition at H.Q. 207, after ways as before cancelled up to time of relief by Queen Victoria Rifles & Tower[?] Finch S.A. bombarders by trench mortar in afternoon and at night from old Boche [?] front of O.C. 60 shots all short – no damage done. Trenches 36-41 relieved by Q.V. Rifles & two platoons at H.Q. Gr. Bng. out by the Royal West Kent Relief completed by mid-night – Battn relieved to huts on VLAMERTINGHE – OUDERDOM – Road.<br>Strength of Battn 33 Officers 928. O'Ranks | [signature]<br>LIEUT. COLONEL.<br>Commanding 1/6th (Rifle) Battn. "The King's"<br>(L'pool. Regt.) |

15th Bde.
5th Div.

1/6th LIVERPOOLS

APRIL

1 9 1 5

On His Majesty's Service.

Army Form C. 2118.

# WAR DIARY
## or INTELLIGENCE SUMMARY
(Erase heading not required.)

Instructions regarding War Diaries and Intelligence Summaries are contained in F. S. Regs., Part II. and the Staff Manual respectively. Title pages will be prepared in manuscript.

| Hour, Date, Place | Summary of Events and Information | Remarks and references to Appendices |
|---|---|---|
| 1.4.15 VLAMERTINGHE | Pm: Riding on huts at VLAMERTINGHE | |
| 5.4. ROSENTAL CHATEAU | a.m. Left VLAMERTINGHE. Left Ypres [Lille Gate] detachments at 10 minute interval. H.Qrs & B. & D. Cys. at Chateau ROSENTAL. "A" Coy in Dugouts at CHESTER-FARM and from a 50 men for Canal Post. "C" Coy in Dugouts along Canal Road Q.7 and Canal Bridge Post of 50 men is supplied 9 & 10 by day with two machine guns. | |
| 6.4.15 ROSENTAL CHATEAU | Battn in Support as above. Nothing to report. Casualties to hour 1 Wounded. | [signature] LIEUT. COLONEL Commanding Batln. (King's) (Liverpool Regt.) |

# WAR DIARY
## or
## INTELLIGENCE SUMMARY
*(Erase heading not required.)*

Army Form C. 2118.

| Hour, Date, Place | Summary of Events and Information | Remarks and references to Appendices |
|---|---|---|
| 7-4-15<br>YPRES.<br>(ROSENTAL) | as for 6th Carvallies nil. Baths returns at night. "A" By by Manchesters By & "C" By by A.C.L.I. relief complete by 1 a.m. Baths went into Huts at ROZENHILL. | |
| 8-4-15 | Baths working at ROSENHILL. Nothing to Report. | |
| 9-4-15<br>ROSEN HILL | | |
| 10-4-15 | Baths less "B" & "D" Coys [Capt Huts and marched] to YPRES. going into Billets there. "B" & "D" Coys altgether a to 1st Norfolks and marched with them at 8.15 pm | |

Signed ............... LIEUT COLONEL
........... Rifle Bgde. "The King's"
(.......Regt.)

# WAR DIARY
## INTELLIGENCE SUMMARY
(Erase heading not required.)

Army Form C. 2118.

| Hour, Date, Place | Summary of Events and Information | Remarks and references to Appendices |
|---|---|---|
| 16. 4. 15 YPRES | Battn in billets at YPRES. Notification received from Brigade that D.C.M. had been awarded to L/Cpl. Bevelin W.C. (2061) and Rfmn Phillips. J. (2350) Casualties 1 killed 1 wounded. Strength of Battn: 30 Officers 935 OR. | Examined 1/6 feb [signature] H.R. Cane |
| 17-4-15 YPRES | Battn: less B "C" Coys moved into old Cavalry in ramparts of town. 4.P.M. heavy gplosion German mine under Hill 60. heavy bombardment during night. | |
| 18-4-15 YPRES | Battn. remained in reserve as above. Casualties with Companies attached to Norfolks & Bedfs 4 wounded carrying materiels fromd artyving to Granges Sandbags &c to 13" Brigade HQrs. +8 hrs Return sent up for "C" Coy was outside POSTE-DE-LILLE Dunsfryn killed. Lieut park Poole 1 killed Duntin Maurice killed | |

Army Form C. 2118.

# WAR DIARY
## or
## INTELLIGENCE SUMMARY

*(Erase heading not required.)*

Instructions regarding War Diaries and Intelligence Summaries are contained in F. S. Regs., Part II. and the Staff Manual respectively. Title pages will be prepared in manuscript.

| Hour, Date, Place | Summary of Events and Information | Remarks and references to Appendices |
|---|---|---|
| 11.4.15 YPRES. | Bath Cos. "B" & "D" Coys. billeted in YPRES Barracks. 6 men, 2 wounded. | |
| 12.4.15 YPRES. | as above. Barracks. 1 man wounded. | |
| 13.4.15 YPRES. | as above. Barracks. nil. | |
| 14.4.15 YPRES. | "C" Coy. relieved "D" Coy. with 1st Rifle Bde. Barracks. 1 man wounded. | |
| 15.4.15 YPRES | as above. Telephone message received from Brigade at 5.30 pm. Coys. ordered to hold themselves in readiness to man all armaments in trenches all quiet during night. | ✻ BM.471. |

LIEUT. COLONEL.
Commanding 1st (Rifle) Battn. "The King's"
(Liverpool Regt.)

Army Form C. 2118.

# WAR DIARY
## or
## INTELLIGENCE SUMMARY
*(Erase heading not required.)*

Instructions regarding War Diaries and Intelligence Summaries are contained in F. S. Regs., Part II. and the Staff Manual respectively. Title pages will be prepared in manuscript.

| Hour, Date, Place | Summary of Events and Information | Remarks and references to Appendices |
|---|---|---|
| 19. 4. 15 YPRES. | H.Qrs. 14 & D. Coys in Casemate. Town shelled w. heavy artillery continuously. Carrying parties found at night. 3 other ranks killed, nine wounded. | |
| 20. 4. 15 YPRES. | As above. Orders received at 7-30 PM to move into dugouts in Railway Embankment near 15th Brigade Headquarters. H.Qrs. 14 H.) Coys in position by 9 PM. All men employed on carrying parties for Belfort Wks: Day break. 2nd Lt. Rowe wounded. 1 other rank wounded. | |
| 21. 4. 15 YPRES. | As above. Carrying parties found at night. Casualties 2 other ranks killed. 21 other ranks wounded. | |
| 22. 4. 15 YPRES. | As above. Carrying parties at night. Casualties 5 other ranks wounded. | [signature] LIEUT. COLONEL Commanding 1/6th King's Batt. "The King's" (Liverpool Regt.) |

# WAR DIARY
## or
## INTELLIGENCE SUMMARY

(Erase heading not required.)

Army Form C. 2118.

| Hour, Date, Place | Summary of Events and Information | Remarks and references to Appendices |
|---|---|---|
| 23.4.15 YPRES | As above. Carrying parties at night. Casualties. 3 other ranks wounded | |
| 24.4.15 YPRES | As above. Working parties sent out under R.E. at 9 P.M. to construct a new switch. Work on trench from VERBRANDENMOLEN to Railway Cutting near Sniper's Hut in I 28 B. Casualties. 2 other ranks wounded | |
| 25.4.15 YPRES | As above. Work on switch continued. 3 other ranks wounded | |
| 26.4.15 YPRES | Work on switch also continued. Party employed in running second line trench in T 20 D. Work interfered with by shelling. Casualties. 1 other rank wounded | |
| 27.4.15 YPRES | As above. Carrying parties at night. French wounded carried up to Sandown Support. Casualties. 2nd R.F. Stones | |

Lieut. Colonel
Commanding 1/4th (Ring Bn.) "The King's"
(L/pool Regt.)

Army Form C. 2118.

# WAR DIARY
## or
## INTELLIGENCE SUMMARY

*(Erase heading not required.)*

Instructions regarding War Diaries and Intelligence Summaries are contained in F. S. Regs., Part II. and the Staff Manual respectively. Title pages will be prepared in manuscript.

| Hour, Date, Place | Summary of Events and Information | Remarks and references to Appendices |
|---|---|---|
| 28. 4. 15 | As above. Carrying Parties. Casualties. Nil | |
| 29. 4. 15 | As above. Carrying Parties. 1 Other rank wounded | |
| 30. 4. 15 YPRES | 5 Other ranks wounded. As above. Carrying parties. Casualties. | |
| 1. 5. 15 | 2 killed 11 wounded | |

(1)(foot page)
Commanding 1/4th (Extra) Battn. "The King's"
LIEUT. COLONEL.

15th Bde.
5th Div.

1/6th LIVERPOOLS.

MAY

1915

On His Majesty's Service.

Army Form C. 2118.

# WAR DIARY
## or
## INTELLIGENCE SUMMARY

*(Erase heading not required.)*

Instructions regarding War Diaries and Intelligence Summaries are contained in F.S. Regs., Part II. and the Staff Manual respectively. Title pages will be prepared in manuscript.

| Hour, Date, Place | Summary of Events and Information | Remarks and references to Appendices |
|---|---|---|
| 1. 5-15 YPRES | Headquarters (A.D Corps.) in dugouts in Railway Embankment near 15 Brigade H.Qrs. 1, 20 A, B, D, 21.C. All men employed on carrying parties for Devons & with day light. | |
| 2. 5-15 YPRES | 2-30 a.m. 40 men sent up with stretchers to Railway Cutting I 29 C. R.A.M.C. & carrying men of Devons & suffering from effects of poisonous gas. 4 a.m. Orders received to send 1 Company (D) to Larchwood in Railway Cutting I 29 C to report to O.C. Devons. Company moved off in small parties. Duet King Effort 3-30 a.m. Casualties 1st 20 other ranks wounded. 2 " 1 other rank wounded. | |
| 3. 5-15 YPRES | As above. Carrying parties at night. Casualties nil. | |

[signature]
LIEUT. COLONEL
Commanding 1/6th (Service) Battn. "The King's" (L'pool Regt.)

Army Form C. 2118.

# WAR DIARY
## or
## INTELLIGENCE SUMMARY
(Erase heading not required.)

Instructions regarding War Diaries and Intelligence Summaries are contained in F.S. Regs, Part II. and the Staff Manual respectively. Title pages will be prepared in manuscript.

| Hour, Date, Place | Summary of Events and Information | Remarks and references to Appendices |
|---|---|---|
| 4-5-15 YPRES | Orders received for Battalion to assemble at Battalion Headquarters and proceed into Divisional Reserve H.23.B. Companies moved as relieved commencing at 9 P.M. Move completed by 6-30 A.M. Casualties 4 other ranks wounded. 4-7-10 P.M. | AP. I. |
| 5-5-15 YPRES | 9-30 A.M. Orders received for Battalion to move up to Brigade Headquarters. Battalion moved off at 10-15 A.M. by Companies. "A" Company immediately on arrival ordered to report to O.C. Cheshires on Railway Cutting T.29.C. "B" Company ordered to proceed & take up position in trenches (& railway near same) near this actual T.28.B. "C" Company received orders direct from Brigadier to move to ZILLEBEKE VILLAGE via Blanc de Zillebeke and to attack in direction of trench 42 except north ZILLEBEKE - KLEIN - ZILLEBEKE Road as Centre. 4-20 P.M. received that B Company had been ordered to move up | AP. II. AP. III. AP. IV |

LIEUT. COLONEL
Commanding 1/6th (Rifle) Battn. "The King's"
(L'pool Regt.)

# WAR DIARY
## INTELLIGENCE SUMMARY

*(Erase heading not required.)*

Army Form C. 2118.

| Hour, Date, Place | Summary of Events and Information | Remarks and references to Appendices |
|---|---|---|
| 5-5-15<br>YPRES. | to Enclenorm. 7.29 C. and report to O.C. Cheshires. 2-20 P.M. Orders received for Headquarters and "D"Company to move to S.W. END of ETANG-DE-ZILLEBEKE and to take cover in the Borrow pit.<br>No report having been received from "C" Company regarding their attack D Company orders to send out patrols to establish communication.<br>See report from Commander of A.I.C.D. Companies on the operations carried out by them attached.<br>Casualties. Capt E.M.Brocklehurst Lieut E.H.Wilcox killed. Lt R.P.Howell 2ⁿᵈ Lieut R.H. Deasland wounded. 20 other ranks killed & 68 other ranks wounded.<br>9 P.M. Verbal orders received that H.Qrs. & D.Coy. to move to dugouts in railway embankment near R.E. farm. Move not made until 13·3·5 A.M. owing to heavy shelling. | AP I<br><br>AP VI<br>AP VII<br>AP VIII<br>AP IX |

**Army Form C. 2118**

# WAR DIARY
## or
## INTELLIGENCE SUMMARY

*(Erase heading not required.)*

Instructions regarding War Diaries and Intelligence Summaries are contained in F. S. Regs., Part II. and the Staff Manual respectively. Title pages will be prepared in manuscript.

| Hour, Date, Place | Summary of Events and Information | Remarks and references to Appendices |
|---|---|---|
| 6. 5. 15<br>YPRES. | 5.10 PM. Orders received for Battn to proceed after relief to E Camp Ouderdom. D Company move at 9.10 PM. more completed at 6-30 AM | |
| 7. 5. 15<br>Ouderdom. | Lt. A. St Clinstone wounded & 12 other ranks wounded (6A).<br>Battn at E Camp Ouderdom. Strength 25 officers 699 other ranks. | |
| 8. 5. 15<br>do | Battn at E Camp. Nothing to report. | |
| 15. 5. 15<br>E Camp<br>OUDERDOM. | | |
| 15. 5. 15. | Orders received Battn to move at 11.15 PM to bivouac in Square H.23.A. | |

Signed: [signature]
LIEUT. COLONEL
Commanding 5th (Service) Battn. y The King's R
(Liverpool Regt.)

# WAR DIARY
## or
## INTELLIGENCE SUMMARY
(Erase heading not required.)

Army Form C. 2118.

| Hour, Date, Place | Summary of Events and Information | Remarks and references to Appendices |
|---|---|---|
| 15.5.15<br>YPRES. | Orders received at 11.15 A.M. for Battn. to move into Dug outs in H.23.d. Orders received at 12.15 P.M. for working party of 150 men to work on support points in I.22.d.9¼. Party to rendezvous at road junction I.21.d.7/8 at 9.30 P.M. Party found from A & B Companies. The following officers found from 3/6 Bn: Lieuts F. Burkitt, W. Jones, J. Royston, 2nd Lts E.K. Buckley & E.C. Adam. Battalion above working party moved off by Corps at 10 minute interval commencing at 8 P.M. Arrived 9 P.M. | |
| 16.5.15<br>YPRES. | Orders received at 12.15 P.M. to fetch ammunition from Caernot[?] in YPRES & carry it to Dg.1.13.c.3/6 from where it would be taken by motor lorry. At 8 A.M. to Château in H.23.B and placed in stables. Remainder of Bn used for this work. Inpts. party of 90. Rank & file. Maj. Wainwright | |

LIEUT COLONEL
H.F. [signature]
Commanding 1/6th (Rifle) Battn. K.L.R. Regt.
(Upper Right)

# WAR DIARY
## or
## INTELLIGENCE SUMMARY
*(Erase heading not required.)*

Army Form C. 2118.

| Hour, Date, Place | Summary of Events and Information | Remarks and references to Appendices |
|---|---|---|
| 16.5.15 YPRES (Continued) | Left at 3 A.M. and made two journeys bringing up 80 boxes. 2nd party 100 strong under Capt. Bennet left at 6 A.M. 1st lorry load of 82 boxes arrived at Chateau 8.15 A.M. 2nd load of 78 boxes arrived at 9.30. About 400 boxes still on Cocoanut. No casualties. No Noon 1 killed 4 wounded. Orders received noon for ZILLEBEKE POND dug out on west side of Bn to come under Commencing at 8 P.M. Bn to come under orders of O.B. Company. 2 men Command sent on an afternoon to Report to O.C. H.Q. and to reconnoitre trenches that Bn might have to occupy. Orders received 3-45 P.M. for working party of 400 men to work on S. Section of VERBRANDEN MOLEN – ZILLEBEKE line. To rendezvous at Davidson dug out at 10 P.M. More commenced at 8 P.M. Completed by 9-30 P.M. Working party went out. Staff 19. O.R. arrived from hospital etc. | LIEUT. COLONEL, H. S. Barnes. Commanding 1/6th (Rifle) Battn. "The King's" (L'pool. Regt.) |

**Army Form C. 2118.**

# WAR DIARY
## or
## INTELLIGENCE SUMMARY
*(Erase heading not required.)*

Instructions regarding War Diaries and Intelligence Summaries are contained in F.S. Regs., Part II. and the Staff Manual respectively. Title pages will be prepared in manuscript.

| Hour, Date, Place | Summary of Events and Information | Remarks and references to Appendices |
|---|---|---|
| 17.5.15 YPRES | Battalion dug out WEST side of ZILLEBEKE LAKE. Remained to noon the. 3-30PM Orders received for working party of 400 men to work on S. Sect. of VERBRANDENMOLEN ZILLEBEKE line, working parties to return to E. Camp Ouderdom on completion. Remainder of Battalion to move there commencing at 6.30PM. to be relieved in B.13 &B.9. H.Q. & details moved at 6.30P.M. to OUDERDOM. Working parties arrived about 3-30AM. | |
| 18.5.15 E. Camp OUDERDOM | | |
| 19.5.15 E. Camp Ouderdom | Battalion resting in huts. Nothing to report | |

LIEUT. COLONEL
Commanding 1/5th (Rifle) Battn. "The King's" (Lpool. Regt.)
[signature]

Army Form C. 2118.

# WAR DIARY
## or
## INTELLIGENCE SUMMARY

*(Erase heading not required.)*

Instructions regarding War Diaries and Intelligence Summaries are contained in F. S. Regs., Part II. and the Staff Manual respectively. Title pages will be prepared in manuscript.

| Hour, Date, Place | Summary of Events and Information | Remarks and references to Appendices |
|---|---|---|
| E. Camp OUDERDOM 20th May 1915 | Brigade moved up to trenches. Battn. left hunts at 7.15 p.m. and marched via KRUISTRAAT to dug outs on W. side of ETANG de ZILLEBEKE. In Brigade Reserve | |
| W. Side ETANG de ZILLEBEKE 21st May | Casualties to noon 1 O.R. wounded. Whole Bn. employed at night on carrying parties. | |
| 22nd May | Casualties to noon O.R. 1 killed 3 wounded. Carrying parties at night. | |
| 23rd May | Casualties to noon NIL. D Coy's M.G's sent to 1st Norfolks at 6.30 p.m. | |
| 24th May 1.50 a.m. 6. P.M. | Gas was noticed proceeding on our left about MENIN ROAD. Stragglers from various Regiments arrived at W. end of dug outs about 5. a.m. Handed over to Brigade. Not Our Casualties to noon NIL. Gas again felt. Respirators adjusted no ill effect. Carrying parties at night. | |

Commanding ........ Unit.
(*Erase heading*)

Army Form C. 2118.

# WAR DIARY
## or
## INTELLIGENCE SUMMARY.
(Erase heading not required.)

| Place | Date | Hour | Summary of Events and Information | Remarks and references to Appendices |
|---|---|---|---|---|
| ETANG de ZILLEBEKE | 25 May | | Casualties to Noon Nil. Dug outs shelled with 6"Hzy. Explosion in afternoon. Enemy planes at night | |
| | 26 May | | Enemy planes at night | |
| | 27 May | | Casualties to noon O.R. 1 Killed 10 Wounded. Enemy and Turkey Trenches at night. Fall in. | |
| | 28 May | | Casualties to noon O.R. 1 Wounded. Enemy planes at night | |
| | 29 May | | Casualties to noon O.R. 2 Wounded. Enemy planes at night | |
| | 30 May | | Casualties to noon Nil. Enemy planes at night | |
| | 31 May | | Casualties to noon Nil. Enemy planes at night. Casualties to noon O.R. 3 Wounded. Enemy planes at night | Fitzmaurice |

"A" Form.  Army Form
**MESSAGES AND SIGNALS.**  No. of Message_____

| Prefix____ Code____ m. | Words. | Charge. | This message is on a/c of: | Recd. at_____ m. |
| Office of Origin and Service Instructions. | dp. I | | | Date_____ |
| | Sent | | _____Service. | From_____ |
| | At_____ m. | | | |
| | To_____ | | (Signature of "Franking Officer.") | By_____ |
| | By_____ | | | |

TO { 6th Liverpools

| Sender's Number | Day of Month | In reply to Number | AAA |
| BM 841 | 4th | | |

Duke of Wellingtons to relieve Devons Trenches 38 39 40 43 45 and on DUMP tonight AAA Duke of Wellingtons to be at 15th Bde Hd Qrs by companies at half hour intervals commencing at 10 pm where guides from Devons will meet them & take them on to Trenches AAA 14th Bde take over trench No 34 and its supports trench from 15th Bde tonight AAA Norfolks will be relieved in these trenches by East Surreys and will also hand over to E Surreys accomodation in reserve dugouts sufficient for one company AAA 6th Liverpools will be

From
Place
Time

The above may be forwarded as now corrected. (Z)

Censor. Signature of Addressee or person authorised to telegraph in his name

* This line should be erased if not required.

## MESSAGES

relieved tonight and assemble at Liverpools Bn Hd Qrs whence they will be guided to new billeting area under Bn arrangements AAA They will there be in divisional reserve AAA Devons after relief by Duke of Wellingtons will assemble by companies at 15th Bde Hd Qrs where guides will be waiting to lead them back to billets AAA Acknowledge

From 15th Inf Bde
Time 4.5pm

"A" Form.
**MESSAGES AND SIGNALS.** No. of Message_____

Prefix____ Code____ m. Words. Charge. _App III_ This message is on a/c of: Recd. at____ m.
Office of Origin and Service Instructions. Sent Date____
At____ m. ____Service. From____
To____ 
By____ (Signature of "Franking Officer.") By____

TO: O C 6th Liverpools

Sender's Number: BM 878  Day of Month: 5th  In reply to Number: ____  AAA

Three companies of your batt<sup>n</sup> will proceed to Railway Embankment dig outs near 15th Bde Hd Qrs AAA One company will move forward to LARCH plantation behind Hill 60 and report to Colonel SCOTT O.C. CHESHIRES at his Hd Qrs in Railway Cutting

From 15th Bde
Place
Time 11.20 a.m.

"A" Form.  Army Form C. 2121.
## MESSAGES AND SIGNALS.  No. of Message_____

| Prefix____Code____m. | Words. | Charge. | This message is on a/c of: | Recd. at____m. |
| Office of Origin and Service Instructions. | Ap 11 | | | Date____ |
| | Sent At____m. | | D2 Service. | From____ |
| | To | | | By____ |
| | By | | (Signature of "Franking Officer.") | |

TO { 6th Liverpools

| Sender's Number | Day of Month | In reply to Number | AAA |
| BM 862 | 5th | | |

Move up with your batt=
to 15th Bn Sd Qrs
as soon as possible

15th Bn

Time 9.16 a.m

The above may be forwarded as now corrected.  (Z)   WH

Censor.  Signature of Addressee or person authorised to telegraph in his name
* This line should be erased if not required.

**MESSAGES AND SIGNALS.** Army Form C. 2121.

TO: 6th Liverpools

Sender's Number: Bm 900. Day of Month: 5th

The Company of yours which is astride railway near Gayers(?) that has been ordered to push on to Lepot(?) wood and report to O.C. Chelsea(?)

From: 4.10 pm

"A" Form.

## MESSAGES AND SIGNALS.

TO: 6th Lincolns

Sender's Number: B.M. 303
Day of Month: 5

move your remaining company and
Hd Qrs to the south west
end of the ETANG de
la "EKE taking cover in the
pit there

From: 15th Bde.
Time: 2.15 pm

6/8ᵗʰ. MAY. 5ᵗʰ

A Co.   Ordered to dug-outs on Railway Cutting – to report to O.C. 1/22ⁿᵈ.
        12.15 p.m.
        Moved along N side of Railway as far as ZILLEBEKE STA under Shrapnel fire; thence moved across open to LAKE. to to ZILLEBEKE as Railway was open to view from Hill 60
        From ZILLEBEKE the Co. made its way to Dug Outs coming under M.G. fire – having about 20 casualties in reaching H⁴ᵈʳˢ of 1/22ⁿᵈ
        Co. was then ordered to trench 42 to support 1/22ⁿᵈ, 2/25ᵗʰ who were holding 29 & 40. Enemy seemed to have penetrated nearly to 42 A
        Co. held on to pos⁵ where it was joined about 7. p.m by C co who had worked across from the L

        During night pos⁵ was improved – dug outs connected up into a trench
        Held on all 6ᵗʰ – relieved by 50ᵗʰ at 9. p.m.

B Co.   Ordered to ganger's hut in I 28 B: came under fire on reaching ZILLEBEKE Station but pushed on by small rushes. Two platoons reached trench in this way, losing about 20: later on they moved to dug outs in LARCH WOOD, remained there being joined by rest of Co. wh. had halted at ZILLE-BEKE Station.
        Co. remained in support till relieved 11.30 p.m 6ᵗʰ by 9ᵗʰ L.R.

C. Co.  [Gives two maps.]
        Received orders to move about 10.45 & reached H.Q. at RAILWAY ARCH about 12.30 p.m: were ordered to get to ZILLEBEKE, extend across road to Kl. 2 & advance as far as possible, enemy being expected to be working forward down the road.

        Advanced along S of LAKE under fire, enemy being on ridge above 42 A. Some had got as far
        Nos. 10 & 12 firing line, 9 & 11 supports      || forward as Farm X (E of road, marked as "Ruin" on larger map.)
        Firing line deployed. began to push forward coming under heavy fire, making rushes in sections of 10 ; O.C. No 10 killed & losses were severe; N. 12 more fortunate, being W of road
        During this advance enemy evacuated Farm X & some of A co. 1/22ⁿᵈ were seen to occupy trench 42, entering it from R – this masked fire of our men, though a good shot in No. 12 platoon silenced a sniper. forced on the ridge
        Enemy retired from ridge on R or R (according to plan about 3. p.m) but as fire from L front was v. heavy troops dug in & lay low, being then just N of Farm X
        About 7. p.m. No 12 platoon managed to work forward along a shallow valley & joined A co in No. 42 A. An hour later No. 10 reinforced by No 9 were brought forward from E of road & reached 42 A by same route.
        By the time Nos 9,10 & 12 reached 42 A   No 11 was already there, having already apparently worked forward on L, using cover of a hedge to a ruined farm & way between the enemy & Farm X. then made their way across covered by another hedge. Appearance of this platoon on L helped to cause enemy's retreat. [N.B. their fire would not have been masked.]
        Co. wh. had had 2 + 13 K. 1 + 44 W   was relieved about 5.30 p.m 6ᵗʰ

D. Co.  Followed C co keeping W of road: patrols found C co held up about 5.30 p.m D Co then took up pos⁵ to support C Co in case of a hostile advance.   About 1.30 AM 6ᵗʰ D co was recalled to Bttn HQ. as K 3. W. 5

ap VI                    3

A Coy

The Battalion having received orders to proceed from rest camp and report at Brigade Hdqrs 15th Brigade, on arrival at this point A Coy were ordered to make their way to the Davidson' Dug out Railway cutting and obtain orders from the OC Cheshire Regt. The company commander was informed that the enemy having gained the whole line of the 15th Brigade were in possession of Hill 60 trench 45 and probably parts of trench 40. Orders were given that platoon commanders were to bring their platoons at intervals of 5 to 10 minutes on whatever route was chosen by the Coy commander. That the company was to press on at all speed and all costs, not waiting for wounded, and that the destination was the Davidson Dugout where reinforcements were probably urgently required.

The company moved off at about 12·15 pm & started along the N side of the railway line which runs from Ypres past the Brigade (15) Hdqrs to Hill 60. A fairly heavy shrapnel fire was directed on this line but as the effect was very local the company were able to proceed in safety. On arrival of the head of the column at Zillebeke Station the railway line appeared to be more unsafe

4

as shrapnell was bursting in the line and whizz bangs were flying across more frequently, also the above I ring, the line in full view of Hill 60 & also is flanked by trench 45.

The company was halted under shelter of the embankment at Zillebeke Station and rested. No 1 & 2 platoons were then turned about & filed across the open towards the embankment of Zillebeke Lank where they found shelter & were able to make their way under cover to the outskirts of Zillebeke village. No 3 & 4 platoons led by Captain Turner carried out a similar manoeuvre at an interval of some 15 minutes and the whole company reached this spot without casualty.

From this point 1 & 2 platoons made their way by the route originally used by the battalion in marching from and to the Davidson Dug out previous to our capture of Hill 60. After crossing the plank bridge & sheltering from view behind a hedge it became necessary to cross the open & make for the cutting at the point where the gangers hut is situated. For this 200 yards the 2 platoons were subjected to a very heavy machine gun fire and company Sergt Major Beechey was badly wounded, twelve more riflemen were wounded and two killed. Considering that this line was only 400 yds from trench 45 and in view of Knoll 40 and Hill 60 from each of which a heavy fire was directed the casualties do not appear heavy excessive. The two platoons were placed in shelter in the railway cutting and a number of RAMC men were informed that we had left wounded in the field. Later on Capt Turner with No 3 & 4 platoons made his way into Zillebeke village & chose a line more concealed from view of trench 45 but where it was necessary to cross the open it was nearer to the enemy. At this time Lt Stenhouse went out to try and find a safer road of approach and was wounded.

Capt Turner was obliged to go out himself in order to find a safe means of approach and calling for a volunteer to help him Rifleman Hart at once responded and shewed great coolness under heavy fire.

No 3 & 4 platoons suffered about the same casualties as 1 & 2 and finally reported at the Davidson Dug out. On arrival at this place the Headquarters of the 1st Cheshire Regt with written orders from the Brigade to the commanding officer it was found that this officer had most unfortunately just received a mortal wound whilst making his dispositions for an attack. A Coy received orders to proceed to trench 42 A in support of trenches 39 & 40 which were partly held by Cheshires and KOSBs. No information was available of exactly what trenches were held by Germans but Hill 60 & trench 45 and part of 40 were known to be in their possession. Whilst placing the men in different trenches & dugouts and whilst a platoon of the Cheshires were making their way toward 42A

6

Lt Cavanagh was wounded and also one of the
Cshires was hit in what appeared to be absolutely dead
ground just behind the centre of 42 A trenches.
Later on it transpired that these casualties were
inflicted by a party of the enemy who had penetrated
as far as 42 A and down to the edge of the Larch
plantation and no doubt this party were responsible
for the death of the CO of the Cheshires.
Immediately in front of 42 A was a thick belt of
flowering weeds which excluded all field of fire
beyond about 15 yds and it was unfortunate that
it was not brought to the notice of the company
commander before late in the evening that this
party had been observed and had retired to this
cover. Word was passed along the line that the
Devons on our left had been forced to retire and
that a large party of Germans had broken through.
This news was reported to the OC Cheshires and we
had orders to hold on to our position at all costs.
The company therefore had orders to "stand to"
with bayonets fixed and magazines charged.
About 7 pm troops were observed on our left making
their way to our rear and on sending to intercept
and question them they turned out to be "C" Coy
6th Liverpool who had made their way across
country & reinforced our position. The earlier
stages of their advance had been plainly visible
to us. Lt Ronald reported on his arrival that
a small party of the enemy had fired on them

OUDERDOM  ap VII 3
11th May 1915

The Adjutant
 6th Liverpool.

Sir,
On arrival at Brigade HQrs on the morning of 5th May I recieved verbal orders from the OC to proceed with my Company to the trenches dug on both sides of line by Ganger's Hut at Railway Crossing in Square 128 B. I ordered No 5 Platoon to proceed to this position followed by No 7, No 8, No 6 platoons —

No 5 Platoon moved to ZILLEBEKE STATION & came under maxim & rifle fire, extended to the right & advanced in rushes of small parties of about 5 men under an NCO. until they reached trench, they remained there until they recieved further orders to proceed to dugouts in LARCH WOOD just north of DAVIDSON DUGOUT, they arrived there about 6.30. P.M.

This platoon lost 1 killed & 7 wounded on the advance —

No 7 Platoon conformed with the movements of No 5 & occupied the trench, they lost on the day they had in 12 wounded in this advance.

No 6 & 8 Platoon were in support at ZILLEBEKE STATION until they received orders for me to join up with 5 & 7 at LARCHWOOD North of

from the scrub just in front of the trenches with a
machine gun. Mr Ronald who alone knew these support
trenches took out a reconnoitring party but could only find
4 dead bodies. Next morning Mr Ronald again went
out and searched through the scrub and brought back
badges for identification. Mr Ronald also visited the various
trenches and was able to give valuable information both
to the OC Cheshires and an Officer of the West Kent Regt who
was collecting information for carrying out an attack.
During the night of the 5/6th the dug outs were connected
by a trench & the trenches improved. During the 6th nothing
special happened. The trench was shelled by high explosive
shrapnell & whizz bangs and wounded 2 men of "A" and
7 of "C". Early in the morning of the 6th Lance Corpl Hargraves
Rifm Gladwinfield & Burbage reported that five of
our wounded had been left out all night one having
died and that they had moved them to shelter and
remained with them. On sending an officer down to the
cutting he was able to induce the stretcher party to go
out to them and carry them to the dressing station.
A man of "C" Company was lying wounded in a very
exposed position across the Zillebeke Klein Zillebeke Rd
Mr Brownell volunteered to carry water to this man although
the spot was continually shelled and closely covered by a
trench the Germans were holding in the region of 45.
As this man could not be moved except by stretcher there
seemed no object in risking further loss. At 9 pm the
Corps were relieved by the R West Kents and reached the 15th
Brigade Hdqrs without further loss.

B H Wedgwood Capt.
6th K.S.L.I. Regt.

No 2.

DAVIDSON DUGOUT which they did without loss.

I reported myself to O/C CHESHIRES on arrival & remained in support there with my Company until I was relieved by the QUEEN VICTORIA RIFLES at 11.30 P.M on the 6th May.

I received orders to proceed to E Camp OUDERDOM where I arrived with my Company at 6.30 AM on the 7th May.

R Wainwright.
Major
O/C B Company.
8th Liverpool.

Appendix to War Diary Ap. VIII

"C" Coy.    5.5.15.

Captain Brocklehurst.

On the morning of 5.5.15 about 10.45 am the Company which had been bivouacing in a wood near KRUISSTRAAT Chateau since 3.30 AM on the same morning started to return to the H.Q. at the Railway ARCH near ZILLEBEKE.

The morning was warm and the few if any of the men had had breakfast & were tired after their previous 23 days in the trenches.

The RAILWAY ARCH was reached about 12.30 P.M.

Orders were immediately received, in writing, by Captain Brocklehurst "to proceed to ZILLEBEKE VILLAGE by way of the S side of "ZILLEBEKE LAKE and to extend on the far side of the village "on either side of the ZILLEBEKE — KLEIN ZILLEBEKE "road and to push on as far as possible"

Information was also given by the Bgde Major, Capt. Barrett that the enemy were believed to be proceeding down the road towards ZILLEBEKE and that the Coy might expect to come under fire near the E end of the lake.

The advance to ZILLEBEKE was carried out rapidly without difficulty in Indian file & with suitable intervals. At the end of the lake & before reaching the village the fire was fairly hot as the Company was in view of the enemy on the ridge behind 42 A.

Captain Brocklehurst There were No 10 Platoon (Lieut. Wilson) & No 12 Platoon (Lieut. Ronald) had been told off as the firing line — No 9 Platoon (2nd Lieut. Oxenbould) & No 11 Platoon (Lieut. Blackledge) as supports.

Captain Brocklehurst was with the supports.

1.

The ~~ground along the road the~~ firing line platoons were halted under cover in the ruins of ZILLEBEKE & the best approach & way of deployment reconnoitred.

The ground over wh the advance was to be made was quite open & bare with a few old dug outs & shell holes in it. Some of the enemy were observed as far down as the farm house marked x on the sketch map.

They were also seen on the sky line immediately behind 42 A dug outs.

Lieut. Wilson was ordered to take the left of the road & 2nd Lieut Ronald the right.

The firing line platoons were very ably handled by these officers and they deployed out of the village without attracting the notice of the enemy.

A point of two riflemen were left in the village with orders to guide up the Supports & point the direction to them.

The firing line then commenced its advance with great spirit & soon came under a terrific fire from a M.G. & rifles from the ridge behind 42. A and also from M.G.S from the left front.

The men held on with the greatest determination in spite of their losses which in No 10 platoon were heavy. At this point Lieut Wilson was shot dead while leading a rush of a section.

Rushes were made in sections of 10.

No 12 suffered less, apparently receiving less fire from the left front as the ground fell away a little towards the right.

2.

About this time the enemy disappeared from the road near the farm × and some of our men who turned out to be A Coy & some Cheshires were seen to ~~enter~~ enter 42a from the right.

The enemy were on the ridge immediately above 42a & the firing line in its advance dare not ~~return~~ return their fire for fear of hitting or disturbing our own troops.

Lieut. Ronald was able to make use of a good shot in his platoon, L/Cpl Pennington, to put down a conspicuous Sniper & was making arrangements to fire on the enemy's M.G. on the ridge when it was withdrawn together with their infantry there.

A terrific fire was still coming in from the left front & ~~the~~ it appeared futile to advance further especially as the enemy had retired from the road & the ridge & orders were given to dig in & lie low till the light failed.

The men dug themselves in with their intrenching tools & swords & many fine deeds were done in getting the wounded into shell holes & in getting them out of fire altogether as will be found in the other appendices.

About this time Corporal Teague was killed. He was in the first line & was shot in passing a message having raised himself on his elbow. He had acted in the most gallant manner during the advance & took a very active part in leading the men on.

3.                                (Back)

The position of the firing line was just a few yards N of Farm X, the right platoon lying in a patch of beets in wh there were numerous shell holes.

The enemy shelled the whole ground very heavily with whiz bangs and coal boxes throughout the afternoon and any movement at once attracted rifle fire.

About 7. P.M., the light having failed somewhat Lieut. Ronald was ordered to advance by making a movement to the right flank and by way of the shallow valley between the road & the Railway to join A. Coy in 42 a. This was carried out very ably & without any confusion or loss.

About 8. P.M. the remains of No 10 platoon and No. 9 which had lost Lieut Okeulmet wounded were ordered to move across the road & were collected in the shallow valley & led up to 42.a to join A. Coy. Capt. Wedgewood in Command. Men were left with the wounded who could not be removed.

It is impossible to say too much of the conduct of these men who did their utmost to collect & bring in the wounded in a situation of the greatest danger & under a heavy fire. An account of their proceedings will be found in another appendix.

Mention must be made of Sergt Melton whose conduct was most cool. Also Cpl Beaumir & Cpl. Ridge.

The men were excellently in hand at all times & there never was any question of retreat.

4.

After the Coy's arrival in 42.a., Lieut Ronald rendered very valuable service in patrolling the communication trenches between 42a & 39 in which there were thought to be some Germans. He was acquainted with these trenches & was able to make a map & was generally of the greatest assistance. All next day

During the night, the Coy stood to arms in 42 a in company with A. Coy. The position was heavily shelled from time to time & 7 more men were wounded including Sgt Millar by a shell which burst over their dug out.

When No 9, 10 & 12 Platoons arrived in 42.a they found No 11 which had come up on the left under Lieut Blacker. It would seem that the appearance of this platoon on the left contributed to the retirement of the enemy from the road.

Captain Brocklehurst it appeared had been killed on the road leading out of ZILLEBEKE towards the direction of MENIN at the very outset of the operations. He had been conducting a reconnaissance the exact object of which has not been ascertained.

(following the attack) Lieut Ronald at the close of the day went down with a stretcher party to bring in Rifleman Lloyd who was lying wounded in a shell hole & who was discovered by field glasses. He effected this in a brief interval in the shelling & got the man safely to the dressing station in the Ry cutting.

A. & C. Coys were relieved about 8.30 PM on the 6th inst by a Coy of the Royal West Kents. & proceeded to the Ry arch without loss & thence to E camp OUDERDOM (for C Coy)

The Casualties during the two days were:—

15 Killed
45 Wounded
60

J. McKay
Captain C Coy.

Appendix to War Diary

D Company          5th May 1915.

About 1pm I received orders to get into touch with O.C. "E" Company who had proceeded through ZILLEBEKE Village along the KLEIN ZILLEBEKE road with instructions to find out by whom trench 42 was occupied. I moved the Company from Railway Embankment Dugouts along the South side of ZILLEBEKE Lake to the South East corner where the Company halted. Lieut Buckley then dispatched two patrols to endeavour to get into touch with "E" Company. Both patrols returned without getting in touch. Lieut Buckley then proceeded with one platoon having ZILLEBEKE on his left & advanced some 500 yds across the fields on the south side of the KLEIN ZILLEBEKE Road to an old trench & one platoon under Lieut Warburton moved up into ~~Zill Sh~~ ZILLEBEKE. Lieut Buckley having found some of "E" Company wounded proceeded

24

forward with a patrol & found Capt. McKaig on the North side of the Road where he had dug himself in being unable to make further progress owing to the heavy rifle & machine gun fire. At 5.30pm, I received a message from Lieut Buckley reporting that 'C' Coy were held up & were unable to say who was in 42 trench. I reported to Col Davison & at 6 p.m. & received orders to work up in support of 'C' Company & occupy positions to prevent any further advance of the Enemy down the road. This I proceeded to do. At the same time I received orders that the West Kent Regt would attack the Salient at 10pm.

At ~~1.30~~ 1.30 A M on the 6th I received orders to retire to the Railway Dugouts arriving there about 2.30 AM.

Casualties. 3 killed 5 wounded

W.K. Bennet Capt.

N ←

TO KLEIN ZILLEBEKE

60

ZILLEBEKE

TO YPRES

DUMP

VERBRANDE MOLEN

ETANG.

H.Q.

Hill 60.

ZILLEBEKE.

REFERENCE.
McK → Route taken by Capt. McKaig
W. → " " " Lieut Wilson
R. → " " " 2/L Ronald
→Ox→ " " " 2/L Oxenbould
→→→ " " " 2/L Blackledge
ooooo Positions occupied.
Ba. = German Barricade.

15th Bde.
5th Div.

1/6th L I V E R P O O L S.

J U N E

1 9 1 5

Army Form C. 2118.

# WAR DIARY
## or
## INTELLIGENCE SUMMARY.

(Erase heading not required.)

Instructions regarding War Diaries and Intelligence Summaries are contained in F. S. Regs., Part II. and the Staff Manual respectively. Title pages will be prepared in manuscript.

| Place | Date | Hour | Summary of Events and Information | Remarks and references to Appendices |
|---|---|---|---|---|
| | 1st June | | Casualties to noon NIL. Enemy digging trenches at night | |
| | 2nd June | " | Casualties to noon O.R. 1 Wounded. Enemy quiet during night | |
| | 2nd June | " | Casualties to noon NIL. Enemy working during night. A Coy relieved C Coy with 1st Brigade at 9 p.m. | |

1247 W 3299 200,000 (E) 8/14 J.B.C. & A. Forms/C. 2118/11.

Army Form C. 2118.

# WAR DIARY
## or
## INTELLIGENCE SUMMARY
*(Erase heading not required.)*

Instructions regarding War Diaries and Intelligence Summaries are contained in F. S. Regs., Part II. and the Staff Manual respectively. Title pages will be prepared in manuscript.

| Hour, Date, Place | Summary of Events and Information | Remarks and references to Appendices |
|---|---|---|
| E'TANG de ZILLEBEKE | | |
| 4th June | Casualties to noon NIL. Enemy shelling at night | |
| 5th June | As above | |
| 6th June | Casualties O.R. 1 wounded as above | |
| 7th June | Casualties to noon NIL. Enemy shelling at night | |
| 8th June | Casualties to noon O.R. 2 wounded. Enemy shelled in trenches with high explosive 80's dug out very heavy in Enemy trenches at night | |
| 9th June | Casualties to noon O.R. 1 wounded. Enemy shelling trenches at night | |
| 10th June | Casualties to noon NIL. Enemy firing 110 shells in 35 mins was very heavy at night | |
| 11th June | Casualties to noon O.R. 1 wounded Enemy shelled at night | |
| 12th June | Casualties to noon NIL. Enemy shelling trenches at night 2nd Lieuts Bunnell & Mackerton knew to now 2nd Lieutents 8t & Bryant | Henner |

1247  W 3259  200,000  (E)  8/14  J.B.C. & A.  Forms/C. 2118/11.

Army Form C. 2118.

# WAR DIARY
## or
## INTELLIGENCE SUMMARY

*(Erase heading not required.)*

Instructions regarding War Diaries and Intelligence Summaries are contained in F. S. Regs., Part II. and the Staff Manual respectively. Title pages will be prepared in manuscript.

| Hour, Date, Place | Summary of Events and Information | Remarks and references to Appendices |
|---|---|---|
| ETANG de ZILLEBEKE | | |
| 13th June. | Casualties to noon 1 wounded. Carrying parties at noon and night. | |
| 14th June. | Casualties to noon Nil. Working party for 62 found. Carrying parties at night. | |
| 15th June. | Casualties to noon Nil. | |
| 16th June. | Casualties to noon Nil. Carrying parties at night. | H.J. Gunn |

Army Form C. 2118.

# WAR DIARY or INTELLIGENCE SUMMARY

(Erase heading not required.)

Instructions regarding War Diaries and Intelligence Summaries are contained in F. S. Regs., Part II. and the Staff Manual respectively. Title pages will be prepared in manuscript.

| Hour, Date, Place | Summary of Events and Information | Remarks and references to Appendices |
|---|---|---|
| ETANG de ZILLEBEKE 16/6/15 | Casualties to Noon NIL. Carrying parties at night. Heavy cannonading during day away to attack J.5 + 6/S9 on our left in neighbourhood of Hooge Chateau. | |
| " 17/6/15 | Casualties to Noon O.R. 1 Wounded. Carrying parties at night all quiet. | |
| " 18/6/15 | Casualties to Noon O.R. 6 Wounded. Carrying parties at night. | |
| " 19/6/15 | Casualties to Noon O.R. 1 Wounded. Carrying > Working parties at night. | |
| " 20/6/15 | Casualties to Noon Nil. Carrying > Working parties at night. | |
| " 21/6/15 | Casualties to Noon Lieut. F.S.E. BARDSLEY (O.S.H. ORteam) O.R. 1 Wounded. Working + carrying parties at night. | |
| " 22/6/15 | Casualties to Noon O.R. 1 Wounded. (Slightly Wounded at Duty) Orders received for Grenadiers under Lieut Roberdeye to be act at detached Ad June I at 1st Gloster for Bombing at 3/6 an see notes attached. Bombardment of our artillery from 7.30 pm to 8.15 pm. Carrying parties at night. | Ap June I |
| " 23/6/15 | Casualties to Noon O.R. 2 Wounded. 1 slightly wounded at duty. Carrying parties at night. | |
| " 24/6/15 | Casualties to Noon O.R. 1 Wounded. Bn. took over trenches 47, 47 S, 48 Ryfles. Pvt. Jackson 1st Glosters at 11.15 am also brought German Pte Kuphhard found in trench on I.29.6. | Ap June II |

Army Form C. 2118.

# WAR DIARY
## or
## INTELLIGENCE SUMMARY
*(Erase heading not required.)*

Instructions regarding War Diaries and Intelligence Summaries are contained in F. S. Regs., Part II. and the Staff Manual respectively. Title pages will be prepared in manuscript.

| Hour, Date, Place | Summary of Events and Information | Remarks and references to Appendices |
|---|---|---|
| ÉTANG de ZILLEBEKE 24.6.15 | B.C. Coys found Garrisons. Bnys Messenghton assumed of Sector. Kent Guards with Bricks at DAVIDSON DUGOUT in railway cutting. Garrisons as follows: <br> 47 Front 40 men ⎱ B.G. <br> 47 Support 60 " ⎰ <br> 48 Front 35 " ⎱ E.G. <br> Rifle Pits 35 " ⎰ <br> Support Point 20 " <br> 1.2.G. | |
| 25.6.15 | Bn. distributed as above. Carrying parties at night. | Casualties to Noon 1 O.R Killed |
| 26.6.15 | Casualties to Noon O.R. 1 wounded <br> A&D Companies relieved B.C in trenches, handing over at 8.30 p.m. Relief completed at 12 Midnight. All Quiet at night | |
| 27.6.15 | | Casualties to noon 1. O.R wounded. Carrying parties at night J Coys relieving A&D |
| 28.6.15 | Casualties to noon O.R 1 killed 2 wounded B. & C. Companies relieved A&D in trenches. all quiet | |
| 29.6.15 | Casualties to noon O.R 1 wounded. Quiet | |

1247  W 3290  200,000  (E) 8/14  J.B.C. & A.  Forms/C2118/11.

# WAR DIARY

## INTELLIGENCE SUMMARY

*(Erase heading not required.)*

Army Form C. 2118.

| Hour, Date, Place | Summary of Events and Information | Remarks and references to Appendices |
|---|---|---|
| ETANG de ZILLEBEKE. 30/6/15 | A & D Companies relieved B & C. All quiet. Casualties K. n.o.m O.R. 5 wounded. Garrison of trenches as follows:— <br><br> 47 Trench    40 men  } A Coy. <br> 47 Support   60 " <br> 48 Trench    35 " <br> Raft P.its     45 "  } D Coy. <br> Woori I Trpt   30 " | |

To the Adjutant  
6th Bn K.L.R.

ap I/  
23/4/15

Sir,

I have the honour to report the following facts with regard to last night's bombing demonstration.

The Grenadiers of the 6th Liverpool Regt were placed at the disposal of the C.O. 1st Cheshires and in accordance with orders received from him I paraded the battalion grenadiers at 6pm. They were split up into small parties to avoid artillery observation and followed the route NE side of ZILLEBEKE LAKE to 51 Support, where they were met by C.O. 1st Cheshires who gave me his orders. These were to make no advance but to cause as much inconvenience as possible to the enemy by bombing 46 Support from the communication trench from 47 to 46. This was done over the barricade.

Time being short, as many bombs as possible were prepared and I went to the position indicated with twenty men and two lance corpls

On arrival at the spot I found that it was impossible to use the heavy types of hand grenades with which I was provided to any great effect as the German trench (the old 46 support trench) was from 35 to 40 yards away. The trench was cleared for about 50 yds each side of the point from which the grenades were to be thrown and brought the throwers up in parties of four. About 25 hand grenades were thrown and five rifle grenades were also fired. Of the hand grenades one which reached the enemies' trench failed to explode and was returned by the German without effect. Of the remaining hand grenades I should judge about ten to have been wholly or partially effective, the rest falling short. Of the rifle grenades one fell in the vicinity, though slightly beyond the enemy's trench the other two being difficult to observe owing to the enemy's snipers becoming active. None of the German bodies, of which about

**"A" Form.**     Army Form C. 2121.

## MESSAGES AND SIGNALS.  No. of Message_____

| Prefix___ Code___ m/ | Words | Charge | This message is on a/c of | Recd. at_____ m. |
|---|---|---|---|---|
| Office of Origin and Service Instructions | | | Service | Date_____ |
| | Sent At___ m. To___ By___ | | (Signature of "Franking Officer.") | From_____ By_____ |

TO { 6th Liverpools

| Sender's Number. | Day of Month. | In reply to Number | AAA |
|---|---|---|---|
| BM 581 | 23. | | |

6th Liverpools will take over trenches 47, 47S
48 and rifle pits tomorrow night AAA Cheshire
Coy on relief will withdraw to dug outs along
ZILLEBEKE Lake AAA Garrison of 47S now
formed by Dorsets will withdraw on relief
to 42 AAA Arrangements regarding relief
will be fixed by Battalion Commanders
concerned AAA New sector thus formed
will be under Command of O.C. 6th Liverpools

A H Ransome Capt
Bde Major

From 15th Inf Bde
Place
Time 6 55 pm

ten to fifteen were thrown, failed to reach our bombing point, the only casualty being one very slight wound on the arm caused by a German bomb which fell near the front parapet.

The party remained in the trench till 11:30 pm when, as nothing further came, we left and returned to billets at ZILLEBEKE LAKE at 12:15 a.m. the 23rd without further casualties.

I have the honour to be
Sir,
Y'r obedient Servant
G Glyn Blackledge 2Lt
O C Grenadiers

5th Division

15th Infantry Bde

1/6 Liverpools

July To December

1915

To 165 Bde
55 DIV

15th Bde.
5th Div.

1/6th LIVERPOOLS.

JULY

1915

On His Majesty's Service.

# CONFIDENTIAL

War Diary

of

1/8th (Rifle) Battn. "The Kings"
(Lpool Regt.)

From 1st July 1915
to 31st July 1915

# WAR DIARY or INTELLIGENCE SUMMARY

Army Form C. 2118.

Instructions regarding War Diaries and Intelligence Summaries are contained in F.S. Regs., Part II. and the Staff Manual respectively. Title pages will be prepared in manuscript.

(Erase heading not required.)

| Hour, Date, Place | Summary of Events and Information | Remarks and references to Appendices |
|---|---|---|
| ETANG de ZILLEBEKE 1/7/15 | Work done during night on building a parados to 46 T S. Some bombs thrown by enemy in old 46 T & 47 T. All bombs shot. Two grenades thrown from our Grenadiers at 46 T. One bust in Trench. Enemy went away after the Casualties to men. Officers Capt. by G H Teall slightly wounded (Not Duty) Other Ranks 1 Killed. 1 Wounded | |
| 2/7/15 | Some Fire still heard near ZILLEBEKE DUG OUTS on enemy. Enemy very methodical for some hours + 10 P.M. Casualties to noon O.R. 3 Wounded. B. C. Coy relieved A & D Coys in trenches about night 2nd Lieut Brownell went out from 47 T and inspected to within about 15 yards of supposed German left running from old 46 T Lunnates 47 S. He concealed every loophole and closes it. It was and one closed 12 leaves. | |

1247 W.3299 200,000 (E) 8/14 J.P.C. & A. Forms/C. 2118/11.

# WAR DIARY or INTELLIGENCE SUMMARY

Army Form C. 2118.

(Erase heading not required.)

Instructions regarding War Diaries and Intelligence Summaries are contained in F. S. Regs., Part II. and the Staff Manual respectively. Title pages will be prepared in manuscript.

| Hour, Date, Place | Summary of Events and Information | Remarks and references to Appendices |
|---|---|---|
| ETANG de ZILLEBEKE 3/7/15 | Casualties to Noon O.R. 1 wounded. Report to Bde on minor happened on 4/5 Transport part of the trench entirely among the dugouts | |
| 4/7/15 | Casualties to Noon NIL A & D Coys relieved B.C. in trenches at night | |
| 5/7/15 | Casualties to Noon NIL All quiet | |
| 6/7/15 | Casualties to Noon O.R. 3 Wounded B.C. Coys relieved A & D Coys in trenches at night | |
| 7/7/15 | Casualties to Noon O.R. 2 Wounded | |
| 8/8/15 | Casualties to Noon NIL Bays on trenches relieved. L.1 Shropshires at Brigade reserve complete at 1.15 p.m. Bn less 4 Coy intact reserve at ZILLEBEKE. Dug outs occupied to Huts at R.E. HINGE ST. | |
| 9/7/15 | In Huts at PERIN R & REST ST. ① Say nearly to Infidel accompt as evening party the wooden flue (?) | |
| 10/8/15 | As above | |
| 11/8/15 | As above | |

# WAR DIARY or INTELLIGENCE SUMMARY

*(Erase heading not required.)*

Army Form C. 2118.

| Hour, Date, Place | Summary of Events and Information | Remarks and references to Appendices |
|---|---|---|
| REMINGHELST 12/7/15 | Hd Qrs & B. C Coys at REMINGHELST. A Coy in dug outs on ZILLEBEKE LANE north//Rhodders. D Coy with 1st Norfolks in support dug outs in wood near Perfect Hedges. Orders recd that Bat should be relieved by 1/8 Mx Regt. Batt on night of 12/13 & 13/14. Batt to move to BOESCHEPE on 13/7/15. | |
| " 13. | Orders for move to BOESCHEPE cancelled. A + D Companies joined remainder of Battalion at REMINGHELST | |
| " 14. | at REMINGHELST | |
| " 15. | " Lieut Oliver & 2nd Lt Kruger arrived | |
| " 16. | " from England | |
| " 17. | Battalion moves in the evening. A + C Coys to a wood near DICKEBUSCH, B + D Coys to woods round ROSENDAHL CHATEAU Accoutrements, dug outs + bivouacs were much and damp dug outs. Took over from the 1st Cheshire Regt. | |

Army Form C. 2118.

# WAR DIARY
## or
## INTELLIGENCE SUMMARY
*(Erase heading not required.)*

Instructions regarding War Diaries and Intelligence Summaries are contained in F. S. Regs., Part II. and the Staff Manual respectively. Title pages will be prepared in manuscript.

| Hour, Date, Place | | Summary of Events and Information | Remarks and references to Appendices |
|---|---|---|---|
| DIEKEBUSCH + ROSENDAHL | 18.7.15 | Carrying parties from B & D Coys in the morning & afternoon. Whole Battalion on carrying parties at night. No casualties. | |
| | 19. | Battalion moves back to ROSENHILL REST CAMP near REMINGHELST after dusk. | |
| ROSENHILL | 20. | At ROSENHILL CAMP. | |
| ABEELE | 21. | Battalion moves with the 152 Brigade at night westward through BOESCHEPE to billets in farms between ABEELE and GODESWAERVELDE. | |
| | 22 | Draft of 10 men (each returned from ROUEN) and a 2nd Lieut. Burton (from England) s/o Rumport) arrive at POPERINGHE and join Battalion in its passage through REMINGHEIST. Distance of march about 9 miles. Billets comfortable. In billets near ABEELE. | |
| | 23 | At some place. An inspection of the 15th Inf. Bgde. Buttalion was left the 2 Army, was held at Brigade Headquarters by Corps Army Commander, General Plumer. Strength 9 Hutton too prirate 24 officers 580 other ranks | |

1247 W 3299 200,000 (E) 8/14 J.B.C. & A. Forms/C. 2118/11.

**Army Form C. 2118.**

# WAR DIARY
## or
## INTELLIGENCE SUMMARY
*(Erase heading not required.)*

Instructions regarding War Diaries and Intelligence Summaries are contained in F.S. Regs., Part II. and the Staff Manual respectively. Title pages will be prepared in manuscript.

| Hour, Date, Place | Summary of Events and Information | Remarks and references to Appendices |
|---|---|---|
| GODEWAERSVELDE 24.7.15 25.7.15 26.7.15 27.7.15 28.7.15 | Battn in Billets. nothing to report | |
| 29.7.15 | Maj Harman, Lieutenants & 578 &Os on Fatigue party. Left by train from GODEWAERSVELDE Stn at 14.45 o'clock | |
| 30.7.15 | The Battn, strength 27 Officers 615 Other ranks, 74 Horses & Mules, 23 Vehicles, 9 Bicycles entrained at GODEWAERSVELDE Station, left there at 10.30 o'clock. Route via CAESTRE, HAZEBROUCK CALAIS, ABBEVILLE AMIENS to CORBIE arriving there 23.40 o'clock | |
| LAHOUSSOYE 31.7.15 | Detrained there and marched to LAHOUSSOYE. Army constructed of guards from fatigue party Battn billeted there. Report sent to E. Adamson that Batram arm'l arm completed at 3.15 o'clock am. Sewn Inhabs had d.I at busy Sends On reserve in Billets | |

15th Bde.
5th Div.

1/6th LIVERPOOLS

AUGUST

1915

On His Majesty's Service.

Confidential.

War Diary of

1/6th (Rifle) Battn. "The King's" Liverpool Regiment.

From 1st August 1915 to 31st August 1915.

Army Form C. 2118

# WAR DIARY
or
## INTELLIGENCE SUMMARY
(Erase heading not required.)

Instructions regarding War Diaries and Intelligence Summaries are contained in F.S. Regs, Part II. and the Staff Manual respectively. Title pages will be prepared in manuscript.

| Hour, Date, Place | | Summary of Events and Information | Remarks and references to Appendices |
|---|---|---|---|
| LAHOUSSOYE | 1/8/15 | Battn billeted nothing to report | |
| " | 2/8/15 | " | |
| " | 3/8/15 | Battn marched at 6.30 a.m. and proceeded to DERNANCOURT. Settled in Billets at 10 a.m | |
| DERNANCOURT | 4/8/15 | Sr killed at DERNANCOURT | |
| | | Its Hons Lieut Col H Donovan to Hospital on account of horse accident on march. He stays however Brign General assumed command | |
| | 5/8/15 | As above nothing to report | |
| | 6/8/15 | The Battn less B Sy proceeded to MÉAULTE at 8 p.m. and moved into billets here. B Sy proceeded to Plateau M from transfer and came under orders of that Battn. | |
| MEAULTE | 7/8/15 | 2nd Lieut Buckley and 2 No platoon C Sy proceeded at 5.30 a.m. to Point 91 by motor transport for fatigues carried to 12 a Battery. Battn on fatigues. Nothing to report. | |
| | 8/8/15 | Casualties Nil Nothing very strong. | |

Army Form C. 2118

# WAR DIARY
or
## INTELLIGENCE SUMMARY

*(Erase heading not required.)*

Instructions regarding War Diaries and Intelligence Summaries are contained in F. S. Regs., Part II. and the Staff Manual respectively. Title pages will be prepared in manuscript.

| Hour, Date, Place | Summary of Events and Information | Remarks and references to Appendices |
|---|---|---|
| MEAULTE. 8/8/15 (contd.) | Strength of 116 O. Ranks arrived from England | |
| " 9/8/15 | Batln. in billets as above. Meaulte MK. Working party of 100 men for NORFOLKS always. | |
| " 10/8/15 | As about. Trenches wired C. Sy relieve B. Sy on C¹ Sector at night and came under orders of L. Smith. Heavy Turkish fire at night. | |
| " 11/8/15 | As above. Meaulte MK. Heavy Turkish fire at night | |
| " 12/8/15 | As above. Meaulte MK. Shortly Turkish men attempted to take up entrenchment of Road towards Sant. Cam ..... I arrived | |
| " 13/8/15 | As above Meaulte MK | |
| " 14/8/15 | As above Meaulte MK. A Coy relieves C Coy next Donald on sector C1. D Coy proceeds to Bedford HQ. concentrates orders of O.C. Bedfords | |

# WAR DIARY or INTELLIGENCE SUMMARY

Army Form C. 2118

*(Erase heading not required.)*

Instructions regarding War Diaries and Intelligence Summaries are contained in F. S. Regs., Part II. and the Staff Manual respectively. Title pages will be prepared in manuscript.

| Hour, Date, Place | Summary of Events and Information | Remarks and references to Appendices |
|---|---|---|
| MEAULTE 15/6/15 | As above Casualties NIL | |
| 16/6/15 | As above Casualties NIL | |
| 17/8/15 | do | |
| 18/8/15 | Had quarters moved at 8p.m to stay out near Bt 107. C By moved at same hour to Morlancourt and came under their orders. Casualties NIL | |
| 19/8/15 | As above. B By from 107 stay out stood to By in reserve C 1 inch statue Casualties NIL | |
| 20/8/15 | As above Casualties NIL | |
| 21/8/15 | Casualties NIL. Had quarters moved at 9 p.m from 107 stay out to MEAULTE C By from sector C3 were relieved of By in Morlets and D By from sector C2 were relieved of By in Begious and have motored to MEAULTE all night. Transport to Mr Muldoons moved at 9 p.m. from DERNANCOURT to MORLANCOURT. | MM |

Army Form C. 2118.

# WAR DIARY or INTELLIGENCE SUMMARY

(Erase heading not required.)

Instructions regarding War Diaries and Intelligence Summaries are contained in F. S. Regs., Part II. and the Staff Manual respectively. Title pages will be prepared in manuscript.

| Hour, Date, Place | Summary of Events and Information | Remarks and references to Appendices |
|---|---|---|
| MEAULTE 22/8/15 | Bn distributed as follows Hd Qrs & C & D Coys at MEAULTE A Coy at 107 dug outs B Coy at 71 dug outs Casualties Nil M. Guns in Sectors C.2 & C.3 were relieved at 11.50 a.m. by M. Guns of 8 Royal Sussex (Pioneers) | |
| 23/8/15 | Head Qrs & C & D Coys marched at 7.45 p.m. from MEAULTE to MORLANCOURT arriving there at 8.40 p.m. and went into Billets there. A & D Coys moved from 71 & 107 dug outs & 71 dug outs on relief of 7 "Buffs" at 11.15 p.m. and marched to MORLANCOURT arriving 1.0 a.m. Machine Guns from C.1 sector were relieved by M.G. of 8 R.W.K. (Royal West Kents) at 11 p.m. and marched to MORLANCOURT arriving at 2 p.m. (Casualties Nil) | |
| MORLANCOURT 24/8/15 | | |
| " 25/8/15 | Battn at MORLANCOURT nothing to report | |

**WAR DIARY** or **INTELLIGENCE SUMMARY**

*(Erase heading not required.)*

Army Form C. 2118.

| Hour, Date, Place | Summary of Events and Information | Remarks and references to Appendices |
|---|---|---|
| MORLANCOURT 26.8.15 | Battln. in Billets nothing to report. B.O's two fog. Therm. meters proposed to themselves to inspect these to be taken over of Buttln. | |
| 27.8.15 | As along nothing to report. Working party of 375 O.R. found for R.E. Coy to Love | |
| 28.8.15 | As above nothing to report. Working Party as before | |
| 29.8.15 | As above nothing to report | |
| 30.8.15 | As above nothing to report. Working Party of 300. Other ranks found | |
| 31.8.15 | As above nothing to report | |

Instructions regarding War Diaries and Intelligence Summaries are contained in F. S. Regs., Part II. and the Staff Manual respectively. Title pages will be prepared in manuscript.

15th Bde.
5th Div.

1/6th LIVERPOOLS

SEPTEMBER

1915

On His Majesty's Service.

Confidential

War Diary
of
1/10 (Rifle) Battn. The Kings Liverpool Regt.

from.
to.

1st Sept 1915.
30 Sept 1915.

Army Form C. 2118.

# WAR DIARY or INTELLIGENCE SUMMARY

(Erase heading not required.)

Instructions regarding War Diaries and Intelligence Summaries are contained in F.S. Regs., Part II. and the Staff Manual respectively. Title pages will be prepared in manuscript.

| Hour, Date, Place | Summary of Events and Information | Remarks and references to Appendices |
|---|---|---|
| MORLANCOURT 1/9/15 | The Battn moved to SUZANNE. Marched at 9 p.m. | |
| SUZANNE 2/9/15 | Major Campbell started 1.15 p.m. to COO H.Q. 4th Bn. 3 motor guns attd to B. Bn. billeted A 2 Scots.<br>The Battn relieved the 1/5th Cheshires on Sects. A.I.<br>East Tower 1/5 Cheshires C Coy relf SUZANNE at 3.30 am.<br>Proceeded to VAUX to relieve see below relief lasted on the morning of 1/9.<br>The Battn had two platoons C Coy moved at 7.00 am.<br>Artillery were as follows:<br>B. Coy under Capt Murray the BOIS de VAUX & the communication trench W.E of SUZANNE<br>Adjgt & remainder of Battn less 3 machine guns see SUZANNE CARREFOUR ECLUSIER Rd.<br>D Coy under Subaltern Buckley was supplied at ECLUSIER. the remainder of the Battn proceeded to VAUX.<br>Relief completed & reported to Brigade by W/T at 10.35 p.m.<br>Distribution of Battn.<br>DRAGONS<br>D. Coy Trenches Pools 1–3. between ECLUSIER & ROYAL<br>B. Coy Trenches 4–6 on BOIS du VAUX<br>C. Coy Trenches, Listening Posts 7–9 in VAUX & Edge of Wood<br>Head Quarters in VAUX<br>1 M Gm BOIS du VAUX in the Wood Saw on VAUX<br>Relief of 1/5 Cheshires (Lieut Col R.A. S.R.) removed to Batn Reserve until new Lent brought | |

# WAR DIARY or INTELLIGENCE SUMMARY

(Erase heading not required.)

Army Form C. 2118.

Instructions regarding War Diaries and Intelligence Summaries are contained in F. S. Regs., Part II. and the Staff Manual respectively. Title pages will be prepared in manuscript.

| Hour, Date, Place | Summary of Events and Information | Remarks and references to Appendices |
|---|---|---|
| VAUX 3/9/15 | Situation report at 5 a.m. All quiet. Patrols during night found no sign of hostile patrols. Casualties Lance N/L. | |
| | Situation report at 5 p.m. all quiet during day. No infantry fire seen. Patrol under 2/Lt Barnes & 1/Lieut… reconnoitred T.R. Barnes & 1/Lieut… in conjunction went out at 10 a.m. through the trench to FRISE returning via ECCUSIERS at 1.15 a.m. No enemy patrols encountered. All quiet during night. Very heavy rain. Patrol went out from 7.45 p.m. – 10 p.m. No hostile patrols encountered. | |
| 4/9/15 | Situation report at 5 a.m. all quiet. Patrols in evening found no signs of enemy. Casualties Nil. | |
| 5/9/15 | Situation report at morning and evening all good. Patrols found no signs of enemy. Casualty 1 O.R. killed accidentally through his own rifle discharging. Went down cellar to hide revolver from men. when the rifle went off | |

Army Form C. 2118.

# WAR DIARY
## INTELLIGENCE SUMMARY
*(Erase heading not required.)*

Instructions regarding War Diaries and Intelligence Summaries are contained in F.S. Regs., Part II. and the Staff Manual respectively. Title pages will be prepared in manuscript.

| Hour, Date, Place | Summary of Events and Information | Remarks and references to Appendices |
|---|---|---|
| VAUX Sedan A1 6.9.15 | Relieving reports moving and moving all quiet. Patrols found no trace of enemy. Were continued on terrain, addresses. Distribution of garrisons as follows: Trench 1, 2, 3 D.Sy 5 Officers 113 Other Ranks. Trenches 4, 5, 6 B.Sy 5 Officers 124 Other Ranks. Trenches 7, 8, 9 { C.Sy 4 Officers 195 Other Ranks { A 25 Other Ranks | |
| 7.9.15 | Patrol sent 1 Officer and 28 Other Ranks Grenadiers in VAUX 1 Officer 10 Other Ranks. Read Gas in VAUX. 9.45 A6B. (3rd Other Ranks Peter Power Rumbold) 9. reces in VAUX VILLAGE 3 Officers H.Q. 2 Officers 81 Other Ranks. Casualties Nil. | |
| 8.9.15 | Batln as above all quiet. Casualties 1 O. Ra wounded. nothing to report | |
| | Batln as above all quiet Casualties nil. and German aeroplane shelled. | |
| | | |
| 9.9.15 9pm | All quiet. Regiment Nil. Batln relieved on Relief of Dutch 70.5 and returning from Essarts | |

Army Form C. 2118.

# WAR DIARY
## or
## INTELLIGENCE SUMMARY

(Erase heading not required.)

Instructions regarding War Diaries and Intelligence Summaries are contained in F. S. Regs., Part II. and the Staff Manual respectively. Title pages will be prepared in manuscript.

| Hour, Date, Place | Summary of Events and Information | Remarks and references to Appendices |
|---|---|---|
| SUZANNE 10.9.15 | Pouring rain in afternoon. Relay race which was reported to Brigade at 8.30 p.m. Batn. marched from to Billets in SUZANNE | |
| 11/9/15 | Batn. at SUZANNE. Town Guard 1 Officer 40 other ranks found. Batn. as above. Following working parties found:- 100 O.R. for work on intermediate line. 40 O.R. for work on Quarry BRAY-CAPPY ROAD 50 O.R. for work under R.E. at 8 am & 2 pm 150 O.R. for work at BRONFAY farm. | |
| 12/9/15 | Batn. as above. Major P.J. Harrison admitted to Hospital sick Captain G.H. Teale assumes Command of the Batn. Following working parties found:- 40 O.R. as above 100 O.R. for work under Brigade Signalling Officer. | |
| 13/9/15 | Batn. as above. Following working parties found:- 100 O.R. for work under Brigade Signalling Officer 100 O.R. " " at BRONFAY. | |
| 14/9/15 | Batn. as above. Batn. proceeded by Companies to BRAY for baths. 2 parties each of 210.R. for work at BRAY under R.E. | |

G.H.T.

**WAR DIARY** or **INTELLIGENCE SUMMARY**

*(Erase heading not required.)*

Army Form C. 2118.

Instructions regarding War Diaries and Intelligence Summaries are contained in F. S. Regs., Part II. and the Staff Manual respectively. Title pages will be prepared in manuscript.

| Hour, Date, Place | Summary of Events and Information | Remarks and references to Appendices |
|---|---|---|
| SUZANNE 15/9/15 | Baths at SUZANNE. Working parties of 3 Officers & 280 O.R. provided. Bomb proof Shelters for Baths commenced | |
| " 16/9/15 | Baths as above. Working parties of 3 Officers & 200 O.R. provided. Bomb proof Shelters continued | |
| " 17/9/15 | Baths as above. Working parties of 4 Officers & 280 O.R. provided. Bomb proving Shelters continued | |
| " 18/9/15 | Baths as above. Working parties of 4 Officers & 242 O.R. provided. Bomb proof Shelters continued | |
| " 19/9/15 | Baths as above. Working parties of 5 Officers & 245 O.R. provided | |
| " 20/9/15 | Baths as above. Working parties of 4 Officers & 292 O.R. provided. Lieut. V.G. Hatch & 7 Sr. N.C.O.s returned from 15th Bn. Kings & Fort Regt attached to 1st East Lancs for 7 days for instruction in Trench duties. Bomb proof Shelters continued | |
| " 21/9/15 | Baths as above. Town guard of 1 Officer & 110 O.R. found for 6 A.C.s on 10th Sept relieved by number party of 3 Company. Working parties of 3 Officers & 290 O.R. provided | QRB |

**Army Form C. 2118.**

# WAR DIARY
## or
## INTELLIGENCE SUMMARY
*(Erase heading not required.)*

Instructions regarding War Diaries and Intelligence Summaries are contained in F.S. Regs., Part II. and the Staff Manual respectively. Title pages will be prepared in manuscript.

| Hour, Date, Place | Summary of Events and Information | Remarks and references to Appendices |
|---|---|---|
| SUZANNE 22/9/15 | The Battn relieved the 1/5th Cheshires in Sector A1.  Relieving left SUZANNE WOOD DUCK POST park 2&2. 3pm to take over lealning posts in front by day. D Company under Lt Gordon left SUZANNE for ECLUSIER at 6pm. Lt Phillips D Company & duty post left SUZANNE at 7pm 1st Relieve. B Company under Capt Beatty left SUZANNE for BOIS DE VAUX or 6pm marching by detorm via farm French N.E. of SUZANNE. A & C Companies & Head Quarters left SUZANNE for VAUX at 6.15 pm marching via ECLUSIER. Relief Completed reported to Brigade H.Q. 2nd at 9.15 pm. Distribution of Batn:- D Coy Trenches & posts 1-3 between ECLUSIER & ROYAL DRAGONS. B Coy Trenches 4-6 in BOIS DE VAUX. C Coy Trenches & Redoubt PO6.7-9 in VAUX redge & moat. A Coy in reserve at VAUX. HdQrs in VAUX. | PCGB |

Army Form C. 2118.

# WAR DIARY
## or
## INTELLIGENCE SUMMARY

(Erase heading not required.)

Instructions regarding War Diaries and Intelligence Summaries are contained in F. S. Regs., Part II. and the Staff Manual respectively. Title pages will be prepared in manuscript.

| Hour, Date, Place | Summary of Events and Information | Remarks and references to Appendices |
|---|---|---|
| VAUX 22/9/15 | 1 M.G in BOIS de VAUX on high ground over VAUX. Lt Harris & 2/Lt Cooper return from East Survey to Enemy wire Baln. | |
| VAUX 23/9/15 | Situation Report at 5 am All quiet. Patrols during night found no signs of hostile patrols. Casualties to noon NIL. Situation Report at 5 pm All quiet during day. Patrol under 2/Lt Greenhalgh went out at 11am through the Marsh to CURLU returning at 1.30pm no hostile patrols encountered. 2/Lt Dundas patrol went out at 3 P.M. Reconnoitred road from 9.30 to 11pm no hostile patrols encountered. All Quiet during night. Heavy rain. | |
| VAUX 24/9/15 | Situation Report at 5am. All Quiet. Patrols during night encountered no enemy patrols. Casualties to noon NIL. Situation Report at 5pm All quiet during day. Patrols went out at 2.30pm returning at 5pm. 6pm to 8pm. 10pm at 6pm returning at 8pm. no hostile patrols encountered. All Quiet during night. Weather dull & showery. | P.C.A.B. |

**Army Form C. 2118.**

# WAR DIARY
## or
## INTELLIGENCE SUMMARY
(Erase heading not required.)

Instructions regarding War Diaries and Intelligence Summaries are contained in F. S. Regs., Part II. and the Staff Manual respectively. Title pages will be prepared in manuscript.

| Hour, Date, Place | Summary of Events and Information | Remarks and references to Appendices |
|---|---|---|
| VAUX 26th September 1915 | Situation Report at 5 a.m. All Quiet. Patrols during night encountered no hostile patrols. Casualties to noon NIL. About 2.30 pm 2/Lieut M.L. GREENHALGH and nine other ranks went out to patrol the marsh. They proceeded via 1st Plantation, 2nd Wood, 2nd Plantation to 4th wood which is near CURLU. Here the point was fired on from the centre of the wood. The Patrol extended and lay down but did not reply owing to the difire as the point was still inside. And owing to the density of the undergrowth the enemy could not be seen. After about 5 minutes the enemy started to advance when a brisk fire was opened on them & they retired to their original position. The Point then fell back on to our ambush. Here they found that 2/Lieut GREENHALGH the Scout Sergeant, one Lance Cpl & rifleman were missing. Shortly afterwards Cpl BLACKLEDGE arrived with reinforcements immediately pushed forward to No 4 WOOD where he found 2/LIEUT. GREENHALGH dying & the dead bodies of the Sergeant & rifleman. The body of the L/Cpl could not be | V.B. |

Army Form C. 2118.

# WAR DIARY
## or
## INTELLIGENCE SUMMARY

(Erase heading not required.)

Instructions regarding War Diaries and Intelligence Summaries are contained in F. S. Regs., Part II. and the Staff Manual respectively. Title pages will be prepared in manuscript.

| Hour, Date, Place | Summary of Events and Information | Remarks and references to Appendices |
|---|---|---|
| VAUX 25th Sept 1915 | Found. The enemy left behind a quantity of material. Waterproof sheets &c. Lt. BLACKLEDGE withdrew his men about 6.30 pm bringing in the 3 bodies. The strength of the enemy appeared to be about 30 men. All Quiet during the night. | |
| " 26th Sept 1915 | Situation Report at 5 a.m. all quiet Casualties to noon 1 Officer & 2 O.R. killed, 1 O.R. missing Relieved wounded 1 Prisoner officer. Situation report at 5 p.m. all quiet. | |
| " 27th September 1915 | Situation Report at 5 a.m. all quiet. 60 men under Lieuts Blackledge & Warburton formed an Ambush at dawn - Lt Warburton withdrew with 30 men at 1.70 a.m. Casualties 16 noon NIL. Ambush relieved 5 pm. Situation Report 5 pm. quiet day. All quiet during night. Weather cold. wet. | |
| " 28th September 1915 | Situation Report at 5 a.m. All quiet. Casualties to noon NIL. Situation Report at 5 pm all quiet. Ambush sent out no signs of enemy. | W.G.B |

Army Form C. 2118.

# WAR DIARY
## or
## INTELLIGENCE SUMMARY
(Erase heading not required.)

Instructions regarding War Diaries and Intelligence Summaries are contained in F.S. Regs., Part II. and the Staff Manual respectively. Title pages will be prepared in manuscript.

| Hour, Date, Place | Summary of Events and Information | Remarks and references to Appendices |
|---|---|---|
| VAUX 29th Sept/15 | Situation Report at 5pm All Quiet. Combusch withdrew at 5.30 a.m. Casualties to noon Nil. Situation Report at 5pm All Quiet. All quiet during night. Weather cold & windy. | |
| VAUX 30th Sept 1915 | Situation Report at 8 a.m. All Quiet. Casualties to noon Nil. At 2 p.m. a party of 3 men crept out. Bleenten went out onto the main T about 4 p.m. Enemy patrol in 4th trench. Brisk fighting ensued in which we lost one O.R. killed & one O.R. wounded. From an examination rifle loved it was evident at least two Germans had been hit, one of them probably killed. Outpost withdrew about 5.45pm bringing in two German helmets of 12 Bavarian Regt, 2 German rifles & other clothes. Elsewhere in the Sector all was Quiet. | DCalb |

15th Bde.
5th Div.

1/6th LIVERPOOLS

OCTOBER

1 9 1 5

On His Majesty's Service.

"Confidential"

War Diary

of

1/6 (Rifle) Batn the Kings Liverpool Regt

From 1st October 1915    To 31st October 1915

Army Form C. 2118.

# WAR DIARY
## or
## INTELLIGENCE SUMMARY

(Erase heading not required.)

Instructions regarding War Diaries and Intelligence Summaries are contained in F. S. Regs., Part II. and the Staff Manual respectively. Title pages will be prepared in manuscript.

| Hour, Date, Place | Summary of Events and Information | Remarks and references to Appendices |
|---|---|---|
| VAUX 1st October 1915 | Situation Report 5 a.m all Quiet<br>Casualties to Noon NIL<br>Situation Report 5 p.m. all Quiet. Quiet throughout night | |
| " 2nd " " | Situation Report 5 a.m all quiet<br>Casualties to Noon NIL<br>Situation Report 5 p.m. all Quiet. Quiet throughout night | |
| " 3rd " " | Situation Report 5 a.m. all Quiet<br>Casualties to NOON NIL<br>Situation Report 5 p.m. all Quiet. Quiet throughout night. | |
| " 4th " " | Situation Report 5 a.m all Quiet<br>Casualties to NOON NIL<br>Situation Report 5 p.m all Quiet | |
| " 5th " " | Situation Report 5 a.m. all Quiet<br>Casualties to NOON NIL<br>Situation Report 5 p.m. all Quiet. Ambush which had been continuously laid in 4th Ward since the 2nd withdrawn at 6 p.m. as there were no signs of the enemy. | J.D. |
| " 6th " | All Quiet to Situation Report 6 a.m. all Quiet<br>Casualties to Noon NIL<br>Strong Patrol under Lt BLACKLEDGE with Mr Watenton Mr. Adams made thorough reconnaissance of approaches into woods from CURLU<br>No enemy encountered.<br>Situation Report 5 p.m. all Quiet | |

1247 W 3299 200,000 (E) 8/14 J.B.C. & A. Forms/C. 2118/11.

Army Form C. 2118.

# WAR DIARY or INTELLIGENCE SUMMARY

(Erase heading not required.)

Instructions regarding War Diaries and Intelligence Summaries are contained in F. S. Regs., Part II. and the Staff Manual respectively. Title pages will be prepared in manuscript.

| Hour, Date, Place | Summary of Events and Information | Remarks and references to Appendices |
|---|---|---|
| VAUX 7th October 1915 | Situation Report 5 a.m. all quiet. Patrols on march encounter no enemy patrols. Casualties to noon NIL Situation Report 5 p.m. all quiet. | |
| " 8th October 1915 | Situation Report 5 a.m. all quiet. Patrols on march proceed to FARGNY CAUSEWAY no sign of enemy patrols. Casualties to noon NIL Situation Report 5 p.m. all quiet. | |
| " 9th October 1915 | Situation Report 5 a.m. all quiet. Casualties to noon NIL Situation Report 5 p.m. all quiet. Patrol on march at 6 p.m. no enemy encountered. | |
| " 10th October 1915 | Situation Report 5 a.m. all quiet. Casualties to noon 1 O.R. accidentally killed 1 O.R. accidentally wounded. Situation Report 5 p.m. all quiet. | |
| " 11th October 1915 | Situation Report 5 a.m. all quiet. Casualties to noon NIL Situation Report 5 p.m. all quiet | |
| " 12th October 1915 | Situation Report 5 a.m. all quiet. Casualties to noon NIL Situation Report 5 p.m. all quiet. | Lt Col E.J. Harrison Reserves Commanded |

# WAR DIARY or INTELLIGENCE SUMMARY

Army Form C. 2118.

(Erase heading not required.)

Instructions regarding War Diaries and Intelligence Summaries are contained in F. S. Regs., Part II. and the Staff Manual respectively. Title pages will be prepared in manuscript.

| Hour, Date, Place | Summary of Events and Information | Remarks and references to Appendices |
|---|---|---|
| VAUX 19th October 1915 | Situation report 5 am all quiet. Casualties to noon Nil. Situation report 7pm all quiet. Ambush withdrawn at dark, no signs of enemy | |
| 20th October 1915 | Situation Report 5am all quiet. Casualties to noon Nil. Patrols in woods of FRISE encountered no hostile patrols. Situation report 7pm. all quiet. | |
| 21st October 1915 | Situation Report 5am all quiet. Casualties to noon Nil. Patrols on marsh encountered no hostile patrols. Situation 7pm. all quiet | |
| 22nd October 1915 | Situation Report 5am all quiet. Casualties to noon Nil. Ambush laid at dawn returned at 6 pm. without seeing enemy. Situation Report 5pm all quiet | |
| 23rd October 1915 | Situation Report 5am. all quiet. Casualties to noon Nil. Ambush laid at dawn returned at 6 pm without seeing enemy. Situation Report 5pm all quiet | |

Army Form C. 2118.

# WAR DIARY
## or
## INTELLIGENCE SUMMARY

*(Erase heading not required.)*

Instructions regarding War Diaries and Intelligence Summaries are contained in F. S. Regs., Part II. and the Staff Manual respectively. Title pages will be prepared in manuscript.

| Hour, Date, Place | Summary of Events and Information | Remarks and references to Appendices |
|---|---|---|
| VAUX 13th October 1915 | Situation Report 5 am all quiet<br>Casualties to noon NIL<br>Situation Report 5pm all quiet | |
| " 14th October 1915 | Situation Report 5 am all quiet<br>Casualties to noon NIL<br>Situation Report 5pm all quiet | |
| " 15th October 1915 | Situation Report 5 am all quiet<br>Casualties to noon NIL<br>Situation Report 5pm all quiet | |
| " 16th October 1915 | Situation Report 5 am all quiet<br>Casualties to noon NIL<br>Situation Report 5pm all quiet<br>Patrols encountered no hostile patrols | |
| " 17th October 1915 | Situation Report 5 am all quiet<br>Casualties to noon NIL<br>Patrol to FRISE, no enemy encountered<br>Situation Report 5pm all quiet<br>Ambush laid at dawn | |
| " 18th October 1915 | Situation Report 5 am all quiet<br>Casualties to noon NIL<br>Situation Report 5pm all quiet | |

Army Form C. 2118.

# WAR DIARY
## or
## INTELLIGENCE SUMMARY
(Erase heading not required.)

| Hour, Date, Place | Summary of Events and Information | Remarks and references to Appendices |
|---|---|---|
| VAUX<br>24th October 1915. | Situation Report 5 AM - all quiet.<br>Casualties to noon nil<br>Patrol to FRISE, started 3.0 PM returned 5.0 PM - examining no enemy<br>Situation Report 5 PM all quiet. | |
| 25th October 1915. | Situation Report 5 AM all quiet.<br>Casualties to noon nil<br>Patrol in woods - Examining no enemy<br>Situation report 5 PM all quiet. relieved at Frise by 3rd Batt. 119. Regt. (3 coys)<br>Situation report 5 AM all quiet. | |
| 26th October 1915. | Casualties to noon nil<br>Patrol to Frise. Interval French Commander.<br>Casualties noon nil<br>Situation report 5 PM all quiet. | |
| 27th October 1915. | Situation Report 5 AM - all quiet.<br>Casualties to Noon - Nil.<br>Patrol in woods 9 AM - 1.0 PM No enemy encountered<br>Situation Report 5 PM - all quiet. | |
| 28th October 1915. | Situation Report 5 AM - all quiet.<br>Casualties to Noon - Nil<br>Patrol to Frise 2.30 PM - No enemy encountered<br>Situation Report 5 PM - all quiet. | W.R.B. |

Army Form C. 2118.

# WAR DIARY
## or
## INTELLIGENCE SUMMARY

(Erase heading not required.)

Instructions regarding War Diaries and Intelligence Summaries are contained in F. S. Regs., Part II. and the Staff Manual respectively. Title pages will be prepared in manuscript.

| Hour, Date, Place | Summary of Events and Information | Remarks and references to Appendices |
|---|---|---|
| VAUX Oct. 29th 1915. | Situation Report 5 A.M. all quiet. Casualties 5 Noon - Nil. Patrol through hard towards FRIDE 2.15pm - 5pm - No Enemy encountered. Situation Report 5pm all quiet. Reinforcements Draft of 79 men arrived from England | |
| Oct. 30th 1915. | Situation Report 5am - Nil. Casualties to noon - Nil. Brigadier General commanding 14th Brigade inspected new Trench in Bois de Vaux 11 am Situation report 5pm - "all quiet". Patrol escorts March to PAIN 11 am - Returned 1 pm No enemy seen | |
| Oct. 31st 1915. | Situation report 5 A.M. all quiet. Casualties to noon - Nil. Rather more Gun fire than usual but otherwise the day passed quietly. | |

15th Bde.
5th Div.

Became Third Army Troops 17.11.15.

1/6th LIVERPOOLS

NOVEMBER

1 9 1 5

On His Majesty's Service.

Army Form C. 2118.

**WAR DIARY**
or
**INTELLIGENCE SUMMARY.**
(Erase heading not required.)

1st Kings Own ... B E F

| Place | Date | Hour | Summary of Events and Information | Remarks and references to Appendices |
|---|---|---|---|---|
| VAUX | 31/10/15 | | Observation was impossible after 3 P.M owing to the mist. | REF. MAP ALBERT 1/40000 |
| | 1/11/15 | 8.15 AM | A working party of about 20 men was seen in the trench running N. from H.10. B. 4-7. At 8.20 A.M. a cart came along the road, stopped at the end of the French, and was unloaded. The load appeared to consist of tools. At 8.30 a large party of 150/150 men were seen moving N along the Clery/Maurepas road, with a continuation of the French seemed to above, no being carried on. Work has been going on all day in A.29. D. 9-7. | |
| | | 12.30 PM | German Artillery put two heavy shells on Forgny Mill & also to the N of the Mill. Then put three shells on the same section at 1.45. P.M. & at 12.45 P.M. The 119th shelled the CHAPEAU DE GENDARMES at 2 P.M. They shelled the German Vedenny post between Forgny Mill and the CHAPEAU | |
| | | Evening | No trains have been seen to-day owing to the bad lights at Clery | |
| | | Sunday | The village has been unusually quiet to-day | |
| | | Route | No transport has been seen on the roads to-day. | |

E. V. Wynne 2nd Lieut
6th (attd 1st Bn.) K. L. R.

Army Form C. 2118.

# WAR DIARY
## or
## INTELLIGENCE SUMMARY.
(Erase heading not required.)

| Place | Date | Hour | Summary of Events and Information | Remarks and references to Appendices |
|---|---|---|---|---|
| VAUX | 1/11/15 | 3.50 p.m. | Our artillery shelled the German communication trench running from the Bouchavesnes to the Bois de Mercourt. Further observation was impossible owing to bad light. | REF. MAP ALBERT 1/40,000 |
| | 2/11/15 | 8.5 a.m. | About 80 men came along the Clery road towards Herm & went into the trench running S from H. 10. B. 4-7. At 9.55 A.M. 26 men came along & went into the same trench. About 150 men were engaged on the northern portion of this trench running N from the Peronne/Maricourt road. This battery moved off at 11.45 A.M. The French artillery shelled this line of trench at intervals from 9.55 A.M to 11.15. A.M. | |
| Trains | | | Trains were seen passing S through CLERY at 10.55 A.M and 12.45. P.M. | |
| Bois de Mercourt | | | A lot of patrols were seen going into this wood during the day. | |
| Roads | | | An unusual amount of transport has been seen on the road to-day. 17 were going S from Mt. 32 Q in an hour, also N from Mt. 52 Q. westwards Manicha Clery. This number of groups was so large no estimates that a reliable was taken. Motor cars, bicycles and mounted men have been seen going to and from the places referred to. | |
| Civilian March. | | | The village has been quiet all day. A patrol went out at 9.30. A.M as far as the Targny Causeway but saw nothing to report. | 2nd Lieut. K.L.R. |

Army Form C. 2118.

# WAR DIARY
## OF
## INTELLIGENCE SUMMARY.
*(Erase heading not required.)*

Instructions regarding War Diaries and Intelligence Summaries are contained in F. S. Regs., Part II. and the Staff Manual respectively. Title pages will be prepared in manuscript.

| Place | Date | Hour | Summary of Events and Information | Remarks and references to Appendices |
|---|---|---|---|---|
| VAUX. | 2/11/15 | | Observation was impossible after 3 P.M. owing to mist and rain. | Hd/Mqr ALBERT #4000. |
| | 3/11/15 | 8.26am | A train was seen going N through CLERY, and at 11.40 A.M. a train was seen going S through CLERY | |
| | | 9.20am | The road working parties were seen on the left of the PERONNE/MARI-court road in H.4.B&D, and also on the right of the CLERY/HEM road in H.10.B. The French artillery fired two shells about 11.30 A.M. and did not the working parties, which stood on the sunken road, & marched back to CLERY. There were only about 50 men working to-day, and the part of the French which we saw on occ. appears to be nearly completed. | |
| ROADS | | | A number of transport wagons were seen on the MAYREPAS road going into CLERY. The traffic on the other roads was normal. | |
| CURLU | | | The village has been quiet all day. A patrol under 2nd Lieut. Odam went along the running to FRISE, and have nothing to report. | |
| | Artillery | | The Germans from the direction of HEM shelled our French trenches at 10.40 A.M. and again at 11.30 A.M. They shelled FARGNY and the trenches to the N of it. Our artillery have replied on "Y" wood, CHAPEAU DE GENDARMES, the trenches to the N of FARGNY. | E.V. H. ny Lio 2nd Lieut. 6th (Rifle) Batt. K.L.R |

Army Form C. 2118.

# WAR DIARY
## or
## INTELLIGENCE SUMMARY.
(Erase heading not required.)

| Place | Date | Hour | Summary of Events and Information | Remarks and references to Appendices |
|---|---|---|---|---|
| VAUX | 3/11/15 | 3.15 p.m | Our artillery shelled the German batteries hyd between FARGNY, & the CHAPEAU DE GENDARME, the CHATEAU about, & north of CLERY. | REF. MAP ALBERT 1/40000 |
| | 4/11/15 | 8 A.M | A man was seen passing N through CLERY. | |
| | | 8.45 A.M | Working parties were again observed on the N side of the PERONNE/MARICOURT road in H.4, A & B and also on the S side of the CLERY/HEM road in H.10.B.D | |
| | | | At 10.40 A.M the French artillery fired 4 rounds of shrapnel on the trench at H.10.B and scattered the party. There have been several small parties going to and from the line of trench all day. Work has been going on all day in A.29.D, G.7. Considerable activity has been noticed to-day between H.2 A.4-7. and H.2 A.7.0. | |
| CURLU | | | There has been more activity than usual to-day amongst the civilian population. | |
| ROADS | | | There has been no transport on the roads under observation during to-day. | |
| ARTILLERY | | Between 10.10 A.M & 11.50 A.M | The German artillery put several shells over FARGNY. Our artillery replied on the CHAPEAU DE GENDARME and trench above. | |
| DEMOLITION | | | The Germans in CURLU are again pulling down houses at the N & S ends of the village. | |

F.N. Hughes 2nd Lieut
6th (Nights) Batt. K.L.R.

Army Form C. 2118.

# WAR DIARY
# of
# INTELLIGENCE SUMMARY.
(Erase heading not required.)

Instructions regarding War Diaries and Intelligence Summaries are contained in F.S. Regs., Part II. and the Staff Manual respectively. Title pages will be prepared in manuscript.

| Place | Date | Hour | Summary of Events and Information | Remarks and references to Appendices |
|---|---|---|---|---|
| VAUX | 4/11/15 | 3.25 P.M. | A small working party was seen at H.10.B.4.7 returning to CLERY. | REF. MAP. ALBERT 1/40000 |
| | | | Between 6.10 P.M & 6.20 P.M. three flares were sent up from the CHAPEAU DE GEND<sup>me</sup> | |
| | 5/11/15 | 10.15. A.M. | A working party was seen in A.29.D.8-9. | |
| | | 10.40 A.M. | The usual working party was seen N and S of Mt. PERONNE/MARICOURT road NW H.4.A & B. At 11.35. A.M. the French artillery sent some shells near the part of the French adjacent to the CLERY/HEM road. | |
| | | 11.17 A.M | A train was seen travelling S through CLERY. At 11.48 A.M. a train went N through CLERY. | |
| | | 12.50 P.M. | A large party of Germans came over the ridge near G<sup>me</sup> BOUCHERT entered the W3 on the Mercencourt. | |
| | | CURLU | The village has been very quiet to-day. | |
| | | ROADS | There has been practically no traffic on the roads to-day. | |
| | | LISTENING POST | Men have been seen going in and out of the post near the East Suzerje Post. | |
| | | | A new observation post is in course of construction near the top of the CHAPEAU DE GENDARME | |

6<sup>th</sup> (K.Riffes) B<sup>att</sup><sup>n</sup> K.L.R.
L<sup>t</sup> S. Hughes 2<sup>nd</sup> Lieut

Army Form C. 2118.

# WAR DIARY
## INTELLIGENCE SUMMARY.
*(Erase heading not required.)*

Instructions regarding War Diaries and Intelligence Summaries are contained in F.S. Regs., Part II. and the Staff Manual respectively. Title pages will be prepared in manuscript.

| Place | Date | Hour | Summary of Events and Information | Remarks and references to Appendices |
|---|---|---|---|---|
| VAUX. | 5/11/15 | 3.27AM | A.L. was seen going N. through CLERY | REF MAP. ALBERT 1/40,000 |
| | | 3.57 PM | German artillery seen firing S.W. into the N.W. of VAUX | |
| | | 4.07 PM | A relief is observed taking place at the German lake my post by the East Snipers post. | |
| | 6/11/15 | | Observation Limited was impossible all day owing to the mist. Patrols has been out in the woods in | |
| | | MARSH | A Patrol under 2nd Lieut [?] in the direction of CURLU. The Patrol had nothing to report. | |
| | | | | 6th (Service) Bn 2nd Lieut H.W. K.L.R. |

# WAR DIARY
## or
## INTELLIGENCE SUMMARY.

Army Form C. 2118.

| Place | Date | Hour | Summary of Events and Information | Remarks and references to Appendices |
|---|---|---|---|---|
| AU X | 6/11/15 | P.M. 3.25 | A considerable amount of activity on Trench at LA GRENOUILLÈRE at G.18.D. The advanced trench at H.19.A, no action was taken by them. | R of H ALBERT |
| | | 7.10 | A red light was observed coming from the direction of the dugouts at the base of the CHATEAU DE GENDARME. | |
| | 7/11/15 | 6.0 | Observation has been impossible to-day owing to the mist. It has been noticed that the communication trench running from H.19.A.5.6 to the G.ne BOUCHER is being converted into a reserve fire trench. The parapet has been levelled, and loopholes are being inserted. | |

6/Kings Liverpool R.

Army Form C. 2118.

# WAR DIARY
## or
## INTELLIGENCE SUMMARY.
(Erase heading not required.)

| Place | Date | Hour | Summary of Events and Information | Remarks and references to Appendices |
|---|---|---|---|---|
| VAUX. | 7/11/15 | P.M. 3.10/3.35. | Two of our aeroplanes in the sector about ECLUSIER were shelled by the German guns at MAUREPAS. | REF. MAP. ALBERT 1/40000 |
| | | 3.30. | Our artillery shelled the German trench at the house of the CHATEAU DE GEN | |
| | 8/11/15 | A.M. 10.35. | Work is taking place at the house on the CLERY/HEM road, in H.I.G.). Appears to be that an observation post is being made in the roof. | |
| | | 10.40. | The usual working party was seen on the French adjacent to the PERONNE/ MARICOURT road in H.H.D. The party consisted of about 50 men, and they moved off at 11.50 A.M in the direction of HEM. | |
| | | P.M. 12.50 | A large party of Germans came over the ridge from HERBECOURT, & went into the BOIS DE MERCEAUCOURT. | |
| | | 1.2. | A train was seen going N through CLERY, & was followed by another one at 2.23. P.M. | |
| | | | CURLU The village has been quiet all day. | |
| | | | ROADS No transport has been observed on the roads to-day. | |
| | | | MARSH. There is nothing to report to-day. | |

S.F. (Rifle) Hughes. 2nd Lieut.
W. Balfour, K.L.R.

# WAR DIARY
## or
## INTELLIGENCE SUMMARY.
(Erase heading not required.)

Army Form C. 2118.

| Place | Date | Hour | Summary of Events and Information | Remarks and references to Appendices |
|---|---|---|---|---|
| VAUX. | 8/11/15 | P.M. 3.22 | A train was seen travelling N. through CLERY. During the afternoon French artillery shelled the German trench at LA GRENOUILLERE. | REF. MAP. ALBERT 1/40000 |
| | 9/11/15 | A.M. 9.45. | A working party was seen at H.I.B. 6-2. They worked up to 12.30 P.M. | |
| | | 11.0. | A train was observed passing through CLERY. At 11.10 A.M. a long train could be distinctly seen on the CLERY/PERONNE line in I.14.D. | |
| | | P.M. 12.40 | A large party of Germans crossed the ridge from HERBECOURT and entered the Bois de MERCEAUCOURT. | |
| Artillery | | | During the day our artillery shelled the house on the CURLU/HEM road returned to yesterday and also the enemy trenches near LA GRENOUILLERE. | |
| ROADS | | | A very transport has been seen to-day on the roads under our observation. At 1.30. P.M. several mounted men were observed coming down the road from PERONNE into CLERY. They were followed closely by 26 transport wagons with a small guard of infantry. | |
| CURLU | | | The village has been quiet all day. German artillery registered on several points to-day around the ROYAL DRAGONS & BOIS DE VAUX. | |

C.F.(W.Wylie) 2nd Lieut
6th Battn K.L.R

Army Form C. 2118.

# WAR DIARY
## or
## INTELLIGENCE SUMMARY.
(Erase heading not required.)

| Place | Date | Hour | Summary of Events and Information | Remarks and references to Appendices |
|---|---|---|---|---|
| VAUX. | 9/11/15 | P.M. 3.45 | Our artillery shelled the house on the CURLU/HEM road near H.1.C.5-7. | REF MAP ALBERT 1/40000 |
| | | 4.0 | Transport was seen entering CLERY on the road from MT. ST. QUENTIN | |
| | | 6.7 | A light was seen at the base of the CHAPEAU DE GENDARME. Further | |
| | | | queries have been made during the night | |
| | 10/11/15 | A.M. 8.30 | Two large squadrons of cavalry were observed drilling in the fields in front of MT. ST. QUENTIN | |
| | | 9.20 | Small sections of infantry were seen doing extended order drill on the left of the cavalry | |
| | | 9.57 | A train went N through CLERY. At 10.7 A.M another train passed S. Other trains through CLERY to-day were as follows:- 10.15 A.M. going S. 12.43. P.M. going N, 12.43 P.M going S, 1.13 P.M going N, 2.12 P.M going N, 2.24 P.M going S. | |
| | | ROADS | The amount of traffic on the roads under our observation has been very heavy all day. Transport wagons and cars have been observed practically the whole of the day on the CLERY/HEM; CLERY/MT ST QUENTIN; MAUREPAS/CLERY. Most of the traffic was going in an easterly direction | |

| Place | Date | Hour | Summary of Events and Information | Remarks and references to Appendices |
|---|---|---|---|---|
| Vaux | 10/11/15 | A.M. 10.10 | Continued. A mine was blown up and appeared to explode about between the fire trenches N of GNE HOSPICE. After a short interval our artillery shelled the fire and communication trenches in this sector. The enemy only sent over a few shells. The explosion too made a large crater. EARLY Further demolition work has been done at the N end of the village. The village has been quiet all day. Our artillery during this afternoon shelled and partly demolished the house at H.I.C. 5-7. Men have been seen there all day and it is evident that they must have had some casualties as no one left the building when it was struck. | |

6th (Rifle) Batt. K.L.R.

Lt. V. Hughes 2nd Lieut.

# WAR DIARY
## INTELLIGENCE SUMMARY

Army Form C. 2118.

| Place | Date | Hour | Summary of Events and Information | Remarks and references to Appendices |
|---|---|---|---|---|
| VAUX | 10/11/15 | P.M. 3.0 | Nine transport wagons were observed on the road from Peronne going to Mt. St. Quentin. | REF. MAP ALBERT. 1/40000. |
| | | 3.5 & 3.30. | The 119th Batt'y shelled the house at H.I.C. 5-6. During the night of the 10/11th this damage has been partly repaired, and at 6 A.M. this morning a number of men were seen in the house. The artillery have not shelled it to-day, although no reported this to them. | |
| | 11/11/15 | | TRAINS. Three trains were seen to-day morning S through CLERY. They passed through at 9.3. A.M, 12.40. P.M, & 1.18 P.M. | |
| | | | ROADS. There has been considerable activity on the roads to-day. A number of transport wagons have come into CLERY from Mt. St. QUENTIN. At 2.30 P.M. a battalion of German infantry was seen leaving CLERY in close order. They moved about east towards Mt. St. QUENTIN. We found this and the 9th Siege Batt'y who had not registered on the road, unable to get the Highland Batt'y on the telephone. | |
| | | | Small working parties were again seen nr. H.10 and also the E. of FEUILLERES. They moved off at noon in sections of 10. The 9th Siege Batt'y fired without effect. | |
| CURLU | | | The village has been quiet to-day. | |

E. K. Hughes 2nd Lieut.
6th (W:Ple) Batt. K. L. R

Army Form C. 2118.

# WAR DIARY
# INTELLIGENCE SUMMARY.

(Erase heading not required.)

Instructions regarding War Diaries and Intelligence Summaries are contained in F. S. Regs. Part II. and the Staff Manual respectively. Title pages will be prepared in manuscript.

| Place | Date | Hour | Summary of Events and Information | Remarks and references to Appendices |
|---|---|---|---|---|
| VAUX. | 11/10/15 | P.M. 3.10 | Four officers were seen inspecting the new trench adjacent to the MARICOURT road on H.4. They appeared to mark out a new trench between MARICOURT road and the northern edge of CLERY. | PERONNE REF MAP ALBERT 1/40000 |
| | | 4.0. | This was reported to, and the whole of CLERY. A train was observed passing S. through CLERY | |
| | 12/11/15 | TRAINS | The following trains were seen to-day passing through CLERY:- 8.10.A.M. going S, 9.40 A.M. going N, 2.35 P.M. going N. | |
| | | WORKING PARTIES | were observed in the trench to the N.W. of the PERONNE/MARICOURT road and also appeared in the trench to the N.E. of that one. They engaged on a new trench. About 25 men were working, and an earthwork by the French moved off at 11.50 A.M. About 35 men were working and were relieved at 11.20 A.M. by the 9th Siege & Highland Batt. trench in H.10.B. They had also working parties in several parts of the centre of the village | |
| | | CURLU | Demolition is now taking place in several parts of the centre of the village | |
| | | ROADS | A large number of transports have been seen going towards MT ST. QUENTIN from CLERY & FEUILLERES. 19 nav. Poops on to be noticed on the MAUREPAS/FEUILLERES road. At 1.55. P.M. about 250 men went out from CLERY towards MT. ST. QUENTIN. At 2.20 P.M. about 350 men appeared from N and went into CLERY. | |
| | | | German artillery sent a few light shells into the BOIS DE VAUX at 9.40 A.M. and at 10.50 P.M. They sent some H.E. near the guns of the 119th Batt? | 6th (Rifle) Batt K.L.R. Hughes 2nd Lieut |

# WAR DIARY
## of
## INTELLIGENCE SUMMARY.
(Erase heading not required.)

Army Form C. 2118.

| Place | Date | Hour | Summary of Events and Information | Remarks and references to Appendices |
|---|---|---|---|---|
| VAUX. | 12/11/15 | P.M. 3.0 | About 50 Germans left CLERY in a N.E. direction, but returned shortly afterwards. | R.E.F. MAP. ALBERT 1/40000 |
| | | 4.0 | Several transports came into CLERY via the MAUREPAS road, & others went towards MT ST QUENTIN & PERONNE. | |
| | | 4.5 | Our artillery shelled the new trench cut in front on the S. side of the PERONNE RD. | |
| | 13/11/15 | TRAINS | Two trains were seen going N. through CLERY to-day: 9.35 A.M and 2.14 P.M. | |
| | | WORKING PARTIES) | A small working party was seen in the communication trench running from CURLU to the CHATEAU DE GENDARME. There were only about 12 men working in the trench adjacent to the PERONNE/MARICOURT road, but a considerable amount of work has been done there during the night of the 12/13th. | |
| | | CURLU | Further demolition has taken place during the night & at the N end of the village. | |
| | | ROADS | At 11.35 A.M about 150 men left CLERY in the direction of MT. ST. QUENTIN. The MAUREPAS/CLERY road has been used to-day very frequently by transports. It has been noticed that use of the CLERY/HEM road by day has been gradually abandoned. | |
| | | H.I.C. 5.6 | The howr. at this point is still being used. The artillery went one shell close to it to-day. The place still appears to be used as an observation post. | |

6th (Rifles) E.V. 14 eighteen 2nd Lieut.
W. aff. K. L. R.

# WAR DIARY
## INTELLIGENCE SUMMARY.
*(Erase heading not required.)*

Army Form C. 2118.

| Place | Date | Hour | Summary of Events and Information | Remarks and references to Appendices |
|---|---|---|---|---|
| VAUX | 13/11/15 | P.m 3.0 | A small party of men was observed working on the trench in H.4.B. | REF MAP ALBERT / #0000 |
| | | 3.18 | A train passed N through CLERY. | |
| | 14/11/15 | TRAINS | The following trains were seen to-day passing through CLERY:- 9.8 A.M going N, 9.45 A.M going N, 11.6 A.M going S, 1.45 P.M going N, | |
| | | H.1.C.6.6. | Work has been going on inside this building to-day. Our artillery firing demolished the roof this morning, but further work has been done this afternoon. | |
| | | WORKING PARTIES | A few men were working on the trench adjacent to the PERONNE/MARI- COURT road during the morning, and also near the FEUILLERES end of the road running from there to HEM. | |
| | | CURLU | No further demolition seems to have taken place during the night, but men were seen to-day carrying wood away from the ruins to the trenches | |
| | | ROADS | There has been practically no traffic on the roads to-day | |
| | | MARSH | A patrol under 2nd Lieut. E.C. ADAM has been out in the direction of CURLU, but had nothing to report. | |

E.V. Hughes 2nd Lieut.
6th (Rifle) Batt. K.L.R.

Army Form C. 2118.

# WAR DIARY
## or
## INTELLIGENCE SUMMARY.
(Erase heading not required.)

| Place | Date | Hour | Summary of Events and Information | Remarks and references to Appendices |
|---|---|---|---|---|
| VAUX. | 14/11/15 | P.M. 3.45. | A Train was seen moving S. from CLERY and went towards PERONNE | REF: MAP ALBERT 1/40000 |
| | H.I.C.6.6. | | by general wards the trains at this point could be seen during this afternoon | |
| | 15/11/15 | a.m. 11.30. | A working party could be seen in the trench S.W. of the PERONNE/ MARICOURT road in H.4.D.2. Germans were also working on this trench in H.4.D.0.a. and 1b.e.? Shells fell at 11.45 A.M. and again at 12.30 P.M. Some of the shells fell close to some of the men who were working on the trenches. The trench and were not seen again. | |
| | P.M. 2.45 | | A train went N. through CLERY. | |
| | | | CURLU The village has been shelled all day. | |
| | | | MARSH A patrol under 2nd Lieut. E.C.ADAM went along to FRISE, had had nothing to report | |
| | | | ROADS There has been practically no traffic on the roads to-day. Germans and Men? in the direction of the BOIS DE HEM went 11 ch.ffo at 11.25 A.M. on the small between the DUCK POST & VAUX The field to the DUCK POST affixed to be in the direction One sentry rolled to H.I.C.6.6. | |

6th (M.Rifle) Battn "K.L.R."

2nd V. Hughes 2nd Lieut

Army Form C. 2118.

# WAR DIARY
## or
## INTELLIGENCE SUMMARY.
(Erase heading not required.)

Instructions regarding War Diaries and Intelligence Summaries are contained in F.S. Regs., Part II and the Staff Manual respectively. Title pages will be prepared in manuscript.

| Place | Date | Hour | Summary of Events and Information | Remarks and references to Appendices |
|---|---|---|---|---|
| | 15/11/15 | | | REF. MAP. ALBERT 1/40000 |
| VAUX | 15/11/15 | A.M 10.30. | Observation was impossible after 3. P.M owing to the bad light. German artillery from the direction of the BOIS DE HEM shelled No 12 trench to the north of Fargny Mill. There were 27 shells sent over, they were nearly all high explosive. The 119 Ft. Batt<sup>y</sup> replied in the direction of B. 26. | |
| | | 11.30. P.M 12.18 | The 9<sup>th</sup> Siege Batt<sup>y</sup> shelled 4 NTTT. Some transports were seen on the road from MT ST QUENTIN coming into CLERY. | |
| | | 1.22 | A train went N through CLERY. | |
| CURLU | | | Further demolition work has taken place at the N end of the village during the night of the 15<sup>th</sup>/16<sup>th</sup>. Several civilians have been seen moving about in the village to-day. | |

E. V. Hughes 2<sup>nd</sup> Lieut.
6<sup>th</sup> (M<sup>ddx</sup>) Batt<sup>n</sup> K. L. R.

Army Form C. 2118.

# WAR DIARY
## or
## INTELLIGENCE SUMMARY

*(Erase heading not required.)*

Instructions regarding War Diaries and Intelligence Summaries are contained in F. S. Regs., Part II. and the Staff Manual respectively. Title pages will be prepared in manuscript.

| Hour, Date, Place | Summary of Events and Information | Remarks and references to Appendices |
|---|---|---|
| VAUX. November 1st 1915 | Situation Report 5AM. All quiet at 8PM. Casualties nron - Nil. Patrols out - ① 2/Lieut KEMP with 9 men patroled to FRISE, nothing to report. ② Patrol under 2° Lieut. WARBURTON went in direction of CURLU, our from 8PM to 4.30 PM and beard a lot of talk - no enemy encountered. Situation Report 5PM - All quiet. | |
| " November 2d 1915 | Situation Report 5AM. - All quiet. Casualties nron - Nil. Patrol under 2/Lieut. ADAM went nr from 10.30PM to 1 AM returned as far as FACENY. Causeway to FRISE no enemy. Quiet day but our guns fairly active. | |
| " November 3 | Situation Report 5AM. - All quiet. Draft of 8 NCOs from ENGLAND & 21 returned men. Casualties nron NIL. Patrol to FRISE under 2/Lieut ADAM. Nothing to report. Quiet day, some Artillery activity - | R/3/ |
| " November 4th | Situation Report 5AM. - All quiet. Casualties & nron - Nil. Patrol under 2d/ Adam went out nr 3.45PM toward CURLU - nothing to report. Quiet day. | |
| " November 5th | Situation Report 5AM - All quiet. Casualties nron - Nil. Patrol with Sergeant MURPHY towards - nothing to report. Situation 5PM all quiet. | |
| " November 6 | Situation Report 5AM All quiet. Casualties nron - Nil. Patrol in direction of CURLU went out nr 11 AM under 2/Lieut WARBURTON. No enemy encountered. Quiet day except for some activity by our guns during the afternoon. | |

Army Form C. 2118.

# WAR DIARY
## or
## INTELLIGENCE SUMMARY.

(Erase heading not required.)

Instructions regarding War Diaries and Intelligence Summaries are contained in F. S. Regs., Part II. and the Staff Manual respectively. Title pages will be prepared in manuscript.

| Place | Date | Hour | Summary of Events and Information | Remarks and references to Appendices |
|---|---|---|---|---|
| VAUX REF. MAP VAUX G. 4. D. 10. B. | Nov. 7 | 5 am | Situation Report – all quiet. | |
| | | 12 pm | Casualties NIL. 1 man wounded – stray bullet at VOIVE de GOBAIN | |
| | | 2 pm | Patrol to FRISE under Sergt Switzer – accompanied by French Patrol. Nothing to report. | |
| | | 5 pm | Quiet day in all respects. | |
| " | 8 | 5 am | Situation Report – all quiet. | |
| | | 12 pm | Casualties report NIL. | |
| | | 3 pm | Patrol under 2/Lieut Adam as far as 3° mile – Nothing encountered – Returned 4.15 pm. | |
| | | 5 pm | Situation Report all quiet. | |
| " | 9 | 5 am | Situation Report – all quiet. | |
| | | | After Section Left road Royal Dragoon ntrd + N ⁶⁄₇ Corner of Bois de Vaux. No damage. | |
| | | 12 pm | Casualties report NIL. | |
| | | 2 pm | Patrol under Lieut Moss to FRISE. Returned 4 pm. Nothing to report. | |
| | 10 | | Quiet day. | |
| | 11 | | Quiet day. Casualties nil. Nothing to report | |
| | 12 | | Patrols found no sign of enemy on front. Casualties nil. Nothing to report | |

2353  Wt. W2314/1454 700,000 5/15  D. D. & L.  A.D.S.S./Forms/C. 2118.

**Army Form C. 2118.**

# WAR DIARY
## or
## INTELLIGENCE SUMMARY.
*(Erase heading not required.)*

| Place | Date | Hour | Summary of Events and Information | Remarks and references to Appendices |
|---|---|---|---|---|
| VAUX | 13/10 | | Quiet day. November N.E. No sign of enemy's patrols | |
| | 14/10 | | " " | |
| | 15/10 | 10 a.m. | Patrol under Lt Adam to FRISE – nothing to report | |
| | | 12.30pm | About 20 enemy light shells from the direction of BOIS de HEM fell on the river and river front to East road. No damage done | |
| | | | 2nd M.O Casualties. 1.P.B.O. 6 men R.A.M.C. arr to be attached for purpose of carrying wounds from NORTH of FARGNY road | |
| | | 6 p.m | Relief of D Sq by ROYAL DRAGOONS WOOD J a Sq & S Sqdrms commenced | |
| | | | Relief complete 6.65 p.m. | |
| | | 4 p.m. | Workers on river bank near Forge Guard fired at & freed rifle at intervals. Horses moved to front road near hill | |
| | 16/10 | 80 a.m. | Capt BUCKLEY and 80 O.R. proceeded to BRAY. I work march and return of Brody Bus to 3rd Army Rest Quarters, as advanced party for the Regtn. | |
| | | noon | Casualties to noon NIL. | |
| | | 6 pm | Relief of B Sq on BOIS de VAUX and Machine Guns T.S. M. Blockhouse commenced. Relief complete at 7.45 p.m. Relieved Sq. Goes into rest Billets in SURANNE | |

Army Form C. 2118.

# WAR DIARY
## or
## INTELLIGENCE SUMMARY.
(Erase heading not required.)

Instructions regarding War Diaries and Intelligence Summaries are contained in F. S. Regs., Part II. and the Staff Manual respectively. Title pages will be prepared in manuscript.

| Place | Date | Hour | Summary of Events and Information | Remarks and references to Appendices |
|---|---|---|---|---|
| VAUX | 17.11 | | Good night. Lt HUGHES (G) and 50 O.R. proceeded & not reported from SUZANNE to BRAY and left there 4 motor lows for 3rd Army Head Quarters at BEAUQUESNE. Remainder of Battn relieved by 5th Bn Cheshire Regt marched to SUZANNE & billeted there for the night. | |
| V | | | | |
| SUZANNE | 18/11/15 | | Head Quarters & Remainder of Battn all proceeded by route march to BRAY left there by MT. bus for BERTRANCOURT where they went into billets vacated by 2nd Bn Royal Inniskilling Fusiliers. | |
| BERTRANCOURT | 19/11/15 | | Battn in billets. | |
| " | 20/11/15 | | Col J. T. HARRISON proceeded to BEAUQUESNE as Commandant Army Troops Capt G.H. TENILL took over command of Battn. 100 O.R. under CAPT J.R. TRENCH moved into billets at CAUMESNIL. Battn now distributed as follows :-<br>BEAUQUESNE 160 O.R. under Capt E.W.K. BENNET<br>CAUMESNIL 100 O.R. " " J.R. TRENCH<br>BERTRANCOURT Remainder of Battn<br>The following daily working parties were provided from BERTRANCOURT<br>0. 5 N.C.O's 9 men for R.E | |

Army Form C. 2118

# WAR DIARY
## or
## INTELLIGENCE SUMMARY
*(Erase heading not required.)*

Instructions regarding War Diaries and Intelligence Summaries are contained in F. S. Regs., Part II. and the Staff Manual respectively. Title Pages will be prepared in manuscript.

| Place | Date | Hour | Summary of Events and Information | Remarks and references to Appendices |
|---|---|---|---|---|
| BERTRAN COURT | 20/11/15 | | (1) 1 N.C.O. 98 men for R.E. (2) Working parts & every available men for R.E. | |
| " | 21/11/15 22 23 24 25 26 27 28 29 30 | | } In billets in Bertrancourt, usual working parties on Corps line found daily | |

2096

Third Army Troops

Came from 15th Bde. 5th Div. 17/11/15.

## 1/6th LIVERPOOLS

### DECEMBER

### 1 9 1 5

Confidential

War Diary

of

1/6 (Rifle) Battⁿ The King's Liverpool Regt.

From. 1 Dec 1915    To. 31ˢᵗ Dec 1915.

Army Form C. 2118

# WAR DIARY
## or
## INTELLIGENCE SUMMARY
(Erase heading not required.)

| Place | Date | Hour | Summary of Events and Information | Remarks and references to Appendices |
|---|---|---|---|---|
| BERTRAN COURT | 1/12/15 to 23/12/15 | | In Billets at BERTRANCOURT. Working parties of 250 O.R. found daily for work on CORPS LINE | |
| " | 24/12/15 | | 4/Lt. E.V. HUGHES 150 O.R. proceeded to TOUTENCOURT for work under orders of O.C. 10th Labour Battn. Working party of 200 O.R. found for Corps Line. | |
| " | 25/12/15 | | Working party of 250 O.R. Christmas Day. No parties found for Corps Line | |
| " | 26/12/15 | | 2/Lieut W.H.H. DAVIDSON & 50 O.R. proceeded to FAMECHON to work under orders of O.C. 10th Labour Battn. Lieut G.G. BLACKLEDGE & 150 O.R. proceeded to HALLOY to work under orders of R.E. 2/Lieut E.R. BUCKLEY 150 O.R. to AMPLIERS to work under orders of R.E. Working party of 2 Officers & 50 O.R. found at BERTRANCOURT for work on Corps Line. | |
| | 27/12/15 to 31/12/15 | | In Billets at Bertrencourt, working party of 600 O.R. found for R.E. | |

www.ingramcontent.com/pod-product-compliance
Lightning Source LLC
Chambersburg PA
CBHW081423300426
44108CB00016BA/2291